T

Commonwealth Games

THE HISTORY OF ALL THE SPORTS

Bob Phillips

The Parrs Wood Press
MANCHESTER

First Published 2002

THE PARRS WOOD PRESS
St Wilfrid's Enterprise Centre
Royce Road, Manchester, M15 5BJ
www.parrswoodpress.com

© Bob Phillips 2002

ISBN: 1 903158 30 3

This book was produced by The Parrs Wood Press
and Printed in Great Britain by:

MFP Design and Print
Longford Trading Estate
Thomas Street
Stretford
Manchester M32 0JT

CONTENTS

The Sports of the XVIIth Commonwealth Games

Sports previously part of The Commonwealth Games

INTRODUCTION

From 11 countries to 70.
From 400 competitors to 3,638.
The Games have grown just a bit!

The Commonwealth Games have entered their eighth decade, and no doubt the man who can take most credit for their creation would be highly gratified that they have survived so long. It was very much against the odds that Bobby Robinson, who had been manager of the Canadian athletics team at the 1928 Olympics, saw his dream of a gathering of the leading sportsmen (and a few sportswomen) in the British Empire become reality in his home town of Hamilton, Ontario, in 1930.

Some 400 competitors and 50 officials from 11 countries took part in those inaugural Games in six sports - athletics, bowls, boxing, rowing, swimming and wrestling. In Kuala Lumpur in 1998 there were 3,638 competitors, 1,398 officials, 70 countries and 16 sports. The single apparent common factor between those two celebrations - the first and the 16th in the series - is that athletics, boxing and swimming are the only three sports to have always been on the programme.

Even then, of course, there is a World of difference between the athletics and swimming of 1930 and that of almost 70 years later. In Hamilton the hammer throw was won with 47.13 metres by an Englishman who had been an Olympic bronze-medallist; in Kuala Lumpur the event was won with 74.71 metres (an improvement of almost 60 per cent) by an Australian who ranked 44th in the World. In the pool in Hamilton the 400 yards freestyle was won in 4 minutes 39.8 seconds; in Kuala Lumpur the 400 metres freestyle winner would have passed that point en route at even pace in around 3 minutes 25 seconds, representing an improvement of over 25 per cent.

The sterling supporters of that first Games venture were Australia, Bermuda, British Guiana, Canada, England, Ireland, Newfoundland, New Zealand, South Africa, Scotland and Wales. There were no competitors from other parts of Africa; none from Asia, none from elsewhere in the Caribbean; and there were no women except in swimming events. But for the fact that the tireless Bobby Robinson, encouraged by Canada's Olympic Committee-members, had raised 30,000 dollars from Hamilton's city fathers to help pay travelling expenses, those Games may never have taken place at all at a time when the World was in economic recession.

The most successful athlete was David George Brownlow Cecil, the

Lord Burghley and the future Marquess of Exeter, who had been an Olympic champion in 1928 and who was to become a Member of Parliament and then President of the British Olympic Association and of the International Amateur Athletic Federation. The steeplechase, on the other hand, was won by George Bailey, a Derbyshire quarryman, and many other working-class athletes were unable to afford the time off to make the long journey to Canada. In 1998 the great majority of Commonwealth Games champions were unashamedly full-time professionals.

The Games have resisted a multitude of malevolent influences from the very start of their existence. Initially, the English establishment was unenthusiastic but then took on the organisation in 1934 when the Games were moved from South Africa to avoid the scourge of apartheid. The home countries rallied round again to raise the funds to send teams on the four-month voyage to Australia for the 1938 Games and 12 years later - after the disruption of wartime and its aftermath - when the venue was New Zealand.

In more recent years the nadir was reached with a 1986 Games in chilly Edinburgh boycotted by almost all the African and West Indies countries as a protest against continued sporting relations with South Africa. Then, as the more insidious effect of the increasing commercialisation of World-class athletics has threatened to undermine the value of Games competition, the level of interest has somehow been maintained, even if it has meant that sprinters like Linford Christie and Ato Boldon have made only brief appearances before jetting off to lucrative Grand Prix meetings long before the closing ceremony.

A fuller story of the development of the Games was told in my book, "Honour Of Empire, Glory Of Sport", which was published in the year 2000 and which related the history of Games athletics, and it was in the course of research then that it became apparent to me that an over-view of all the sports would be of value in the run-up to the 2002 Games in Manchester.

There was not too great a problem in compiling the results for the athletics events which have been well documented since 1930 - particularly by the universally-acknowledged expert on the subject, Stan Greenberg - though even here there are still a few minor items of in-depth information that are missing. So if any reader does happen to know the first names of one S.G. Bwowe, who figured in the Ugandan 4 x 110 yards relay team which came last in the final in 1958, I would be delighted to hear from them !

For many of the other sports, the task was much more demanding. Though there have been plenty of publications over the years covering one Games or more, few have approached the matter with serious his-

torical intent. A rare exception to this general rule is a pocket-sized paperback entitled "The Guinness Book Of British Empire & Commonwealth Games Records", published in 1966 and edited by Norris & Ross McWhirter, to which both myself and Stan Greenberg contributed. Whilst in Edmonton, Alberta, for the World Athletics Championships I came across an equally valuable booklet with an even longer title, "A Historical Record Of The Games Leading Up To The Commonwealth Games 1978", published by the organisers of that year's Games in Edmonton.

Even so, in many cases the names of individual members of teams, such as in swimming relays, in rowing events, in badminton, fencing or gymnastics, remained unknown, even when they had won gold medals, and this seemed to me to be a major oversight. So I have endeavoured to search all these out, with first names, and have largely been successful, thanks to the willing help of sports enthusiasts and organising bodies Worldwide. I am particularly grateful to the following:

Melvin Beck (South Africa), Mike Burger (South Africa), Geoff Campbell (New Zealand), Josey Corbo (Canada), Les Crouch (Wales), Jon Doig (Scotland), Jeremy Duxbury (Fiji), Diane Gallagher (Australia), Stan Greenberg (England), Matthew Greenwood (England), Earl Hart (New Zealand), Lisa Holton (New Zealand), Paul Ingrouille (Guernsey), Mervyn John (Wales), Kelly Laframboise (Canada), Greta Larmer (New Zealand), Peter Lee (Scotland), Mike Lockhart (Commonwealth Games Federation), Dick McColgan (Northern Ireland), Bruce Miller (Canada), Alex and Gaylene Ongley (New Zealand), David A. Parker (New Zealand), Ann Steele (England), Roger Wood (New Zealand).

The Edmonton Public Library in Sir Winston Churchill Square, in Edmonton, Alberta, and the Central Branch of the Vancouver Public Library on West Georgia Street, in Vancouver, British Columbia, also provided excellent resource material.

THE COMPETING COUNTRIES

At the 1926 Imperial Conference the six existing Dominions of the British Empire, which were Australia, Canada, the Irish Free State, Newfoundland, New Zealand and South Africa, had been established as "autonomous communities within the British Empire, equal in status, in no way subordinate to one another in any aspect of their domestic or external affairs, although united by a common allegiance to the Crown and freely associated as Members of the British Commonwealth of Nations". The Statute of Westminster 1931 gave this declaration legal

standing. Subsequently, no less than 87 countries, some in different guises, have taken part in the Games, and the abbreviations used for them are as follows, indicating the year in which they first competed:

Aden 1962 Ade (South Arabia in 1966), Anguilla 1998 Ang, Antigua & Barbuda 1966 Ant, Australia 1930 Aus, Bahamas 1954 Bah, Bangladesh 1978 Ban, Barbados 1958 Bar, Bermuda 1930 Ber, British Guiana 1930 BG (Guyana from 1966), British Honduras 1962 BH (Belize from 1973), Belize 1978 Blz (formerly British Honduras), Botswana 1974 Bot, Brunei 1994 Bru, British Virgin Islands 1990 BVI, Canada 1930 Can, Cameroon 1998 Cam, Cayman Islands 1978 Cay, Ceylon 1938 Cey (Sri Lanka from 1972), Cook Islands 1974 CkI, Cyprus 1978 Cyp, Dominica 1994 Dom, England 1930 Eng, Falkland Islands 1990 Fal, Fiji 1950 Fij, Gambia 1970 Gam, Ghana 1958 Gha (formerly Gold Coast), Gibraltar 1958 Gib, Gold Coast 1954 GC (Ghana from 1957), Grenada 1970 Gre, Guernsey 1970 Gue, Guyana 1966 Guy (formerly British Guiana), Hong Kong`1954 HK, India 1934 Ind, Ireland 1930 Ire, Irish Free State 1934 IFS, Isle of Man 1958 IoM, Jamaica 1934 Jam, Jersey 1958 Jer, Kenya 1954 Ken, Lesotho 1974 Les, Malawi 1970 Mlw, Malaya 1950 Mal (Malaysia from 1965), Malaysia 1966 Mal, Maldives 1994 Mld, Malta 1994 Mlt, Mauritius 1958 Mau, Montserrat 1994 Mon, Mozambique 1998 Moz, Namibia 1994 Nam, Nauru 1994 Nau, Newfoundland 1930 NF (Canada from 1949), New Zealand 1930 NZ, Nigeria 1950 Nig, Norfolk Islands 1990 Nor, North Borneo 1958 NB (Malaya from 1963), Northern Ireland 1934 NI, Northern Rhodesia 1954 NR (Zambia from 1964), Pakistan 1954 Pak, Papua New Guinea 1966 PNG, Rhodesia 1934 Rho (Northern Rhodesia from 1954), Rhodesia & Nyasaland 1962 Rho (Zambia from 1964), St Helena 1962 StH, St Kitts & Nevis 1978 StK, St Lucia 1958 StL, St Vincent & the Grenadines 1958 StV, Sarawak 1958 Sar (Malaya from 1963), Scotland 1930 Sco, Seychelles 1990 Sey, Sierra Leone 1958 SL, Singapore 1958 Sin, Solomon Islands 1982 Sol, South Africa 1930 SA, South Arabia 1966 SAr (formerly Aden), Southern Rhodesia 1934 SR (Zimbabwe from 1980), Sri Lanka 1972 SriL (formerly Ceylon), Swaziland 1970 Swa, Tanganyika 1958 Tan (Tanzania from 1964), Tanzania 1970 Tan (formerly Tanganyika), Tonga 1974 Ton, Trinidad & Tobago 1934 Tri, Turks & Caicos Islands 1978 TCI, Uganda 1954 Uga, Vanuatu 1982 Van, Wales 1934 Wal, Western Samoa 1974 WS, Zambia 1966 Zam (formerly Northern Rhodesia), Zimbabwe 1982 Zim (formerly Southern Rhodesia).

THE GAMES VENUES AND SPORTS

The title of the Games has changed as follows: 1930-1950, British Empire Games; 1954-1966, British Empire & Commonwealth Games; 1970-1974, British Commonwealth Games; 1978 onwards, Commonwealth Games.

1930: CANADA - HAMILTON, ONTARIO, 16-23 AUGUST.
11 countries, 400 competitors.
Six sports - Athletics, Bowls, Boxing, Rowing, Swimming, Wrestling.

1934: ENGLAND - LONDON, 4-11 AUGUST.
16 countries, 500 competitors.
Seven sports - Athletics, Bowls, Boxing, Cycling, Rowing, Swimming, Wrestling.

1938: AUSTRALIA - SYDNEY, 5-12 FEBRUARY.
15 countries, 464 competitors.
Seven sports - Athletics, Bowls, Boxing, Cycling, Rowing, Swimming, Wrestling.

1950: NEW ZEALAND - AUCKLAND, 4-11 FEBRUARY.
12 countries, 590 competitors.
Nine sports - Athletics, Bowls, Boxing, Cycling, Fencing, Rowing, Swimming, Weightlifting, Wrestling.

1954: CANADA - VANCOUVER, 30 JULY-7 AUGUST.
24 countries, 662 competitors.
Nine sports - Athletics, Bowls, Boxing, Cycling, Fencing, Rowing, Swimming, Weightlifting, Wrestling.

1958: WALES - CARDIFF, 17-26 JULY.
35 countries, 1,130 competitors.
Nine sports - Athletics, Bowls, Boxing, Cycling, Fencing, Rowing, Swimming, Weightlifting, Wrestling.

1962: AUSTRALIA - PERTH,
21 NOVEMBER-1 DECEMBER.

35 countries, 863 competitors.
Nine sports - Athletics, Bowls, Boxing, Cycling, Fencing, Rowing,
Swimming, Weightlifting, Wrestling.

1966: JAMAICA - KINGSTON,
4-13 AUGUST.

34 countries, 1,050 competitors.
Nine sports - Athletics, Badminton, Boxing, Cycling, Fencing, Shooting,
Swimming, Weightlifting, Wrestling.

1970: SCOTLAND - EDINBURGH,
16-25 JULY.

42 countries, 1,383 competitors.
Nine sports - Athletics, Badminton, Bowls, Boxing, Cycling, Shooting,
Swimming, Weightlifting, Wrestling.

1974: NEW ZEALAND - CHRISTCHURCH,
24 JANUARY- 2 FEBRUARY.

39 countries, 1,276 competitors.
Nine sports - Athletics, Badminton, Bowls, Bowling, Cycling, Shooting,
Swimming, Weightlifting, Wrestling.

1978: CANADA - EDMONTON, ALBERTA,
3-12 AUGUST.

46 countries, 1,519 competitors.
10 sports - Athletics, Badminton, Bowls, Boxing, Cycling, Gymnastics
(Artistic), Shooting, Swimming, Weightlifting, Wrestling.

1982: AUSTRALIA - BRISBANE,
30 SEPTEMBER-9 OCTOBER.

45 countries, 1,583 competitors.
10 sports - Archery, Athletics, Badminton, Bowls, Boxing, Cycling,
Shooting, Swimming, Weightlifting, Wrestling.

1986: SCOTLAND - EDINBURGH,
24 JULY-2 AUGUST.

26 countries, 1,662 competitors.
10 sports - Athletics, Badminton, Bowls, Boxing, Cycling, Rowing,
Shooting, Swimming (including Synchronised), Weightlifting, Wrestling.

1990: NEW ZEALAND - AUCKLAND, 24 JANUARY-3 FEBRUARY.
55 countries, 2,073 competitors.
10 sports - Athletics, Badminton, Bowls, Boxing, Cycling, Gymnastics (Artistic), Judo, Shooting, Swimming, Weightlifting.

1994: CANADA - VICTORIA, BRITISH COLUMBIA, 18-28 AUGUST.
63 countries, 2,557 competitors.
10 sports - Athletics, Badminton, Bowls, Boxing, Cycling, Gymnastics (Artistic), Shooting, Swimming, Weightlifting, Wrestling.

1998: MALAYSIA - KUALA LUMPUR, 11-21 SEPTEMBER.
70 countries, 3,638 competitors.
16 sports - Athletics, Badminton, Bowls, Boxing, Cricket, Cycling, Gymnastics (Artistic and Rhythmic), Hockey, Netball, Rugby Union Sevens, Shooting, Squash, Swimming, Ten-pin Bowls, Weightlifting.

In a few instances some events have been held elsewhere than the main venue; for example, the cycling events in 1934 took place at Fallowfield, Manchester.

THE GOLD MEDALS AND WHERE THEY WENT

The Commonwealth Games are not supposed to be concerned with "league tables" of medals accumulated by the various countries, and for that reason there is no great emphasis on such a subject within the pages of this book. However, the media inevitably puts together such compilations as each Games unfolds, and so for interest's sake the 40 gold-medal-winning countries are listed below:

Australia 564, England 487, Canada 351, New Zealand 105, South Africa 71, Scotland 64, India 50, Kenya 49, Wales 42, Nigeria 30, Jamaica 26, Malaysia 22 (including two as Malaya), Northern Ireland 22, Pakistan 20, Ghana 13, Trinidad & Tobago 8, Uganda 8, Nauru 6, Zimbabwe 5 (including two as Southern Rhodesia), Bahamas 4, Cyprus 4, Hong Kong 5, Singapore 4, Tanzania 4, Guyana 3 (including one as British Guiana), Sri Lanka 3 (including two as Ceylon), Zambia 3 (including one as Northern Rhodesia), Barbados 2, Fiji 2, Isle of Man 2, Bangladesh 1,

Bermuda 1, Guernsey 1, Jersey 1, Lesotho 1, Mauritius 1, Mozambique 1, Namibia 1, Papua New Guinea 1, St Vincent 1.

THE LEADING INDIVIDUAL
GOLD-MEDALLISTS

Any compilation of gold medal-winners is bound to favour participants in those sports where there is a proliferation of related events, particularly including relay and team competitions.

> 10 Susie O'Neill (Aus) - Swimming 1990-98
> 9 Bill Hoskyns (Eng) - Fencing 1958-70
> 9 Mike Wenden (Aus) - Swimming 1970-74
> 8 Allan Jay (Aus/Eng) - Fencing 1950-66
> 7 Marjorie Jackson-Nelson (Aus) - Athletics 1950-54
> 7 René Paul (Eng) - Fencing 1950-58
> 7 Ralph Cooperman (Eng) - Fencing 1962-66
> 7 Raelene Boyle (Aus) - Athletics 1970-82
> 7 Phil Adams (Aus) - Shooting 1982-90
> 7 Lisa Curry-Kenny (Aus) - Swimming 1982-90
> 7 Hayley Lewis (Aus) - Swimming 1990-94

Note: Graham Smith (Can) won six gold medals in swimming, all at the same Games of 1978. The leader in terms of all medals is the pistol marksman, Phil Adams (Aus), with 17 (7 gold, 8 silver, 2 bronze) 1982-94

AQUATICS - SWIMMING

The pool gleams golden for
Australia's water sprites

Judged solely by its spread of medals, swimming would have a difficult job justifying its continued existence at the Commonwealth Games. Australia has won 515 medals, Canada 365, England 290. The other home countries, together with New Zealand and South Africa, have shared all the remainder, with a tiny handful of exceptions.

In every Games but one since 1938 Australia has been the dominant nation - and their lead is now greater than ever. Canada briefly broke the chain in 1978, but the Australians won 27 more medals than any other team in 1990, 29 more in 1994, and 28 more in 1998. In nine individual events in Kuala Lumpur Australia's swimmers finished either 1-2 or 1-2-3. They also won all six relays, and in the 4 x 200 metres freestyle the men touched home almost 12 seconds ahead and the women did so more than six seconds ahead.

You have to go back to the 1930s when William McCatty, from Jamaica, won a breaststroke silver in 1934 and was succeeded in the same event four years later by 36-year-old Walter Spence, of British Guiana. McCatty and his brother, who also competed at the 1934 Games, were students at a university in Canada and had previously earned their living as pearl divers.

The saving grace of what has largely been one-way traffic is that the quality of the swimming has been of the very highest order and has relentlessly improved Games after Games. In Kuala Lumpur 20 Games records were broken, including a World record for that all-conquering Australian men's 4 x 200 team, and Commonwealth records in five other events - all but one by Australians. Ian Thorpe and Susie O'Neill, winners of 10 gold medals between them at those Games, followed in a long and honourable tradition first established in the 1950s by multi-medallists John Henricks, Murray Rose, Jon and Ilsa Konrads and Dawn Fraser.

Olympic gold medals have been won for Australia by Henricks, Rose, John Devitt, Mike Wenden, Kevin Berry, Kieren Perkins and Ian Thorpe, among others, in men's events, and by Fraser, O'Neill, Shane Gould, Lorraine Crapp and Beverley Whitfield, to name but some, in women's events. Other countries, too, have produced outstanding Olympic champions: Alex Baumann, Victor Davis, Mark Tewksbury and Anne Ottenbrite, of Canada; Duncan Goodhew, Adrian Moorhouse, Judy Grinham and Anita Lonsbrough, of England; Danyon Loader, of New Zealand; Joan Harrison, of South Africa.

Swimming was already being practised in Egypt 3000 years ago. In the early 19th Century Lord Byron famously swam the Hellespont and wrote a poem about it. Competitive swimming became organised when the Swimming Association of Great Britain was formed in 1874, and the following year James Trudgen demonstrated a new technique which had been imported from South America and became the origins of the freestyle "crawl" technique. The first English championships were held four years later, with J.S. Moore winning the 100 yards Freestyle in 1min 16¾sec.

Swimming was also included in the programme for the first modern Olympic Games of 1896 and John Jarvis, of Great Britain, was the first champion from an Empire country, winning a 1000 metres freestyle race in 1900. Women's events were introduced at the 1912 Games and two Australian women, Fanny Durack and Wilhelmina Wylie, were 1st and 2nd at 100 metres freestyle. Miss Durack's time was 1min 22.2sec, and on the next occasion that an Australian won that title - Dawn Fraser in 1956 - the winning time was 1min 2sec. Four years later Fraser won again in 59.5sec.

SWIMMING

At the end of the year 2001 Australian men held four individual freestyle World records: Ian Thorpe 1:44.06 at 200 metres, 3:40.17 at 400 metres and 7:39.16 at 800 metres; and Grant Hackett 14:34.56 at 1500 metres. Thorpe's time at 400 metres represented an advance of more than 1min 20sec (approximately 26 per cent) on what Noel Ryan had achieved in becoming Empire champion at 440 yards freestyle in 1934.

Leading countries:
(including swimming, diving and synchronised swimming)

Australia 212 gold medals; Canada 119; England 79; New Zealand 12; Scotland 11; South Africa 7; Wales 4; Zimbabwe 1.

Leading gold-medallists:

Susie O'Neill (Aus) 10 1990-98; Mike Wenden (Aus) 9 1970-74; Lisa Curry-Kenny (Aus) 7 1982-90; Hayley Lewis (Aus) 7 1990-94; Dawn Fraser (Aus) 6 1958-62; Graham Smith (Can) 6 1978; Nicole Livingstone-Stevenson (Aus) 6 1990-98; Matt Dunn (Aus) 6 1994-98; Phyllis Dewar (Can) 5 1934-38; Anita Lonsbrough (Eng) 5 1958-62; Ian O'Brien (Aus) 5 1962-66; Linda Ludgrove (Eng) 5 1962-66; Alex Baumann (Can) 5 1982-86; Andrew Baildon (Aus) 5 1990-94; Chris Fydler (Aus) 5 1990-94; Karen Van Wirdum (Aus) 5 1990-94.

Note: these dates include instances where swimmers took part only in the heats.

Highlights - Games by Games

1930:
Joyce, the versatile mermaid, is England's star

Australia had already produced a super-swimmer in the 1920s. Andrew "Boy" Charlton had won five Olympic medals, including gold at 1500 metres freestyle in 1924, and his successor at the first Empire Games was Noel Ryan, winner of two of the three freestyle races, but Canada and England were by far the most successful countries with 30 medals between them. Joyce Cooper, from the aptly-named Mermaid Swimming Club, won four gold medals for England and had been a double bronze-medallist in the 1928 Olympics at the age of 19. She was also English long-distance champion in 1930, winning a race in the River Thames in 1hr 12min 57sec.

1934:
Ryan's double for Australia,
but Tarzan's record is beyond threat

Noel Ryan repeated his freestyle double for Australia, and the leading woman swimmer this time was 17-year-old Phyllis Dewar, from Moose Jaw, Saskatchewan, with two freestyle wins. Bob Pirie, another Canadian medallist, was the brother of Irene, who was in Canada's 1930 silver-medal relay team, and she married English silver-medallist Freddie Milton in 1935, and their son, Tony, was to swim in the Olympics for Britain. Valerie Davies, backstroke and relay bronze-medallist at the 1932 Olympics, won her fourth medal for Wales, and remains to this day the Principality's most successful Games swimmer. In World terms the leading nations were Japan, the USA and Holland, and Johnny "Tarzan" Weissmuller still held the World record for 440 yards freestyle from 1927 at 4:52.0.

1938:
Still the Empire champions lag
behind the World records

Bob Pirie won two more golds for Canada in the 55-yard North Sydney pool, though his 440 freestyle time was still almost 14 seconds slower than the existing World record held by the Olympic champion, Jack Medica, of the USA. The women's winner at this distance was Dorothy Green, of Australia, and she was more than 17 seconds outside the World record of Holland's Catherina Wagner. The women's breaststroke champion was 18-year-old Doris Storey, from the Montague Burton club in Leeds, who later in the year set a British record of 2:42.4 at 220 yards which was only one second slower than the World record held by another Dutchwoman, Jopie Waalberg.

Walter Spence, at the age of 36, won what was to survive into the 21st Century as the only swimming medal for British Guiana (now Guyana), and John Davies took the breaststroke title using the butterfly technique which had not yet gained separate recognition. Standards generally were not high at the Games as no swimmer from any British Empire country had finished better than 6th at the Berlin Olympics two years before.

1950:
"The best distance prospect that any Empire festival has yet given us"

Empire swimmers had made more of an impression at the 1948 Olympics, with a silver and bronze for John Marshall and a silver for Beatrice Lyons and a bronze for Judy Joy Davies, all of Australia. There were capacity crowds of 5,000 every night at the Auckland Games swimming events, and though the open-air 55-yard Newmarket Olympic pool was shallow and slow the competition was often intensely exciting and nine Games records were broken. John Marshall, a student in the USA, had recently broken the World record for 440 yards freestyle with 4:36.4, but he was an absentee from Auckland and the title went instead to another Australian, Garrick Agnew, in a time which was 13 seconds slower. Agnew's coach, Harry Hay, had also advised Andrew Charlton and Noel Ryan.

John Brockway, a one-man Welsh swimming team, led in the 110 yards backstroke but collided with the ropes towards the end and was passed by the South African, Jackie Wiid. In the women's breaststroke Judy Joy Davies, described as "the best all-round swimmer Australia has produced", edged ahead in the last five yards to get the touch from New Zealand's Jean Stewart. The men's breaststroke title went to 16-year-old Australian butterflier David Hawkins, who paid his own expenses to the Games, with 31 year-old Roy Romain 2nd for England and 14-year-old Ron Sharpe 3rd for Australia.

Another swimmer aged only 14 was South Africa's Joan Harrison, winner of the 440 freestyle, and she was hailed perceptively by one New Zealand reporter as "the best distance prospect among the girls that any Empire festival has yet given us".

1954:
Jack pays his way to Vancouver and comes back with gold in his pocket

Using the Olympic experience as a yardstick, Empire standards were obviously continuing to improve. There had been 18 finalists in Helsinki two years before, including gold medals for Australia's John Davies in the 100 metres breaststroke and for Joan Harrison in the 100 metres backstroke. Davies was not in Vancouver, but Miss Harrison at 18 won her backstroke speciality, and Australia - ominously - had 1-2-3 in the men's 100 yards freestyle, led by Jon Henricks, and a youthful double champion

17

in the women's freestyle events in 15-year-old Lorraine Crapp.

As in 1950 there were full houses every night of 7,000 spectators at the specially-built outdoor pool on the University of British Columbia's campus and they saw repeat wins for Graham Johnston (South Africa) at 1,650 yards freestyle and for Helen Orr Gordon (always known as "Elenor") for Scotland at 220 breaststroke. The men's 220 breaststroke went to an unheralded New Zealander, Jack Doms, who had gone cap in hand round his home town of Waikato to raise the £500 needed to pay his way to the Games after the national selectors dismissed his chances of winning a medal.

1958:
Jon and Ilsa, the record-breaking twins, lead the Australian attack

These Games marked the beginning of Australia's reign of supremacy. Five of their champions (John Devitt, Jon Konrads, John Monckton, Terry Gathercole and Dawn Fraser) were already World record-holders and Australians had won eight titles at the 1956 Melbourne Olympics. In Cardiff Konrads, Latvian-born and aged only 16, won the 440 and 1,650 freestyle and twin sister Ilsa took the women's 440. Australia's men won the freestyle and medley relay finals by margins of 20 seconds and 12 seconds respectively.

Scotland's Ian Black, at butterfly, was the only non-Australian male winner, but the English women made a broader impression with wins for 19-year-old Judy Grinham and 16-year-old Anita Lonsbrough in the breaststroke finals - and, amazingly, no medals for Australia at all in either race.

1962:
Fraser makes it six

A greatly expanded programme of events simply added massively to Australia's score: 41 medals this time, compared with 22 in 1958. Dawn Fraser took her tally of gold medals to six, setting a World record 59.5 for 110 freestyle, and Murray Rose (freestyle), 15-year-old Ian O'Brien (breaststroke) and 17-year-old Kevin Berry (butterfly) were also all double winners in individual events. There was a clean sweep to the delight of the Perth crowd in the men's 440 and 1,650 freestyle finals and Australia won the 4 x 220 relay in World-record time by 29 seconds.

Yet at 110 freestyle a Canadian, Dick Pound, won from a Scot, Bobby McGregor. Graham Sykes, a comparative veteran at 25, won the 110

backstroke for England and two of his women team-mates did even better in similar style - 15-year-old Linda Ludgrove with two golds at backstroke (World record 2:35.2 in the heats which she equalled in the final) and Anita Lonsbrough with three at breaststroke and individual medley (equalling her own World record in the 220 breaststroke heats and beating that by another half-a-second in the final).

1966:
Every Aussie takes a prize,
though Canada's Princess reigns over all

Australia sent 21 swimmers to the Games in Jamaica - and every one of them won at least one medal. The only men's events in which they were beaten were the two butterfly finals (won by Canada and New Zealand) and the medley relay in which they were disqualified. Ian O'Brien, who had won the 1964 Olympic 200 metres breaststroke, repeated his double success of 1962, but that was at least one Australian feat that was matched because England's Linda Ludgrove did the same in the women's backstroke events, as did Brian Phelps in diving.

The pool was heated to 88degF, which was 10deg above the recommended maximum, but it was a fiery furnace which produced a shoal of World records - no less than 14 in all. O'Brien accounted for three of them, including 1:08.5 and 2:28.0 in his respective breaststroke heats, and Kathy Wainwright, also of Australia, broke the 440 freestyle record in her heat (4:39.6) and again in the final. Mike Wenden produced a 1:57.3 "split" for 220 freestyle in the relay final which was another World record.

Yet the unquestioned Princess of the pool was 5ft 2in (1.57m) tall 15-year-old Elaine Tanner, of Canada, who won four gold medals, including both butterfly finals, and set a World record at the longer distance. Her team-mate, 18-year-old Ralph Hutton, established some sort of record for profligacy by racing 13 times in six days and picking up one gold medal, five silvers and two bronzes.

These were the last Games at which swimming events were held at imperial distances, as from 1970 onwards the swimmers, like the athletes, would be going metric. This would leave the men's 440 freestyle winner, Bob Windle, among others, with the consolation that his record time could never be beaten. Windle, one of the finest swimmers of his generation, won in 4min 15.0sec, which was an improvement of 48sec on the time set by his fellow-Australian, Noel Ryan, when the event had first been contested at the Games 32 years before.

1970:
Wenden adds a Commonwealth double to an Olympic double

At the 1968 Olympic Games in Mexico City Mike Wenden had followed up his previous Commonwealth win by taking the 100 and 200 metres freestyle titles. In Edinburgh Wenden won the same two events and took two further golds in the freestyle relays, helping his team to a World record 7:50.77 at 4 x 200. The men's 200 freestyle appeared for the first time at these Games, as did the women's 800 freestyle and the 200 individual medley for both men and women.

Australia's men won all six freestyle individual and relay titles - but nothing else. Bill Mahoney became the first Canadian for 40 years to win a Games breaststroke title, taking both the 100 and 200 metres events, and Canada also won the medley relay. There was even a Canadian 1-2-3 in the 100 butterfly and yet another success for that country at 100 backstroke, where Bill Kennedy beat Mike Richards, of Wales, by a mere 4/100ths of a second. Richards won the 200 final.

Of the 14 women's events all but two went to Australia. Karen Moras won the 200, 400 and 800 freestyle, with a World record 9:02.45 in the last-named, and there were doubles for Lynette Watson at backstroke, Beverley Whitfield at breaststroke and Denise Langford at individual medley. Watson and Langford also each won two relay golds and Whitfield won one.

1974:
Wenden wins again - but Steve, 15, and Jenny, 13, are the next generation

Mike Wenden became the first Games swimmer to win three successive titles in the same individual event (and is still the only one to have done so). From 1966 to 1974 Wenden won 13 medals in all - nine of them gold. Even so, his 15-year-old team-mate, Steve Holland, who had won the World 1500 freestyle title the previous year, created an even greater impression by breaking the 800 metres World record en route to winning the 1500. Altogether, Holland was to set 10 World records over a four-year spell.

Scotland's David Wilkie, also the current World champion, took the 200 breaststroke and 200 individual medley, while there were successes for England's David Leigh at 100 breaststroke and Brian Brinkley at 200 butterfly. Canadian swimmers failed to win any individual titles but took two of the three relays, leaving Mike Wenden in silver-medal position each time.

Jenny Turrall became the youngest Games champion in memory by winning the 400 freestyle at the age of 13, and later in the year she set a World record at 1500 metres. Canada, England, New Zealand and Wales also won women's individual titles and Canada took both relays.

1978:
The Smiths have something to celebrate
in the family

Canada's Graham Smith won both the 100 and 200 breaststroke finals ahead of England's Duncan Goodhew and took the 200 and 400 individual medleys, as his brother, George, had done eight years before. Graham also figured in two winning relay teams, and their sister, Becky, had won a relay gold in 1974. In any circumstances it was a remarkable display of family fortune, but there was poignant cause for special celebration because the venue was the Dr Donald F. Smith Memorial Pool built for the Games and named after their father, who had been a stalwart administrator and who had died of cancer two years before.

Gary Hurring won New Zealand's first (and still their only) men's backstroke gold, which was cause for another extended family celebration. At the 1954 Games his father, Lincoln Hurring, had won two silver medals, losing the backstroke title by 4/10ths of a second; his mother, Jean (nee Stewart), had won silver and bronze in 1950 and 1954 at backstroke; and his uncle, Jack Stewart, had won bronze medals in diving in 1950 and 1954.

Australia's men won five titles, with a double for Ron McKeon at 200 and 400 freestyle, but the finest single performance of the Games was posted by Tracey Wickham, aged 15, who was another double winner for Australia in the women's 400 and 800 freestyle, and broke her own World record with 8:24.62 in the latter event. England's Sharron Davies won both individual medley events, but it was actually the Canadians who were the dominant women's team, winning five individual events and both relays, while a New Zealander, Rebecca Perrott, took the 200 freestyle, having finished last in both her heats at the 1974 Games when she swam for Fiji. For the first time in 40 years Australia were beaten in the medals table: Canada 39, Australia 32.

1982:
Moorhouse, Davis, Ottenbrite and Baumann
head the Olympian parade

At the 1980 Olympics Duncan Goodhew had won breaststroke gold for
Great Britain and Michelle Ford had won freestyle gold for Australia.
Ford won again in Brisbane and it was a vintage Games for champions
of the future. Adrian Moorhouse, Victor Davis and Ann Ottenbrite (all
in breaststroke events) and Alex Baumann (individual medley) won
Commonwealth titles.

Baumann, at 200 and 400 medley, and England's Andy Astbury, at
200 and 400 freestyle, were the only men to win two individual swimming
golds, but Chris Snode maintained an established tradition by becoming
the third successive man to successfully defend both diving titles.
Another Australian, Neil Brooks, was actually the fastest man on view
with a Commonwealth record 51.09 in his 100 metres freestyle heat and
relay "splits" of 50.56 and 50.44 which helped towards two further golds.

June Croft became the first Englishwoman to win the shortest sprint
since Joyce Cooper 52 years previously, and Croft's time of 56.97sec for
100 metres was in a different league to Cooper's 1min 7.0sec for the
much shorter 100 yards (91.44 metres). Croft also won the 200 freestyle
and Tracey Wickham repeated her 400/800 successes of 1978, again
beating a 1980 Olympic champion, Michelle Ford. Lisa Curry won the
100 butterfly and both individual medleys, and she would probably have
had two more golds but for both of the Australian women's relay teams
being disqualified.

1986:
Moorhouse and Davis battle it out
to the hundredths of a second

Alex Baumann had set a World record of 4:17.41 in winning the 1984
Olympic 400 individual medley. He was not quite as fast in Edinburgh
but still took the double in his events for the second successive Games.
His fellow-Canadian, Victor Davis, had also set a World record of 2:13.34
for 200 breaststroke in taking Olympic gold and he won a
Commonwealth title on this occasion at 100 metres.

As had become customary, Australian men won all the freestyle titles,
and the 4 x 200 metres relay team set a Commonwealth record, but
Baumann was the only man to take two individual golds and Canada,

England and New Zealand shared nine titles between them, including relays. The closest rivalry was between breaststroke masters Adrian Moorhouse and Victor Davis: at 100 metres Moorhouse lost to Davis by 8/100ths of a second; at 200 metres Davis lost to Moorhouse by 35/100ths.

Three women each won two swimming events: Sarah Hardcastle at freestyle for England; 13-year-old Allison Higson at breaststroke for Canada; and Suzanne Landells in the individual medleys for Australia, including a Commonwealth record at the longer distance.

1990:
Mrs Kenny returns better than ever,
but little Miss Lewis wins most

Andrew Baildon won a novel double at 100 metres freestyle and butterfly, setting a Commonwealth record 49.80 in the first of these, and Australian men took all the six freestyle titles available to them. Games records were set in 24 of the 32 events and Commonwealth records were also broken by Glen Housman (men's 1500 freestyle) and in women's races by Lisa Curry-Kenny (50 and 100 freestyle and 100 butterfly), Karen Van Wirdum (100 freestyle), Nicole Livingstone (100 backstroke) and Hayley Lewis (400 individual medley). All of them were Australian and another Commonwealth record was set by the 4 x 200 women's freestyle team.

Lisa Curry-Kenny, now 27 and the mother of a young daughter, had already won three golds in 1982 and now added four more. She lost the 100 freestyle final to her team-mate, Karen Van Wirdum, but then beat the latter's record with 56.46 on her stage of the 4 x 100 freestyle relay. Even more prolific was 15-year-old Hayley Lewis, with five gold medals.

England had a solitary winner, but an outstanding one, as Adrian Moorhouse equalled his World record of 1:01.49 for the 100 breaststroke, and his team-mates, James Parrack and Nick Gillingham, made it only the second English clean-sweep in Games history after the 1958 women's 200 breaststroke. Men's backstroke and breaststroke remained something of a problem area for the Australians and in the four finals they won only one medal and Canadians (including Mark Tewksbury again) took the other three golds. Tragically, Canada's Victor Davis had died the previous year after a hit-and-run.

1994:
World record, gold medal
- and another World record in passing

Another batch of records was set by the Australians this time, and the most spectacular of them was by Kieren Perkins, winner of five gold medals, who took the 1500 freestyle with a World record 14:41.66 and set another World record en route of 7:46.00 for 800 metres. The other Commonwealth records to go were in the men's 400 individual medley (Matt Dunn 4:17.01), the women's 100 breaststroke (Samantha Riley 1:08.02) and in the women's 4 x 200 freestyle (Australia 8:08.06). Games records for the team in green-and-gold were fairly modest in number - a mere 22 of them.

The English men also had a good Games with three wins - from Mark Harris and Adam Ruckwood at backstroke and Nick Gillingham at breaststroke - and Danyon Loader took the 200 butterfly for New Zealand, following wins by his compatriot, Anthony Mosse, in the two previous Games. Only one Australian - Kevin Berry in 1962 - had ever won this event at the Games. English-born Stephen Clarke was the winner of the "blue riband" 100 freestyle and received his medal from Sir Roger Bannister but was swimming for his adopted Canada.

There were double wins for four Australian women. Susie O'Neill took the 200 freestyle and 200 butterfly, Nicole Stevenson (nee Livingstone) both backstrokes, Samantha Riley both breaststrokes, and Elli Overton both medleys. England's Karen Pickering, at 100 freestyle, was the only non-Australian woman to take an individual title, but England's quartet (anchored by Pickering) did beat the Australians by half-a-second in the 4 x 100 relay.

The total medals won in all aquatics events were 60 for Australia (including 27 gold), 31 for Canada (eight gold) and 22 for England (also eight gold).

1998:
O'Neill, O'Neill, O'Neill, O'Neill, O'Neill, O'Neill

Six times the name was called out and six times Suzie O'Neill climbed the rostrum to receive a gold medal. That made 10 in all at the Commonwealth Games since her debut as a 17-year-old in 1990, and so she broke the previous record of nine gold medals won by Mike Wenden. She won the 200 and 400 freestyle and 200 butterfly and was in all three relay teams.

Still Suzie might have been left wondering how long the record would last. Ian Thorpe, aged 15, won the 200 (Commonwealth record 1:46.70) and 400 freestyle and was in two gold-medal relay teams (World record 7:11.86 for 4 x 200), causing the veteran Australian team coach, Don Talbot, who had seen more great swimmers than anyone, to remark with typical candour, "You can't believe he's 15. It's genetics gone bloody crazy!" Another Commonwealth record fell to Matt Dunn (200 individual medley), who was also in the World-record relay squad.

Double wins were gained by another Australian, Simon Cowley, at breaststroke and by Canada's Mark Versfeld at backstroke.

Refusing to be overawed by the ubiquitous O'Neill, England's Sue Rolph beat her into 2nd place in the 100 freestyle final and also won the 50 metres event. O'Neill again met her match in another event, the 100 butterfly, where she lost to team-mate Petria Thomas - but then O'Neill did compete 13 times during the Games, covering a total distance of 2,400 metres!

There was little sign of a significant widening of swimming's horizons in Kuala Lumpur. Swimmers from the Bahamas, Malaysia, Trinidad & Tobago and Zimbabwe reached finals, though the highest placing for any of them was 7th, and of the 120 medals on offer in all aquatics events Australia took 58, Canada 30, England 26, New Zealand two, South Africa two, Scotland one and Zimbabwe one.

SWIMMING MEDALLISTS

MEN

Note: automatic timing to one-hundredth of a second, hand-timing to one-tenth of a second.

50 metres Freestyle:
First held 1990
1990: 1 Andrew Baildon (Aus) 22.76, 2 Angus Waddell (Aus) 23.03, 3 Mark Foster (Eng) 23.16.
1994: 1 Mark Foster (Eng) 23.12, 2 Darren Lange (Aus) 23.13, 3 Peter Williams (SA) 23.16.
1998: 1 Mark Foster (Eng) 22.58, 2 Bredon Dedekind (SA) 22.70, 3 Michael Klim (Aus) 22.86.

100 metres Freestyle:
100 yards (91.44 metres) 1930-1934, 110 yards (100.58 metres) 1938-1966
1930: 1 Munro Bourne (Can) 56.0, 2 Norman Brooks (Eng) 56.1, 3 Bert Gibson (Can) -.

1934: 1 George Burleigh (Can) 55.0, 2 George Larson (Can) 55.6, 3 Noel Crump (NZ) 56.2.

1938: 1 Bob Pirie (Can) 59.6, 2 Terry Collard (SA) 1:00.8, 3 Bill Fleming (Aus) 1:01.0.

1950: 1 Peter Salmon (Can) 1:00.4, 2 Frank O'Neill (Aus) 1:00.6, 3 Pat Kendall (Eng) 1:01.8.

1954: 1 Jon Henricks (Aus) 56.5, 2 Cyrus Weld (Aus) 58.5, 3 Rex Aubrey (Aus) 58.7.

1958: 1 John Devitt (Aus) 56.6, 2 Gary Chapman (Aus) 56.6, 3 Geoff Shipton (Aus) 57.0.

1962: 1 Dick Pound (Can) 55.8, 2 Bobby McGregor (Sco) 56.1, 3 David Dickson (Aus) 56.1.

1966: 1 Mike Wenden (Aus) 54.0, 2 Bobby McGregor (Sco) 54.2, 3 David Dickson (Aus) 54.6.

1970: 1 Mike Wenden (Aus) 53.06, 2 Greg Rogers (Aus) 54.26, 3 William Devenish (Aus) 54.28.

1974: 1 Mike Wenden (Aus) 52.73, 2 Bruce Robertson (Can) 53.78, 3 Brian Phillips (Can) 54.11.

1978: 1 Mark Morgan (Aus) 52.70, 2 Bill Sawchuk (Can) 52.81, 3 Gary MacDonald (Can) 52.90.

1982: 1 Neil Brooks (Aus) 51.14, 2 Greg Fasala (Aus) 51.28, 3 Michael Delany (Aus) 51.57.

1986: 1 Greg Fasala (Aus) 50.95, 2 Neil Brooks (Aus) 51.18, 3 Andy Jameson (Eng) 51.21.

1990: 1 Andrew Baildon (Aus) 49.80, 2 Chris Fydler (Aus) 50.49, 3 Mike Fibbens (Eng) 50.76.

1994: 1 Stephen Clarke (Can) 50.21, 2 Chris Fydler (Aus) 50.51, 3 Andrew Baildon (Aus) 50.71.

1998: 1 Michael Klim (Aus) 49.43, 2 Chris Fydler (Aus) 49.51, 3 Gavin Meadows (Eng) 50.14.

200 metres Freestyle:
First held 1970

1970: 1 Mike Wenden (Aus) 1:56.69, 2 Ralph Hutton (Can) 1:58.45, 3 Greg Rogers (Aus) 1:58.63.

1974: 1 Steve Badger (Aus) 1:56.72, 2 Bruce Robertson (Can) 1:57.21, 3 Mike Wenden (Aus) 1:57.83.

1978: 1 Ron McKeon (Aus) 1:52.06, 2 Graeme Brewer (Aus) 1:52.86, 3 Mark Morgan (Aus) 1:53.16.

1982: 1 Andy Astbury (Eng) 1:51.52, 2 Peter Szmidt (Can) 1:51.65, 3 Ron McKeon (Aus) 1:51.71.

1986: 1 Robert Gleria (Aus) 1:50.57, 2 Peter Dale (Aus) 1:51.16, 3 Tom Stachewicz (Aus) 1:51.21.

1990: 1 Martin Roberts (Aus) 1:49.58, 2 Ian Brown (Aus) 1:49.60, 3 Tom Stachewicz (Aus) 1:49.98.

1994: 1 Kieren Perkins (Aus) 1:49.31, 2 Trent Bray (NZ) 1:49.47, 3 Danyon Loader (NZ) 1:49.53.

1998: 1 Ian Thorpe (Aus) 1:46.70, 2 Michael Klim (Aus) 1:48.05, 3 Daniel

Kowalski (Aus) 1:48.26.

400 metres Freestyle:

400 yards (365.76 metres) 1930, 440 yards (402.34 metres) 1934-1966

1930: 1 Noel Ryan (Aus) 4:39.8, 2 Gordon Bridson (NZ) 4:45.8, 3 George Burleigh (Can) -.

1934: 1 Noel Ryan (Aus) 5:03.0, 2 Norman Wainwright (Eng) 5:07.8, 3 Bob Pirie (Can) 5:14.8.

1938: 1 Bob Pirie (Can) 4:54.6, 2 Bobby Leivers (Eng) 4:55.4, 3 Robin Biddulph (Aus) 4:55.5.

1950: 1 Garrick Agnew (Aus) 4:49.4, 2 Graham Johnston (SA) 4:51.3, 3 Fred Lucas (NZ) 5:02.5.

1954: 1 Gary Chapman (Aus) 4:39.8, 2 Jack Wardrop (Sco) 4:41.5, 3 Graham Johnston (SA) 4:43.3.

1958: 1 John Konrads (Aus) 4:25.9, 2 Ian Black (Sco) 4:28.5, 3 Gary Winram (Aus) 4:32.4.

1962: 1 Murray Rose (Aus) 4:20.0, 2 Alan Wood (Aus) 4:22.5, 3 Bob Windle (Aus) 4:23.1.

1966: 1 Bob Windle (Aus) 4:15.0, 2 John Bennett (Aus) 4:15.9, 3 Ralph Hutton (Can) 4:16.1.

1970: 1 Graham White (Aus) 4:08.48, 2 Ralph Hutton (Can) 4:08.77, 3 Greg Brough (Aus) 4:12.16.

1974: 1 John Kulasalu (Aus) 4:01.44, 2 Brad Cooper (Aus) 4:02.12, 3 Steve Badger (Aus) 4:04.07.

1978: 1 Ron McKeon (Aus) 3:54.43, 2 Simon Gray (Eng) 3:56.87, 3 Max Metzker (Aus) 3:58.83.

1982: 1 Andy Astbury (Eng) 3:53.29, 2 Peter Szmidt (Can) 3:53.74, 3 John Davey (Eng) 3:55.52.

1986: 1 Duncan Armstrong (Aus) 3:52.25, 2 Kevin Boyd (Eng) 3:55.00, 3 Michael Davidson (NZ) 3:56.96.

1990: 1 Ian Brown (Aus) 3:49.91, 2 Glen Housman (Aus) 3:53.90, 3 Chris Bowie (Can) 3:54.04.

1994: 1 Kieren Perkins (Aus) 3:45.77, 2 Danyon Loader (NZ) 3:49.65, 3 Daniel Kowalski (Aus) 3:50.41.

1998: 1 Ian Thorpe (Aus) 3:44.35, 2 Grant Hackett (Aus) 3:44.88, 3 Daniel Kowalski (Aus) 3:48.91.

1500 metres Freestyle:

1500 yards (1371.60 metres) 1930-1934, 1650 yards (1508.76 metres) 1938-1966

1930: 1 Noel Ryan (Aus) 18:55.4, 2 Gordon Bridson (NZ) 19:41.0, 3 George Burleigh (Can) -.

1934: 1 Noel Ryan (Aus) 18:25.4, 2 Bob Pirie (Can) 18:28.4, 3 Norman Wainwright (Eng) 18:55.2.

1938: 1 Bobby Leivers (Eng) 19:46.4, 2 Bob Pirie (Can) 19:59.2, 3 Norman Wainwright (Eng) 20:17.4.

1950: 1 Graham Johnston (SA) 19:55.7, 2 Jim Portelance (Can) 20:08.3, 3 Fred

Lucas (NZ) 20:10.1.

1954: 1 Graham Johnston (SA) 19:01.4, 2 Peter Duncan (SA) 19:22.1, 3 Gary Chapman (Aus) 19:28.4.

1958: 1 John Konrads (Aus) 17:45.4, 2 Gary Winram (Aus) 18:17.2, 3 Murray McLachlan (SA) 18:19.2.

1962: 1 Murray Rose (Aus) 17:18.1, 2 Bob Windle (Aus) 17:44.5, 3 Alan Wood (Aus) 17:55.6.

1966: 1 Ron Jackson (Aus) 17:25.9, 2 Sandy Gilchrist (Can) 17:33.9, 3 Ralph Hutton (Can) 17:38.9.

1970: 1 Graham Windeatt (Aus) 16:23.82, 2 Max Travasci (Aus) 16:34.46, 3 Mark Treffers (NZ) 16:44.69.

1974: 1 Steve Holland (Aus) 15:34.73, 2 Mark Treffers (NZ) 15:59.82, 3 Steve Badger (Aus) 16:22.23.

1978: 1 Max Metzker (Aus) 15:31.92, 2 Simon Gray (Eng) 15:39.39, 3 Andy Astbury (Eng) 15:42.89.

1982: 1 Max Metzker (Aus) 15:23.94, 2 Tim Ford (Aus) 15:27.00, 3 Andy Astbury (Eng) 15:34.41.

1986: 1 Jason Plummer (Aus) 15:12.62, 2 Mike McKenzie (Aus) 15:12.62, 3 Chris Chalmers (Can) 15:18.05.

1990: 1 Glen Housman (Aus) 14:55.25, 2 Kieren Perkins (Aus) 14:58.08, 3 Mike McKenzie (Aus) 15:09.95.

1994: 1 Kieren Perkins (Aus) 14:41.66, 2 Daniel Kowalski (Aus) 14:53.61, 3 Glen Housman (Aus) 15:02.59.

1998: 1 Grant Hackett (Aus) 14:50.92, 2 Ryk Neethling (SA) 15:02.88, 3 Kieren Perkins (Aus) 15:03.00.

4 x 100 metres Freestyle Relay:

First held 1962, 4 x 110 yards (100.58 metres) 1962-1966

1962: 1 Australia (Peter Phelps, Murray Rose, Peter Doak, David Dickson) 3:43.9, 2 Canada (Aldwin Meinhardt, John Kelso, Sandy Gilchrist, Dick Pound) 3:48.3, 3 England (Stan Clarke, John Martin-Dye, Rodney Clayden, Peter Kendrew) 3:51.3.

1966: 1 Australia (Mike Wenden, John Ryan, David Dickson, Bob Windle) 3:35.6, 2 Canada (Robert Kasting, Ralph Hutton, Ron Jacks, Sandy Gilchrist) 3:42.3, 3 England (Bobby Lord, John Martin-Dye, Tony Jarvis, Mike Turner) 3:43.7.

1970: 1 Australia (Greg Rogers, William Devenish, Graham White, Mike Wenden) 3:36.02, 2 Canada (Ralph Hutton, George Smith, Ron Jacks, Robert Kasting) 3:37.65, 3 England (Ivan Myall, Malcolm Windeatt, Tony Jarvis, Ray Terrell) 3:41.24.

1974: 1 Canada (Bruce Robertson, Ian Mackenzie, Gary MacDonald, Brian Phillips) 3:33.79, 2 Australia (Ross Paterson, Peter Coughlan, Neil Rogers, Mike Wenden) 3:34.26, 3 England (Colin Cunningham, Keith Walton, Ray Terrell, Brian Brinkley) 3:38.22.

1978: 1 Canada (Bill Sawchuk, Graham Smith, Gary MacDonald, Peter Szmidt) 3:27.94, 2 Australia (Mark Morgan, Ron McKeon, Graeme Brewer, Glenn Patching) 3:28.62, 3 England (Martin Smith, Kevin Burns, David Dunne, Richard Burrell) 3:30.10.

1982: 1 Australia (Greg Fasala, Michael Delany, Graeme Brewer, Neil Brooks)

3:24.17, 2 England (David Lowe, Philip Osborn, Phil Hubble, Richard Burrell) 3:26.98. 3 Canada (Alex Baumann, Blair Hicken, Graham Welbourn, Peter Szmidt) 3:27.74.

1986: 1 Australia (Neil Brooks, Greg Fasala, Matthew Renshaw, Mark Stockwell) 3:21.58, 2 Canada (Alex Baumann, Vlastimil Cerny, Sandy Goss, Blair Hicken) 3:22.98, 3 England (Andy Jameson, Mark Foster, Geoffrey Stewart, Roland Lee) 3:25.01.

1990: 1 Australia (Tom Stachewitz, Matthew Renshaw, Chris Fydler, Andrew Baildon) 3:20.05, 2 England (Mike Fibbens, Neil Metcalfe, Steven Dronsfield, Austyn Shortman) 3:22.61, 3 Canada (Stéphane Hébert, Steven Vander Meulen, Marcel Gery, Darren Ward) 3:22.79.

Note: Jason Cooper and Ian Vander-Wal (both Aus) swam in heat.

1994: 1 Australia (Darren Lange, Andrew Baildon, Dwade Sheehan, Chris Fydler) 3:20.89, 2 New Zealand (John Steel, Nicholas Tongue, Danyon Loader, Trent Bray) 3:21.79, 3 England (Nick Shackell, Mark Foster, Andy Clayton, Mike Fibbens) 3:22.61.

1998: 1 Australia (Michael Klim, Ashley Callus, Ian Thorpe, Chris Fydler) 3:17.83, 2 Canada (Stephen Clarke, Robbie Taylor, Craig Hutchison, Garret Pulle) 3:21.27, 3 England (Nick Shackell, Andy Clayton, Anthony Howard, Mark Stevens) 3:22.13.

Note: Adam Pine, Jeff English and Matt Dunn (all Aus) swam in heat.

4 x 200 metres Freestyle Relay

4 x 200 yards (182.88 metres) 1930-1934, 4 x 220 yards (201.17 metres) 1938-1966

1930: 1 Canada (Munro Bourne, Bert Gibson, George Burleigh, James Thompson) 8:42.4, 2 England (A.G. Watts, Freddie Milton, Norman Brooks, Joe Whiteside) 8:42.8.

Note: only two teams competed.

1934: 1 Canada (George Larson, Bob Hooper, Bob Pirie, George Burleigh) 8:40.6, 2 England (Reg Sutton, Mostyn Ffrench-Williams, Norman Wainwright, Bobby Leivers) 8:52.8, 3 Scotland (William Burns, Merilees Chassels, George Anderson, Henry Cunningham) 9:23.4.

1938: 1 England (Freddy Dove, Mostyn Ffrench-Williams, Bobby Leivers, Norman Wainwright) 9:19.0, 2 Canada (George Burleigh, Bob Hooper, Gordon Devlin, Bob Pirie) 9:20.2, 3 Australia (Noel Ryan, Robert Wilshire, Bill Fleming, Robin Biddulph) 9:32.9.

1950: 1 New Zealand (Lyall Barry, Fred Lucas, Noel Chambers, Michael Amos) 9:27.7, 2 Australia (Frank O'Neill, Garrick Agnew, James Beard, Barrie Kellaway) 9:34.5, 3 England (Ray Legg, Donald Bland, Pat Kendall, Jack Hale) 9:36.8.

1954: 1 Australia (Gary Chapman, Rex Aubrey, David Hawkins, Jon Hendricks) 8:47.6, 2 Canada (Gerald McNamee, Ted Simpson, Sandy Gilchrist, George Park) 8:56.0, 3 South Africa (Dennis Ford, Bill Steuart, Peter Duncan, Graham Johnston) 8:56.3.

1958: 1 Australia (Jon Konrads, Brian Wilkinson, John Devitt, Gary Chapman) 8:33.4, 2 Scotland (Bob Sreenan, James Leiper, Athole Still, Ian Black) 8:54.2, 3 Canada (Kenneth Williams, Peter Bell, Cameron Grout, William Slater) 9:01.8.

1962: 1 Australia (Murray Rose, Alan Wood, Anthony Strahan, Bob Windle) 8:13.4, 2 Canada (John Kelso, Aldwin Meinhardt, Dick Pound, Sandy Gilchrist) 8:42.4, 3 England (Peter Kendrew, Dick Campion, Stan Clarke, John Martin-Dye) 8:46.0.

1966: 1 Australia (Mike Wenden, Peter Reynolds, David Dickson, Bob Windle) 7:59.5, 2 Canada (Robert Kasting, Ralph Hutton, Ron Jacks, Sandy Gilchrist) 8:15.0, 3 England (Mike Turner, Keith Bewley, John Thurley, Tony Jarvis) 8:24.0.

1970: 1 Australia (Greg Rogers, William Devenish, Graham White, Mike Wenden) 7:50.77, 2 Canada (Ralph Hutton, George Smith, Ron Jacks, Robert Kasting) 8:00.69, 3 England (Ivan Myall, John Mills, Ray Terrell, Tony Jarvis) 8:10.60.

1974: 1 Australia (John Kulasalu, Robert Nay, Steve Badger, Mike Wenden) 7:50.13, 2 England (Tony Jarvis, Ivan Myall, Malcolm Windeatt, Ray Terrell) 7:52.90, 3 Canada (Ian Mackenzie, Gary MacDonald, Jim Fowlie, Bruce Robertson) 7:53.38.

1978: 1 Australia (Mark Morgan, Ron McKeon, Max Metzker, Graeme Brewer) 7:34.83, 2 Canada (Bill Sawchuk, Dennis Corcoran, Robert Baylis, Peter Szmidt) 7:36.58, 3 England (David Dunne, Phil Hubble, Martin Smith, Simon Gray) 7:42.02.

1982: 1 Australia (Graeme McGufficke, Ron McKeon, Paul Rowe, Graeme Brewer) 7:28.81, 2 England (Philip Osborn, John Davey, Phil Hubble, Andy Astbury) 7:30.00, 3 Scotland (Douglas Campbell, Neil Cochran, Graeme Wilson, Paul Easter) 7:39.86.

1986: 1 Australia (Duncan Armstrong, Tom Stachewicz, Robert Gleria, Peter Dale) 7:23.49, 2 Canada (Scott Flowers, Sandy Goss, Tom Ponting, Paul Szekula) 7:29.52, 3 England (Kevin Boyd, John Davey, Paul Howe, Jonathan Broughton) 7:33.39.

1990: 1 Australia (Tom Stachewicz, Gary Lord, Ian Brown, Martin Roberts) 7:21.17, 2 Canada (Eddie Parenti, Steven Vander Meulen, Jon Kelly, Turlough O'Hare) 7:25.53, 3 New Zealand (John Steel, Richard Tapper, Anthony Mosse, Ross Anderson) 7:30.10.

1994: 1 Australia (Glen Housman, Matt Dunn, Martin Roberts, Kieren Perkins) 7:20.80, 2 New Zealand (Trent Bray, John Steel, Guy Callaghan, Danyon Loader) 7:21.67, 3 England (Andy Clayton, Steven Mellor, Nick Shackell, James Salter) 7:26.19.

1998: 1 Australia (Ian Thorpe, Daniel Kowalski, Matt Dunn, Michael Klim) 7:11.86, 2 England (Andy Clayton, Gavin Meadows, Paul Palmer, James Salter) 7:23.83, 3 New Zealand (Trent Bray, John Davis, Scott Cameron, Danyon Loader) 7:24.52.

100 metres Backstroke:

100 yards (91.44 metres) 1930-1934, 110 yards (100.58 metres) 1938-1966

1930: 1 James Trippet (Eng) 1:05.4, 2 Willie Francis (Sco) 1:05.8, 3 John Besford (Eng) 1:07.0

1934: 1 Willie Francis (Sco) 1:05.2, 2 John Besford (Eng) 1:05.6, 3 Ben Gazell (Can) 1:06.6.

1938: 1 Percy Oliver (Aus) 1:07.9, 2 Gordon Kerr (Can) 1:09.0, 3 Micky Taylor (Eng) 1:09.3.

1950: 1 Jackie Wiid (SA) 1:07.7, 2 John Brockway (Wal) 1:08.0, 3 Bert Kinnear

(Sco) 1:10.9.

1954: 1 John Brockway (Wal) 1:06.5, 2 Lincoln Hurring (NZ) 1:06.9, 3 Cyrus Weld (Aus) 1:08.6.

1958: 1 John Monckton (Aus) 1:01.7, 2 John Hayres (Aus) 1:03.5, 3 Robert Wheaton (Can) 1:06.5.

1962: 1 Graham Sykes (Eng) 1:04.5, 2 Julian Carroll (Aus) 1:05.4, 3 Wayne Vincent (Aus) 1:06.2.

1966: 1 Peter Reynolds (Aus) 1:02.4, 2 Ralph Hutton (Can) 1:02.7, 3 Neil Jackson (Eng) 1:03.3.

1970: 1 Bill Kennedy (Can) 1:01.65, 2 Mike Richards (Wal) 1:01.69, 3 Erik Fish (Can) 1:02.02.

1974: 1 Mark Tonelli (Aus) 59.65, 2 Steve Pickell (Can) 59.88, 3 Brad Cooper (Aus) 1:00.17.

1978: 1 Glenn Patching (Aus) 57.90, 2 Gary Abraham (Eng) 58.48, 3 Jay Tapp (Can) 59.05.

1982: 1 Mike West (Can) 57.12, 2 Cameron Henning (Can) 57.82, 3 Wade Flemons (Can) 58.38.

1986: 1 Mark Tewksbury (Can) 56.45, 2 Paul Kingsman (NZ) 57.17, 3 Mike West (Can) 57.46.

1990: 1 Mark Tewksbury (Can) 56.07, 2 Gary Anderson (Can) 56.84, 3 Paul Kingsman (NZ) 57.07.

1994: 1 Martin Harris (Eng) 55.77, 2 Steven Dewick (Aus) 56.09, 3 Adam Ruckwood (Eng) 56.52.

1998: 1 Mark Versfeld (Can) 55.52, 2 Josh Watson (Aus) 55.92, 3 Chris Renaud (Can) 55.99.

200 metres Backstroke:

First held 1962, 220 yards (201.17 metres) 1962-1966

1962: 1 Julian Carroll (Aus) 2:20.9, 2 Tony Fingleton (Aus) 2:21.0, 3 Alan Robertson (NZ) 2:23.0.

1966: 1 Peter Reynolds (Aus) 2:12.0, 2 Ralph Hutton (Can) 2:13.5, 3 Karl Byrom (Aus) 2:18.8.

1970: 1 Mike Richards (Wal) 2:14.53, 2 Ray Terrell (Eng) 2:15.48, 3 Neil Rogers (Aus) 2:15.63.

1974: 1 Brad Cooper (Aus) 2:06.31, 2 Mark Tonelli (Aus) 2:09.47, 3 Robert Williams (Aus) 2:09.83.

1978: 1 Gary Hurring (NZ) 2:04.37, 2 Glenn Patching (Aus) 2:05.76, 3 Paul Moorfoot (Aus) 2:05.99.

1982: 1 Cameron Henning (Can) 2:02.58, 2 David Orbell (Aus) 2:03.93, 3 Mike West (Can) 2:04.36.

1986: 1 Sandy Goss (Can) 2:02.55, 2 Paul Kingsman (NZ) 2:02.90, 3 Sean Murphy (Can) 2:03.05.

1990: 1 Gary Anderson (Can) 2:01.69, 2 Paul Kingsman (NZ) 2:01.86, 3 Kevin Draxinger (Can) 2:02.02.

1994: 1 Adam Ruckwood (Eng) 2:00.79, 2 Kevin Draxinger (Can) 2:02.19, 3 Scott Miller (Aus) 2:02.43.

1998: 1 Mark Versfeld (Can) 1:59.67, 2 Adrian Radley (Aus) 2:01.41, 3 Greg Hamm (Can) 2:01.47.

100 metres Breaststroke:

First held 1962, 110 yards (100.58 metres) 1962-1966

1962: 1 Ian O'Brien (Aus) 1:11.4, 2 William Burton (Aus) 1:13.9, 3 Steve Rabinovich (Can) 1:14.1.

1966: 1 Ian O'Brien (Aus) 1:08.2, 2 Hamilton Graham (NZ) 1:12.9, 3 Malcolm Tucker (Eng) 1:13.9.

1970: 1 Bill Mahony (Can) 1:09.0, 2 Peter Cross (Can) 1:09.4, 3 Paul Jarvie (Aus) 1:10.0.

1974: 1 David Leigh (Eng) 1:06.52, 2 David Wilkie (Sco) 1:07.37, 3 Paul Naisby (Eng) 1:08.52.

1978: 1 Graham Smith (Can) 1:03.81, 2 Duncan Goodhew (Eng) 1:04.24, 3 Paul Naisby (Eng) 1:06.36.

1982: 1 Adrian Moorhouse (Eng) 1:02.93, 2 Victor Davis (Can) 1:03.18, 3 Peter Evans (Aus) 1:03.48.

1986: 1 Victor Davis (Can) 1:03.01, 2 Adrian Moorhouse (Eng) 1:03.09, 3 Brett Stocks (Aus) 1:03.75.

1990: 1 Adrian Moorhouse (Eng) 1:01.49, 2 James Parrack (Eng) 1:03.15, 3 Nick Gillingham (Eng) 1:03.16.

1994: 1 Phil Rogers (Aus) 1:02.62, 2 Nick Gillingham (Eng) 1:02.65, 3 Jon Cleveland (Can) 1:03.20.

1998: 1 Simon Cowley (Aus) 1:02.00, 2 Phil Rogers (Aus) 1:02.46, 3 Darren Mew (Eng) 1:02.52.

200 metres Breaststroke:

200 yards (182.88 metres) 1930-1934, 220 yards (201.17 metres) 1938-1966

1930: 1 Jack Aubin (Can) 2:38.4, 2 Stanley Bell (Eng) 2:39.6, 3 Reggie Flint (Eng) 2:44.8.

1934: 1 Norman Hamilton (Sco) 2:41.4, 2 William McCatty (Jam) 2:42.4, 3 Bill Puddy (Can) 2:42.8.

1938: 1 John Davies (Eng) 2:51.9, 2 Walter Spence (BG) 3:00.5, 3 Jimmy Prentice (Can) 3:01.8.

1950: 1 David Hawkins (Aus) 2:54.1, 2 Roy Romain (Eng) 2:54.2, 3 Ron Sharpe (Aus) 2:56.0.

1954: 1 Jack Doms (NZ) 2:52.6, 2 Peter Jervis (Eng) 2:52.6, 3 Alan Hime (Eng) 2:52.8.

1958: 1 Terry Gathercole (Aus) 2:41.6, 2 Peter Rocchi (SA) 2:44.9, 3 Chris Walkden (Eng) 2:47.3.

1962: 1 Ian O'Brien (Aus) 2:38.2, 2 William Burton (Aus) 2:42.1, 3 Neil Nicholson (Eng) 2:42.6.

1966: 1 Ian O'Brien (Aus) 2:29.3, 2 Hamilton Graham (NZ) 2:36.9, 3 Bill Mahony (Can) 2:38.9.

1970: 1 Bill Mahony (Can) 2:30.29, 2 Paul Jarvie (Aus) 2:30.70, 3 David Wilkie (Sco) 2:32.87.

1974: 1 David Wilkie (Sco) 2:24.42, 2 David Leigh (Eng) 2:24.75, 3 Paul Naisby (Eng) 2:27.36.

1978: 1 Graham Smith (Can) 2:20.86, 2 Duncan Goodhew (Eng) 2:21.92, 3 Lindsay Spencer (Aus) 2:22.49.

1982: 1 Victor Davis (Can) 2:16.25, 2 Glenn Beringen (Aus) 2:19.06, 3 Adrian Moorhouse (Eng) 2:19.31.

1986: 1 Adrian Moorhouse (Eng) 2:16.35, 2 Victor Davis (Can) 2:16.70, 3 Nick Gillingham (Eng) 2:20.46.

1990: 1 Jon Cleveland (Can) 2:14.96, 2 Rodney Lawson (Aus) 2:15.68, 3 Nick Gillingham (Eng) 2:16.02.

1994: 1 Nick Gillingham (Eng) 2:12.54, 2 Phil Rogers (Aus) 2:13.56, 3 Jon Cleveland (Can) 2:14.91.

1998: 1 Simon Cowley (Aus) 2:13.13, 2 Ryan Mitchell (Aus) 2:13.20, 3 Adam Whitehead (Eng) 2:14.44.

100 metres Butterfly:

First held 1962, 110 yards (100.58 metres) 1962-1966

1962: 1 Kevin Berry (Aus) 59.5, 2 Neville Hayes (Aus) 1:02.3, 3 Aldwin Meinhardt (Can) 1:02.6.

1966: 1 Ron Jacks (Can) 1:00.3, 2 Graham Dunn (Aus) 1:00.9, 3 Keith Bewley (Eng) 1:01.5.

1970: 1 Byron MacDonald (Can) 58.44, 2 Tom Arusoo (Can) 58.98, 3 Ron Jacks (Can) 59.01.

1974: 1 Neil Rogers (Aus) 56.58, 2 Byron MacDonald (Can) 56.83, 3 Bruce Robertson (Can) 56.84.

1978: 1 Dan Thompson (Can) 55.04, 2 John Mills (Eng) 56.22, 3 Bill Sawchuk (Can) 56.37.

1982: 1 Dan Thompson (Can) 54.71, 2 Phil Hubble (Eng) 55.52, 3 Tom Ponting (Can) 55.64.

1986: 1 Andy Jameson (Eng) 54.07, 2 Anthony Mosse (NZ) 54.31, 3 Tom Ponting (Can) 54.56.

1990: 1 Andrew Baildon (Aus) 53.98, 2 Marcel Gery (Can) 54.42, 3 Jason Cooper (Aus) 54.47.

1994: 1 Scott Miller (Aus) 54.39, 2 Stephen Clarke (Can) 54.45, 3 Adam Pine (Aus) 54.76.

1998: 1 Geoff Huegill (Aus) 52.81, 2 Adam Pine (Aus) 53.09, 3 Michael Klim (Aus) 53.50.

200 metres Butterfly:

First held 1958, 220 yards (201.17 metres) 1958-1966

1958: 1 Ian Black (Sco) 2:22.6, 2 Graham Symonds (Eng) 2:25.5, 3 Brian Wilkinson (Aus) 2:31.0.

1962: 1 Kevin Berry (Aus) 2:10.8, 2 Neville Hayes (Aus) 2:16.3, 3 Brett Hill (Aus) 2:18.7.

1966: 1 David Gerrard (NZ) 2:12.7, 2 Brett Hill (Aus) 2:12.8, 3 Tom Arusoo (Can) 2:14.2.

1970: 1 Tom Arusoo (Can) 2:08.97, 2 Martyn Woodroffe (Wal) 2:09.14, 3 James Findlay (Aus) 2:09.41.

1974: 1 Brian Brinkley (Eng) 2:04.51, 2 Ross Seymour (Aus) 2:06.64, 3 John

Coutts (NZ) 2:07.03.

1978: 1 George Nagy (Can) 2:01.99, 2 Claus Bredschneider (Can) 2:02.49, 3 Phil Hubble (Eng) 2:02.53.

1982: 1 Phil Hubble (Eng) 2:00.98, 2 Paul Rowe (Aus) 2:01.18, 3 Jon Sieben (Aus) 2:01.24.

1986: 1 Anthony Mosse (NZ) 1:57.27, 2 Tom Ponting (Can) 1:58.54, 3 Nick Hodgson (Eng) 2:00.50.

1990: 1 Anthony Mosse (NZ) 1:57.33, 2 Martin Roberts (Aus) 1:59.95, 3 Jon Kelly (Can) 2:00.37.

1994: 1 Danyon Loader (NZ) 1:59.54, 2 Scott Miller (Aus) 1:59.70, 3 James Hickman (Eng) 2:00.87.

1998: 1 James Hickman (Eng) 1:57.11, 2 William Kirby (Aus) 1:59.57, 3 Stephen Parry (Eng) 1:59.63.

200 metres Individual Medley:

First held 1970

1970: 1 George Smith (Can) 2:13.72, 2 Ken Campbell (Can) 2:16.57, 3 Martyn Woodroffe (Wal) 2:16.64.

1974: 1 David Wilkie (Sco) 2:10.11, 2 Brian Brinkley (Eng) 2:21.73, 3 Gary MacDonald (Can) 2:12.98.

1978: 1 Graham Smith (Can) 2:05.25, 2 Bill Sawchuk (Can) 2:05.61, 3 Peter Dawson (Aus) 2:09.05.

1982: 1 Alex Baumann (Can) 2:02.25, 2 Robin Brew (Sco) 2:05.83, 3 Jeffrey Sheehan (Can) 2:07.14.

1986: 1 Alex Baumann (Can) 2:01.80, 2 Rob Woodhouse (Aus) 2:04.19, 3 Neil Cochran (Sco) 2:04.34.

1990: 1 Gary Anderson (Can) 2:02.94, 2 Rob Bruce (Aus) 2:03.78, 3 Martin Roberts (Aus) 2:04.03.

1994: 1 Matt Dunn (Aus) 2:02.28, 2 Curtis Myden (Can) 2:03.47, 3 Fraser Walker (Sco) 2:04.28.

1998: 1 Matt Dunn (Aus) 2:00.26, 2 James Hickman (Eng) 2:01.87, 3 Robert Van der Zandt (Aus) 2:02.73.

400 metres Individual Medley:

First held 1962, 440 yards (402.34 metres) 1962-1966

1962: 1 Alex Alexander (Aus) 5:15.3, 2 John Oravainen (Aus) 5:16.3, 3 John Kelso (Can) 5:16.5.

1966: 1 Peter Reynolds (Aus) 4:50.8, 2 Ralph Hutton (Can) 4:51.8, 3 Sandy Gilchrist (Can) 4:58.7.

1970: 1 George Smith (Can) 4:48.87, 2 Ray Terrell (Eng) 4:49.85, 3 James Findlay (Aus) 4:51.92.

1974: 1 Mark Treffers (NZ) 4:35.90, 2 Brian Brinkley (Eng) 4:41.29, 3 Ray Terrell (Eng) 4:42.94.

1978: 1 Graham Smith (Can) 4:27.34, 2 Simon Gray (Eng) 4:27.70, 3 Bill Sawchuk (Can) 4:27.99.

1982: 1 Alex Baumann (Can) 4:23.53, 2 Steve Poulter (Eng) 4:27.09, 3 John Davey (Eng) 4:27.91.

1986: 1 Alex Baumann (Can) 4:18.29, 2 Rob Woodhouse (Aus) 4:22.51, 3 Steve Poulter (Eng) 4:24.71.

1990: 1 Rob Bruce (Aus) 4:20.26, 2 Rob Woodhouse (Aus) 4:21.79, 3 Jon Kelly (Can) 4:23.96.

1994: 1 Matt Dunn (Aus) 4:17.01, 2 Curtis Myden (Can) 4:17.73, 3 Philip Bryant (Aus) 4:21.34.

1998: 1 Trent Steed (Aus) 4:19.89, 2 James Hickman (Eng) 4:20.17, 3 Zane King (Aus) 4:23.20.

4 x 100 metres Medley Relay:

First held 1934, 3 x 100 yards (91.44 metres) 1934, 3 x 110 yards (100.58 metres) 1938-1954, 4 x 110 yards (100.58 metres) 1958-1966 (Butterfly added)

1934: 1 Canada (Ben Gazell, George Burleigh, Bill Puddy) 3:11.2, 2 Scotland (Willie Francis, Norman Hamilton, Merilees Chassels) 3:15.2, 3 England (John Besford, Alan Summers, Mostyn Ffrench-Williams) 3:16.0.

1938: 1 England (Micky Taylor, John Davies, Freddy Dove) 3:28.2, 2 Canada (Gordon Kerr, Jimmy Prentice, Bob Pirie) 3:30.5, 3 Australia (Percy Oliver, Ernest Hobbs, Bill Fleming) 3:31.8.

1950: 1 England (Jack Hale, Roy Romain, Pat Kendall) 3:26.6, 2 Canada (Lucien Beaumont, Peter Salmon, Sandy Gilchrist) 3:29.4, 3 New Zealand (Peter Mathieson, John Shanahan, Lyall Barry) 3:30.1.

1954: 1 Australia (Cyrus Weld, David Hawkins, Jon Hendricks) 3:22.0, 2 New Zealand (Lincoln Hurring, Jack Doms, Fred Lucas) 3:26.6, 3 Scotland (Bert Wardrop, John Service, Jack Wardrop) 3:27.3.

1958: 1 Australia (John Monckton, Terry Gathercole, Brian Wilkinson, John Devitt) 4:14.2, 2 Canada (Robert Wheaton, Peter Bell, George Park, Cameron Grout) 4:26.3, 3 England (Graham Sykes, Chris Walkden, Graham Symonds, Neil McKechnie) 4:26.4.

Note: Gary Chapman (Aus) swam in heat.

1962: 1 Australia (Julian Carroll, Ian O'Brien, Kevin Berry, David Dickson) 4:12.4, 2 England (Graham Sykes, Neil Nicholson, Terry Glenville, Peter Kendrew) 4:19.9, 3 Canada (John Kelso, Steve Rabinovich, Aldwin Meinhardt, Dick Pound) 4:19.9.

1966: 1 Canada (Ralph Hutton, Leonard Chase, Ron Jacks, Sandy Gilchrist) 4:10.5, 2 England (Neil Jackson, Malcolm Tucker, Keith Bewley, Mike Turner) 4:11.3, 3 New Zealand (Hilton Brown, Hamilton Graham, David Gerrard, Paddy O'Carroll) 4:17.5.

1970: 1 Canada (Bill Kennedy, Bill Mahony, Byron MacDonald, Robert Kasting) 4:01.10, 2 Australia (Neil Rogers, Paul Jarvie, James Findlay, Mike Wenden) 4:04.55, 3 Wales (Mike Richards, Nigel Johnson, Martyn Woodroffe, Kevin Moran) 4:08.05.

1974: 1 Canada (Steve Pickell, Bill Mahony, Bruce Robertson, Brian Phillips) 3:52.93, 2 Australia (Mark Tonelli, Nigel Cluer, Neil Rogers, Mike Wenden) 3:55.76, 3 England (Colin Cunningham, David Leigh, Steve Nash, Brian Brinkley) 4:00.48.

1978: 1 Canada (Jay Tapp, Graham Smith, Dan Thompson, Bill Sawchuk) 3:49.76,

2 England (Gary Abraham, Duncan Goodhew, John Mills, Martin Smith) 3:50.22, 3 Australia (Glenn Patching, Lindsay Spencer, Mark Morgan, Graeme Brewer) 3:53.16.

1982: 1 Australia (David Orbell, Peter Evans, Jon Sieben, Neil Brooks) 3:47.34, 2 England (Steve Harrison, Adrian Moorhouse, Phil Hubble, David Lowe) 3:48.25, 3 Scotland (Douglas Campbell, Iain Campbell, William McGoldrick, Paul Easter) 3:55.45.

1986: 1 Canada (Alex Baumann, Victor Davis, Tom Ponting, Mark Tewksbury) 3:44.00, 2 England (Nick Harper, Adrian Moorhouse, Andy Jameson, Roland Lee) 3:44.85, 3 Australia (Carl Wilson, Brett Stocks, Barry Armstrong, Greg Fasala) 3:45.86.

1990: 1 Canada (Mark Tewksbury, Jon Cleveland, Tom Ponting, Marcel Gery) 3:42.45, 2 England (Gary Binfield, Adrian Moorhouse, Mike Fibbens, Austyn Shortman) 3:43.88, 3 Australia (Tom Stachewicz, Phil Rogers, Andrew Baildon, Chris Fydler) 3:43.91.

1994: 1 Australia (Steven Dewick, Phil Rogers, Scott Miller, Chris Fydler) 3:40.41, 2 Canada (Chris Renaud, Jon Cleveland, Stephen Clarke, Robert Braknis) 3:43.25, 3 England (Martin Harris, Nick Gillingham, James Hickman, Nick Shackell) 3:43.72.

Note: Simon Beqir, Shane Lewis, Adam Pine and Andrew Baildon (all Aus) swam in heat.

1998: 1 Australia (Josh Watson, Simon Cowley, Geoff Huegill, Michael Klim) 3:38.52, 2 England (Neil Willey, Richard Maden, James Hickman, Nick Shackell) 3:40.73, 3 Canada (Mark Versfeld, Andrew Chan, Garret Pulle, Stephen Clarke) 3:42.74.

Note: Adrian Radley and Chris Fydler (both Aus) swam in heat.

WOMEN

50 metres Freestyle:
First held 1990

1990: 1 Lisa Curry-Kenny (Aus) 25.80, 2 Karen Van Wirdum (Aus) 26.00, 3 Andrea Nugent (Can) 26.26.

1994: 1 Karen Van Wirdum (Aus) 25.90, 2 Andrea Nugent (Can) 26.24, 3 Shannon Shakespeare (Can) 26.27.

1998: 1 Sue Rolph (Eng) 25.82, 2 Alison Sheppard (Sco) 25.92, 3 Toni Jeffs (NZ) 26.07.

100 metres Freestyle:
100 yards (91.44 metres) 1930-1934, 110 yards (100.58 metres) 1938-1966

1930: 1 Joyce Cooper (Eng) 1:07.0, 2 Ellen King (Sco) 1:07.4, 3 Valerie Davies (Wal) -.

1934: 1 Phyllis Dewar (Can) 1:03.5, 2 Irene Pirie (Can) 1:03.6, 3 Jean McDowall (Sco) 1:05.8.

1938: 1 Evelyn de Lacy (Aus) 1:10.1, 2 Dorothy Green (Aus) 1:11.1, 3 Dorothy Lyon (Can) 1:12.1.

1950: 1 Marjorie McQuade (Aus) 1:09.0, 2 Margaret Wellington (Eng) 1:09.6,

3 Joan Harrison (SA) 1:09.7.

1954: 1 Lorraine Crapp (Aus) 1:05.8, 2 Virginia Grant (Can) 1:06.3, 3 Joan Harrison (SA) 1:08.2.

1958: 1 Dawn Fraser (Aus) 1:01.4, 2 Lorraine Crapp (Aus) 1:03.8, 3 Alva Colqohoun (Aus) 1:04.0.

1962: 1 Dawn Fraser (Aus) 59.5, 2 Robin Thorn (Aus) 1:03.8, 3 Mary Stewart (Can) 1:04.4.

1966: 1 Marion Lay (Can) 1:02.3, 2 Lynette Bell (Aus) 1:03.2, 3 Jan Murphy (Aus) 1:03.4.

1970: 1 Angela Coughlan (Can) 1:01.22, 2 Lynne Watson (Aus) 1:01.45, 3 Jenny Watts (Aus) 1:01.81.

1974: 1 Sonya Gray (Aus) 59.13, 2 Gail Amundrud (Can) 59.36, 3 Judy Wright (Can) 59.46.

1978: 1 Carol Klimpel (Can) 57.78, 2 Rosemary Brown (Aus) 58.30, 3 Wendy Quirk (Can) 58.41.

1982: 1 June Croft (Eng) 56.97, 2 Angela Russell (Aus) 57.39, 3 Lisa Curry (Aus) 57.68.

1986: 1 Jane Kerr (Can) 57.62, 2 Angela Harris (Aus) 57.64, 3 Nicola Fibbens (Eng) 57.66.

Note: Harris nee Russell.

1990: 1 Karen Van Wirdum (Aus) 56.48, 2 Lisa Curry-Kenny (Aus) 56.61, 3 Trish Noall (Can) 56.67.

Note: Curry-Kenny nee Curry.

1994: 1 Karen Pickering (Eng) 56.20, 2 Karen Van Wirdum (Aus) 56.42, 3 Marianne Limpert (Can) 56.44.

1998: 1 Sue Rolph (Eng) 55.17, 2 Susie O'Neill (Aus) 55.58, 3 Rebecca Creedy (Aus) 56.07.

200 metres Freestyle:

First held 1970

1970: 1 Karen Moras (Aus) 2:09.78, 2 Angela Coughlan (Can) 2:10.83, 3 Alex Jackson (IoM) 2:13.52.

1974: 1 Sonya Gray (Aus) 2:04.27, 2 Jenny Turrall (Aus) 2:06.90, 3 Gail Amundrud (Can) 2:07.03.

1978: 1 Rebecca Perrott (NZ) 2:00.63, 2 Tracey Wickham (Aus) 2:01.50,
3 Michelle Ford (Aus) 2:01.64.

1982: 1 June Croft (Eng) 1:59.74, 2 Tracey Wickham (Aus) 2:00.60, 3 Susie Baumer (Aus) 2:02.29.

1986: 1 Susie Baumer (Aus) 2:00.61, 2 Jane Kerr (Can) 2:03.40, 3 Ruth Gilfillan (Sco) 2:03.88.

1990: 1 Hayley Lewis (Aus) 2:00.79, 2 Jennifer McMahon (Aus) 2:02.43, 3 Trish Noall (Can) 2:02.66.

1994: 1 Susie O'Neill (Aus) 2:00.86, 2 Nicole Stevenson (Aus) 2:01.34, 3 Karen Pickering (Eng) 2:01.50.

1998: 1 Susie O'Neill (Aus) 2:00.24, 2 Karen Pickering (Eng) 2:01.19, 3 Jessica Deglau (Can) 2:01.59.

400 metres Freestyle:

400 yards (365.76 metres) 1930, 440 yards (402.34 metres) 1934-1966

1930: 1 Joyce Cooper (Eng) 5:25.4, 2 Valerie Davies (Wal) 5:28.0, 3 Sarah Stewart (Sco) -.

1934: 1 Phyllis Dewar (Can) 5:45.6, 2 Jennie Maakal (SA) 5:53.0, 3 Irene Pirie (Can) 5:54.4.

1938: 1 Dorothy Green (Aus) 5:39.7, 2 Margaret Jeffrey (Eng) 5:40.2, 3 Mona Leydon (NZ) 5:42.0.

1950: 1 Joan Harrison (SA) 5:26.4, 2 Margaret Wellington (Eng) 5:33.7, 3 Denise Norton (Aus) 5:33.8.

1954: 1 Lorraine Crapp (Aus) 5:11.4, 2 Gladys Priestley (Can) 5:19.6, 3 Margaret Girvan (Sco) 5:21.4.

1958: 1 Ilsa Konrads (Aus) 4:49.4, 2 Dawn Fraser (Aus) 5:00.8, 3 Lorraine Crapp (Aus) 5:06.7.

1962: 1 Dawn Fraser (Aus) 4:51.4, 2 Ilsa Konrads (Aus) 4:55.0, 3 Liz Long (Eng) 5:00.4.

1966: 1 Kathy Wainwright (Aus) 4:38.8, 2 Jenny Thorn (Aus) 4:44.5, 3 Kim Herford (Aus) 4:47.2.

1970: 1 Karen Moras (Aus) 4:27.38, 2 Denise Langford (Aus) 4:31.42, 3 Robyn Risson (Aus) 4:39.75.

1974: 1 Jenny Turrall (Aus) 4:22.09, 2 Wendy Quirk (Can) 4:22.96, 3 Jaynie Parkhouse (NZ) 4:23.09.

1978: 1 Tracey Wickham (Aus) 4:08.45, 2 Michelle Ford (Aus) 4:10.25, 3 Rebecca Perrott (NZ) 4:16.70.

1982: 1 Tracey Wickham (Aus) 4:08.82, 2 Jackie Wilmott (Eng) 4:13.04, 3 June Croft (Eng) 4:13.13.

1986: 1 Sarah Hardcastle (Eng) 4:07.68, 2 Susie Baumer (Aus) 4:12.77, 3 Jenny Burke (Aus) 4:14.22.

1990: 1 Hayley Lewis (Aus) 4:08.89, 2 Julie McDonald (Aus) 4:09.72, 3 Janelle Elford (Aus) 4:10.74.

1994: 1 Hayley Lewis (Aus) 4:12.56, 2 Stacey Gartrell (Aus) 4:13.06, 3 Sarah Hardcastle (Eng) 4:13.29.

1998: 1 Susie O'Neill (Aus) 4:12.39, 2 Vicki Horner (Eng) 4:12.56, 3 Joanne Malar (Can) 4:13.91.

800 metres Freestyle:

First held 1970

1970: 1 Karen Moras (Aus) 9:02.45, 2 Helen Gray (Aus) 9:27.48, 3 Robyn Risson (Aus) 9:37.89.

1974: 1 Jaynie Parkhouse (NZ) 8:58.49, 2 Jenny Turrall (Aus) 8:58.53, 3 Rosemary Milgate (Aus) 8:58.59.

1978: 1 Tracey Wickham (Aus) 8:24.62, 2 Michelle Ford (Aus) 8:25.78, 3 Rebecca Perrott (NZ) 8:44.87.

1982: 1 Tracey Wickham (Aus) 8:29.05, 2 Michelle Ford (Aus) 8:33.74, 3 Jackie Wilmott (Eng) 8:36.66.

1986: 1 Sarah Hardcastle (Eng) 8:24.77, 2 Julie McDonald (Aus) 8:29.52, 3 Jenny Burke (Aus) 8:41.64.

1990: 1 Julie McDonald (Aus) 8:30.27, 2 Janelle Elford (Aus) 8:30.47, 3 Sheridan Burge-Lopez (Aus) 8:36.78.
1994: 1 Stacey Gartrell (Aus) 8:30.18, 2 Hayley Lewis (Aus) 8:30.72, 3 Nikki Dryden (Can) 8:37.70.
1998: 1 Rachel Harris (Aus) 8:42.23, 2 Joanne Malar (Can) 8:43.96, 3 Sarah Collings (Eng) 8:45.56.

4 x 100 metres Freestyle Relay:

4 x 100 yards (91.44 metres) 1930-1934, 4 x 110 yards (100.58 metres) 1938-1966

1930: 1 England (Olive Joynes, Doreen Cooper, Phyllis Harding, Joyce Cooper) 4:32.8, 2 Canada (Irene Pirie, Betty Edwards, Marjorie Linton, Peggy Bailey) 4:33.0, 3 Scotland (Ellen King, Jean McDowall, Cissie Stewart, Jessie McVey) 4:37.0
1934: 1 Canada (Phyllis Dewar, Florence Humble, Irene Pirie, Margaret Hutton) 4:21.8, 2 South Africa (Enid Hayward, Mollie Ryde, Jennie Maakal, Kathleen Russell) 4:34.0, 3 England (Edna Hughes, Beatrice Wolstenholme, Olive Bartle, Margery Hinton) 4:34.4.
1938: 1 Canada (Florence Humble, Dorothy Lyon, Noel Oxenbury, Phyllis Dewar) 4:48.3, 2 Australia (Pat Norton, Margaret Rawson, Dorothy Green, Evelyn de Lacey) 4:49.9, 3 England (Joyce Harrowby, Edna Hughes, Zilpha Grant, Margery Hinton) 4:50.1.
1950: 1 Australia (Denise Spencer, Denise Norton, Judy Joy Davies, Marjorie McQuade) 4:44.9, 2 New Zealand (Kristen Jacobi, Norma Bridson, Winifred Griffin, Joan Hastings) 4:48.7, 3 England (Grace Wood, Helen Yate, Lillian Preece, Margaret Wellington) 4:56.0.
1954: 1 South Africa (Felicity Loveday, Maggie Petzer, Natalie Myburgh, Joan Harrison) 4:33.9, 2 Canada (Virginia Grant, Gladys Priestley, Helen Stewart, Beth Whittall) 4:37.0, 3 England (Fearne Ewart, Valerie Nares-Pillow, Daphne Wilkinson, Jean Botham) 4:41.8.
1958: 1 Australia (Dawn Fraser, Sandra Morgan, Lorraine Crapp, Alva Colquhoun) 4:17.4, 2 Canada (Sara Barber, Margaret Iwasaki, Gladys Priestley, Susan Sangster) 4:30.0, 3 England (Judy Grinham, Beryl Noakes, Anne Marshall, Daphne Wilkinson) 4:31.5.
1962: 1 Australia (Lynette Bell, Ruth Everuss, Robin Thorn, Dawn Fraser) 4:11.0, 2 Canada (Patricia Thomson, Sara Barber, Madeleine Sevigny, Mary Stewart) 4:21.1, 3 England (Sandra Keen, Liz Long, Linda Amos, Diana Wilkinson) 4:21.3.
1966: 1 Canada (Elaine Tanner, Jane Hughes, Louise Kennedy, Marion Lay) 4:10.8, 2 Australia (Jan Murphy, Jenny Steinbeck, Marion Smith, Lynette Bell) 4:11.1. 3 England (Diana Wilkinson, Sue Cope, Jeanette Cave, Pauline Sillett) 4:17.3.
1970: 1 Australia (Lynne Watson, Jenny Watts, Debra Cain, Denise Langford) 4:06.41, 2 Canada (Susan Smith, Linda Hall, Karen James, Angela Coughlan) 4:12.16, 3 England (Kathryn Smith, Lesley Allardyce, Karen Pickering, Diana Sutherland) 4:14.90.
1974: 1 Canada (Gail Amundrud, Becky Smith, Anne Jardin, Judith Wright) 3:57.14, 2 Australia (Jenny Turrall, Debra Cain, Suzy Anderson, Sonya Gray) 4:02.37, 3 England (Alyson Jones, Avis Willington, Susan Edmondson, Lesley

Allardyce) 4:05.59.

1978: 1 Canada (Gail Amundrud, Carol Klimpel, Susan Sloan, Wendy Quirk) 3:50.28, 2 England (Kaye Lovatt, Heidi Turk, Cheryl Brazendale, Sharron Davies) 3:53.27, 3 Australia (Rosemary Brown, Lisa Burnes, Michelle Ford, Tracey Wickham) 3:54.11.

1982: 1 England (June Croft, Nicola Fibbens, Debra Gore, Jackie Wilmott) 3:54.23, 2 Scotland (Sarah Inkson, Cathy Finlay, Alison Hamilton, Nikki Ramsay) 4:01.46, 3 New Zealand (Pamela Croad, Melanie Jones, Kim Dewar, Gail Jonson) 4:07.41.

1986: 1 Canada (Jane Kerr, Trish Noall, Andrea Nugent, Pam Rai) 3:48.45, 2 England (Caroline Cooper, Nicola Fibbens, Zara Long, Annabelle Cripps) 3:49.65, 3 Australia (Jacqueline Grant, Angela Harris, Julie Pugh, Sarah Thorpe) 3:50.06.

1990: 1 Australia (Lisa Curry-Kenny, Susie O'Neill, Angela Mullens, Karen Van Wirdum) 3:46.85, 2 Canada (Allison Higson, Erin Murphy, Kim Paton, Trish Noall) 3:48.69, 3 England (Karen Pickering, Sharron Davies, Zara Long, June Croft) 3:51.26.

1994: 1 England (Sue Rolph, Alex Bennett, Claire Huddart, Karen Pickering) 3:46.23, 2 Australia (Susie O'Neill, Sarah Ryan, Elli Overton, Karen Van Wirdum) 3:46.73, 3 Canada (Marianne Limpert, Shannon Shakespeare, Jessica Amey, Glencora Maughan) 3:47.25.

1998: 1 Australia (Rebecca Creedy, Sarah Ryan, Lori Munz, Susie O'Neill) 3:42.61, 2 England (Sue Rolph, Claire Huddart, Karen Legg, Karen Pickering) 3:43.20, 3 Canada (Laura Nicholls, Marianne Limpert, Jessica Deglau, Nicole Davey) 3:45.48.

4 x 200 metres Freestyle Relay:

First held 1986

1986: 1 Australia (Suzie Baumer, Jennifer Burke, Sarah Thorpe, Michele Pearson) 8:12.09, 2 England (Annabelle Cripps, Sarah Hardcastle, Karen Mellor, Zara Long) 8:13.70, 3 Canada (Sophie Dufour, Jane Kerr, Donna McGinnis, Trish Noall) 8:20.78.

1990: 1 Australia (Hayley Lewis, Jennifer McMahon, Janelle Elford, Julie McDonald) 8:08.95, 2 England (Joanna Coull, Sharron Davies, Judy Lancaster, June Croft) 8:16.31, 3 New Zealand (Michelle Burke, Philippa Langrell, Sharon Hanley, Linda Robinson) 8:22.60.

1994: 1 Australia (Anna Windsor, Nicole Stevenson, Hayley Lewis, Susie O'Neill) 8:08.06, 2 England (Sarah Hardcastle, Claire Huddart, Alex Bennett, Karen Pickering) 8:09.62, 3 Canada (Jessica Amey, Lisa Flood, Beth Hazel, Marianne Limpert) 8:14.97.

1998: 1 Australia (Julia Greville, Susie O'Neill, Anna Windsor, Lori Munz) 8:03.73, 2 England (Claire Huddart, Karen Legg, Lyndsey Cooper, Karen Pickering) 8:10.09, 3 Canada (Jessica Deglau, Andrea Schwartz, Laura Nicholls, Joanne Malar) 8:11.84.

SWIMMING

100 metres Backstroke

100 yards (91.44 metres) 1930-1934, 110 yards (100.58 metres) 1938-1966

1930: 1 Joyce Cooper (Eng) 1:15.0, 2 Valerie Davies (Wal) 1:16.8, 3 Phyllis Harding (Eng) 1:17.6.

1934: 1 Phyllis Harding (Eng) 1:13.8, 2 Margot Hamilton (Sco) 1:15.0, 3 Valerie Davies (Wal) 1:18.2.

1938: 1 Pat Norton (Aus) 1:19.5, 2 Jeanne Greenland (Wal) 1:22.5, 3 Margot Hamilton (Sco) 1:23.2.

1950: 1 Judy-Joy Davies (Aus) 1:18.6, 2 Jean Stewart (NZ) 1:19.1, 3 Helen Yate (Eng) 1:20.5.

1954: 1 Joan Harrison (SA) 1:15.2, 2 Pat Symons (Eng) 1:17.4, 3 Jean Stewart (NZ) 1:17.5.

1958: 1 Judy Grinham (Eng) 1:11.9, 2 Margaret Edwards (Eng) 1:12.6, 3 Philippa Gould (NZ) 1:13.7.

1962: 1 Linda Ludgrove (Eng) 1:11.1, 2 Pam Sergeant (Aus) 1:11.5, 3 Sylvia Lewis (Eng) 1:12.2.

1966: 1 Linda Ludgrove (Eng) 1:09.2, 2 Elaine Tanner (Can) 1:09.9, 3 Janet Franklin (Eng) 1:11.8.

1970: 1 Lynne Watson (Aus) 1:07.10, 2 Debra Cain (Aus) 1:07.73, 3 Donna-Marie Gurr (Can) 1:08.87.

1974: 1 Wendy Cook (Can) 1:06.37, 2 Donna-Marie Gurr (Can) 1:06.55, 3 Linda Young (Aus) 1:07.52.

1978: 1 Debra Forster (Aus) 1:03.97, 2 Hélène Boivin (Can) 1:04.54, 3 Cheryl Gibson (Can) 1:04.68.

1982: 1 Lisa Forrest (Aus) 1:03.48, 2 Georgina Parkes (Aus) 1:03.63, 3 Audrey Moore (Aus) 1:03.91.

1986: 1 Sylvia Hume (NZ) 1:04.00, 2 Georgina Parkes (Aus) 1:04.07, 3 Nicole Livingstone (Aus) 1:04.42.

1990: 1 Nicole Livingstone (Aus) 1:02.46, 2 Anna Simcic (NZ) 1:02.55, 3 Johanna Griggs (Aus) 1:03.69.

1994: 1 Nicole Stevenson (Aus) 1:02.68, 2 Elli Overton (Aus) 1:02.90, 3 Kathy Osher (Eng) 1:03.27.

Note: Stevenson nee Livingstone, Osher nee Read.

1998: 1 Giaan Rooney (Aus) 1:02.43, 2 Kelly Stefanyshyn (Can) 1:02.81, 3 Meredith Smith (Aus) 1:03.19.

200 metres Backstroke:

First held 1962, 220 yards (201.17 metres) 1962-1966

1962: 1 Linda Ludgrove (Eng) 2:35.2, 2 Sylvia Lewis (Eng) 2:36.7, 3 Pam Sergeant (Aus) 2:37.5.

1966: 1 Linda Ludgrove (Eng) 2:28.5, 2 Elaine Tanner (Can) 2:29.7, 3 Margaret McRae (NZ) 2:34.7.

1970: 1 Lynne Watson (Aus) 2:22.86, 2 Donna-Marie Gurr (Can) 2:24.33, 3 Debra Cain (Aus) 2:26.02.

1974: 1 Wendy Cook (Can) 2:20 .37, 2 Sandra Yost (Aus) 2:22.07, 3 Donna-Marie Gurr (Can) 2:23.74.

1978: 1 Cheryl Gibson (Can) 2:16.57, 2 Lisa Forrest (Aus) 2:17.66, 3 Glenda

Robertson (Aus) 2:18.32.

1982: 1 Lisa Forrest (Aus) 2:13.36, 2 Georgina Parkes (Aus) 2:13.95, 3 Cheryl Gibson (Can) 2:15.87.

1986: 1 Georgina Parkes (Aus) 2:14.88, 2 Kathy Read (Eng) 2:16.92, 3 Jodi McGibbon (Aus) 2:17.66.

1990: 1 Anna Simcic (NZ) 2:12.32, 2 Nicole Livingstone (Aus) 2:12.62, 3 Karen Lord (Aus) 2:14.53.

1994: 1 Nicole Stevenson (Aus) 2:12.73, 2 Anna Simcic (NZ) 2:13.94, 3 Elli Overton (Aus) 2:14.96.

Note: Stevenson nee Livingstone.

1998: 1 Katy Sexton (Eng) 2:13.18, 2 Meredith Smith (Aus) 2:13.19, 3 Helen Don Duncan (Eng) 2:13.50.

100 metres Breaststroke:

First held 1962, 110 yards (100.58 metres) 1962-1966

1962: 1 Anita Lonsbrough (Eng) 1:21.3, 2 Vivien Haddon (NZ) 1:21.3, 3 Dorinda Fraser (Eng) 1:21.7.

1966: 1 Diana Harris (Eng) 1:19.7, 2 Jill Slattery (Eng) 1:19.8, 3 Heather Saville (Aus) 1:21.6.

1970: 1 Beverley Whitfield (Aus) 1:17.40, 2 Dorothy Harrison (Eng) 1:17.60, 3 Chris Jarvis (Eng) 1:19.83.

1974: 1 Catherine Gaskell (Eng) 1:16.42, 2 Marion Stuart (Can) 1:16.61, 3 Sandra Dickie (Sco) 1:17.17.

1978: 1 Robin Corsiglia (Can) 1:13.56, 2 Maggie Kelly (Eng) 1:13.69, 3 Marion Stuart (Can) 1:13.72.

1982: 1 Kathy Bald (Can) 1:11.89, 2 Anne Ottenbrite (Can) 1:11.99, 3 Suki Brownsdon (Eng) 1:13.76.

1986: 1 Allison Higson (Can) 1:10.84, 2 Jean Hill (Sco) 1:11.38, 3 Dimity Douglas (Aus) 1:11.98.

1990: 1 Keltie Duggan (Can) 1:10.74, 2 Guylaine Cloutier (Can) 1:11.22, 3 Suki Brownsdon (Eng) 1:11.54.

1994: 1 Samantha Riley (Aus) 1:08.02, 2 Rebecca Brown (Aus) 1:09.40, 3 Penelope Heyns (SA) 1:09.86.

1998: 1 Helen Denman (Aus) 1:08.71, 2 Samantha Riley (Aus) 1:09.08, 3 Lauren Van Oosten (Can) 1:09.11.

200 metres Breaststroke:

200 yards (182.88 metres) 1930-1934, 220 yards (201.17 metres) 1938-1966

1930: 1 Celia Wolstenholme (Eng) 2:54.8, 2 Margery Hinton (Eng) 3:04.2, 3 Ellen King (Sco) -.

1934: 1 Claire Dennis (Aus) 2:50.2, 2 Phyllis Haslam (Can) 2:55.4, 3 Margery Hinton (Eng) 2:58.6.

1938: 1 Doris Storey (Eng) 3:06.3, 2 Carla Gerke (SA) 3:12.1, 3 Joan Langdon (Can) 3:22.2.

1950: 1 Elenor Gordon (Sco) 3:01.7, 2 Nancy Lyons (Aus) 3:03.6, 3 Elizabeth Church (Eng) 3:10.3.

1954: 1 Elenor Gordon (Sco) 2:59.2, 2 Mary Morgan (SA) 3:03.3, 3 Margaret Grundy (Eng) 3:04.5.

1958: 1 Anita Lonsbrough (Eng) 2:53.5, 2 Jackie Dyson (Eng) 2:58.2, 3 Chris Gosden (Eng) 2:58.4.

1962: 1 Anita Lonsbrough (Eng) 2:51.7, 2 Jackie Enfield (Eng) 2:54.7, 3 Vivien Haddon (NZ) 2:56.3.

1966: 1 Jill Slattery (Eng) 2:50.3, 2 Stella Mitchell (Eng) 2:50.3, 3 Vivien Haddon (NZ) 2:53.9.

1970: 1 Beverley Whitfield (Aus) 2:44.12, 2 Dorothy Harrison (Eng) 2:46.18, 3 Amanda Radnage (Eng) 2:50.11.

1974: 1 Pat Beaven (Wal) 2:43.11, 2 Beverley Whitfield (Aus) 2:43.58, 3 Alison Smith (Aus) 2:45.08.

1978: 1 Lisa Borsholt (Can) 2:37.70, 2 Debbie Rudd (Eng) 2:38.07, 3 Maggie Kelly (Eng) 2:38.63.

1982: 1 Anne Ottenbrite (Can) 2:32.07, 2 Kathy Bald (Can) 2:36.06, 3 Katherine Richardson (Can) 2:36.45.

1986: 1 Allison Higson (Can) 2:31.20, 2 Cindy Ounpuu (Can) 2:32.63, 3 Dimity Douglas (Aus) 2:34.54.

1990: 1 Nathalie Giguere (Can) 2:32.15, 2 Guylaine Cloutier (Can) 2:32.91, 3 Helen Morris (Aus) 2:33.57.

1994: 1 Samantha Riley (Aus) 2:25.53, 2 Rebecca Brown (Aus) 2:30.24, 3 Lisa Flood (Can) 2:31.85.

1998: 1 Samantha Riley (Aus) 2:27.30, 2 Courtenay Chuy (Can) 2:29.23, 3 Lauren Van Oosten (Can) 2:29.58.

100 metres Butterfly:

First held 1958, 110 yards (100.58 metres) 1958-1966

1958: 1 Beverley Bainbridge (Aus) 1:13.5, 2 Tessa Staveley (NZ) 1:14.4, 3 Margaret Iwasaki (Can) 1:15.9.

1962: 1 Mary Stewart (Can) 1:10.1, 2 Anne Cotterill (Can) 1:11.2, 3 Linda McGill (Aus) 1:11.6.

1966: 1 Elaine Tanner (Can) 1:06.8, 2 Judy Gegan (Eng) 1:09.3, 3 Ann Barner (Eng) 1:09.7.

1970: 1 Diane Lansley (Eng) 1:07.90, 2 Susan Smith (Can) 1:08.18, 3 Allyson Mabb (Aus) 1:08.67.

1974: 1 Patti Stenhouse (Can) 1:05.38, 2 Kim Wickham (Sco) 1:05.96, 3 Sandra Yost (Aus) 1:06.04.

1978: 1 Wendy Quirk (Can) 1:01.92, 2 Penny McCarthy (NZ) 1:02.27, 3 Linda Hanel (Aus) 1:02.69.

1982: 1 Lisa Curry (Aus) 1:01.22, 2 Janet Tibbits (Aus) 1:01.70, 3 Michelle MacPherson (Can) 1:01.93.

1986: 1 Caroline Cooper (Eng) 1:02.12, 2 Caroline Foot (Eng) 1:02.30, 3 Samantha Purvis (Eng) 1:02.49.

1990: 1 Lisa Curry-Kenny (Aus) 1:00.55, 2 Susie O'Neill (Aus) 1:01.03, 3 Madeleine Scarborough (Eng) 1:01.44.

Note: Curry-Kenny nee Curry.

1994: 1 Petria Thomas (Aus) 1:00.21, 2 Susie O'Neill (Aus) 1:00.24, 3 Elli Overton (Aus) 1:01.88.

1998: 1 Petria Thomas (Aus) 59.42, 2 Susie O'Neill (Aus) 59.61, 3 Kathryn Godfrey (Aus) 1:00.14.

200 metres Butterfly:
First held 1966, 220 yards (201.17 metres) 1966
1966: 1 Elaine Tanner (Can) 2:29.9, 2 Marilyn Carson (Can) 2:34.8, 3 Ann Barner (Eng) 2:35.0.
1970: 1 Maree Robinson (Aus) 2:24.67, 2 Jane Comerford (Aus) 2:24.95,
3 Allyson Mabb (Aus) 2:31.09.
1974: 1 Sandra Yost (Aus) 2:20.57, 2 Patti Stenhouse (Can) 2:20.66, 3 Gail Neall (Aus) 2:21.66.
1978: 1 Michelle Ford (Aus) 2:11.29, 2 Wendy Quirk (Can) 2:13.65, 3 Linda Hanel (Aus) 2:14.52.
1982: 1 Michelle Ford (Aus) 2:11.89, 2 Janet Tibbits (Aus) 2:13.18, 3 Ann Osgerby (Eng) 2:13.91.
1986: 1 Donna McGinnis (Can) 2:11.97, 2 Karen Phillips (Aus) 2:12.71, 3 Jill Horstead (Can) 2:14.53.
1990: 1 Hayley Lewis (Aus) 2:11.15, 2 Helen Morris (Aus) 2:11.76, 3 Nicole Redford (Aus) 2:13.53.
1994: 1 Susie O'Neill (Aus) 2:09.96, 2 Hayley Lewis (Aus) 2:12.21, 3 Julie Major (Aus) 2:12.43.
1998: 1 Susie O'Neill (Aus) 2:06.60, 2 Petria Thomas (Aus) 2:10.42, 3 Jessica Deglau (Can) 2:11.67.

200 metres Individual Medley:
First held 1970
1970: 1 Denise Langford (Aus) 2:28.89, 2 Shelagh Ratcliffe (Eng) 2:29.65, 3 Diana Rickard (Aus) 2:30.80.
1974: 1 Leslie Cliff (Can) 2:24.13, 2 Becky Smith (Can) 2:25.17, 3 Susan Hunter (NZ) 2:26.18.
1978: 1 Sharron Davies (Eng) 2:18.37, 2 Rebecca Perrott (NZ) 2:18.70, 3 Becky Smith (Can) 2:18.95.
1982: 1 Lisa Curry (Aus) 2:16.94, 2 Cheryl Gibson (Can) 2:19.91, 3 Michele Pearson (Aus) 2:20.19.
1986: 1 Suzanne Landells (Aus) 2:17.02, 2 Jean Hill (Sco) 2:17.21, 3 Jane Kerr (Can) 2:18.73.
1990: 1 Nancy Sweetnam (Can) 2:15.61, 2 Jodie Clatworthy (Aus) 2:17.10,
3 Hayley Lewis (Aus) 2:17.13.
1994: 1 Elli Overton (Aus) 2:15.59, 2 Marianne Limpert (Can) 2:15.97, 3 Nancy Sweetnam (Can) 2:16.67.
1998: 1 Marianne Limpert (Can) 2:15.05, 2 Joanne Malar (Can) 2:15.28, 3 Sue Rolph (Eng) 2:15.39.

400 metres Individual Medley:
First held 1962, 440 yards (402.34 metres) 1962-1966
1962: 1 Anita Lonsbrough (Eng) 5:38.6, 2 Linda McGill (Aus) 5:46.1, 3 Jennifer Corish (Aus) 5:53.0.

1966: 1 Elaine Tanner (Can) 5:26.3, 2 Jan Murphy (Aus) 5:28.1, 3 Jane Hughes (Can) 5:34.1.

1970: 1 Denise Langford (Aus) 5:10.74, 2 Gail Neall (Aus) 5:15.82, 3 Shelagh Ratcliffe (Eng) 5:17.89.

1974: 1 Leslie Cliff (Can) 5:01.35, 2 Becky Smith (Can) 5:03.68, 3 Susan Hunter (NZ) 5:07.20.

1978: 1 Sharron Davies (Eng) 4:52.44, 2 Becky Smith (Can) 4:57.83, 3 Cheryl Gibson (Can) 4:59.39.

1982: 1 Lisa Curry (Aus) 4:51.95, 2 Michele Pearson (Aus) 4:53.73, 3 Michelle MacPherson (Can) 4:55.09.

1986: 1 Suzanne Landells (Aus) 4:45.82, 2 Jodie Clatworthy (Aus) 4:49.67, 3 Sarah Hardcastle (Eng) 4:50.52.

1990: 1 Hayley Lewis (Aus) 4:42.65, 2 Jodie Clatworthy (Aus) 4:47.76, 3 Donna Procter (Aus) 4:47.38.

1994: 1 Elli Overton (Aus) 4:44.01, 2 Nancy Sweetnam (Can) 4:46.20, 3 Hayley Lewis (Aus) 4:46.62.

1998: 1 Joanne Malar (Can) 4:43.74, 2 Elizabeth Warden (Can) 4:47.69, 3 Jennifer Reilly (Aus) 4:48.43.

4 x 100 metres Medley Relay:

First held 1934. 3 x 100 yards (91.44 metres) 1934, 3 x 110 yards (100.58 metres) 1938-1954, 4 x 110 yards 1958-1966 (Butterfly added)

1934: 1 Canada (Margaret Hutton, Phyllis Haslam, Phyllis Dewar) 3:42.0, 2 England (Phyllis Harding, Vera Kingston, Edna Hughes) 3:43.0, 3 Scotland (Margot Hamilton, Margaret McCallum, Jean McDowall) 3:50.0.

1938: 1 England (Lorna Frampton, Doris Storey, Margery Hinton) 3:57.7, 2 South Africa (Hazel Holmes, Carla Gerke, Mollie Ryde) 4:07.5, 3 Australia (Pat Norton, Valerie George, Evelyn de Lacey) 4:10.0.

1950: 1 Australia (Judy-Joy Davies, Nancy Lyons, Marjorie McQuade) 3:53.8, 2 England (Helen Yate, Elizabeth Church, Margaret Wellington) 3:56.6, 3 Scotland (Margaret Girvan, Elenor Gordon, Elizabeth Turner) 3:58.9.

1954: 1 Scotland (Margaret McDowall, Elenor Gordon, Margaret Girvan) 3:51.0, 2 South Africa (Joan Harrison, Mary Morgan, Maggie Petzer) 3:52.7, 3 Australia (Judith Knight, Jann Grier, Lorraine Crapp) 3:55.6.

1958: 1 England (Judy Grinham, Anita Lonsbrough, Chris Gosden, Diana Wilkinson) 4:54.0, 2 Australia (Anne Nelson, Barbara Evans, Beverley Bainbridge, Dawn Fraser) 4:55.1, 3 Canada (Sara Barber, Irene Service, Margaret Iwasaki, Gladys Priestley) 5:01.6.

Note: Gergaynia Beckett and Alva Colquhoun (both Aus) swam in heat.

1962: 1 Australia (Pam Sargeant, Marguerite Ruygrok, Linda McGill, Dawn Fraser) 4:45.9, 2 England (Linda Ludgrove, Anita Lonsbrough, Anne Cotterill, Diana Wilkinson) 4:47.9, 3 Canada (Sara Barber, Alison Glendenning, Mary Stewart, Patricia Thompson) 4:48.1.

1966: 1 England (Linda Ludgrove, Diana Harris, Judy Gegan, Pauline Sillett) 4:40.6, 2 Canada (Louise Kennedy, Donna Ross, Elaine Tanner, Marion Lay) 4:44.5, 3 Australia (Allyson Mabb, Heather Saville, Jill Groeger, Lynette Bell) 4:45.7.

1970: 1 Australia (Lynn Watson, Beverley Whitfield, Allyson Mabb, Denise

Langford) 4:30.66, 2 England (Sylvia Platt, Dorothy Harrison, Diane Lansley, Katie Smith) 4:38.94, 3 Canada (Donna-Marie Gurr, Sylvie Dockerill, Susan Smith, Angela Coughlan) 4:39.65.

1974: 1 Canada (Wendy Cook, Marion Stuart, Patti Stenhouse, Gail Amundrud) 4:24.77, 2 Australia (Linda Young, Beverley Whitfield, Debra Cain, Sonya Gray) 4:30.55, 3 Scotland (Gillian Fordyce, Sandra Dickie, Kim Wickham, Morag McGlashan) 4:31.68.

1978: 1 Canada (Hélène Boivin, Marion Stuart, Wendy Quirk, Carol Klimpel) 4:15.26, 2 Australia (Debra Forster, Lisa Curry, Tracey Wickham, Rosemary Brown) 4:16.75, 3 England (Helen Gilyard, Maggie Kelly, Sue Jenner, Sharron Davies) 4:19.87.

1982: 1 Canada (Cheryl Gibson, Anne Ottenbrite, Michelle MacPherson, Maureen New) 4:14.33, 2 England (Catherine White, Suki Brownsdon, Ann Osgerby, June Croft) 4:19.04, 3 Scotland (Beverley Rose, Nicola Geddes, Cathy Finlay, Nikki Ramsay) 4:25.75.

1986: 1 England (Simone Hindmarch, Suki Brownsdon, Caroline Cooper, Nicola Fibbens) 4:13.48, 2 Canada (Allison Higson, Jane Kerr, Barb McBain, Donna McGinnis) 4:14.89, 3 Australia (Georgina Parkes, Dimity Douglas, Karen Phillips, Angela Harris) 4:15.06.

1990: 1 Australia (Nicole Livingstone, Lara Hooiveld, Lisa Curry-Kenny, Karen Van Wirdum) 4:10.87, 2 England (Joanne Deakins, Suki Brownsdon, Madeleine Scarborough, Karen Pickering) 4:11.88, 3 Canada (Lori Melien, Keltie Duggan, Nancy Sweetnam, Trish Noall) 4:12.20.

Note: Curry-Kenny nee Curry.

1994: 1 Australia (Nicole Stevenson, Samantha Riley, Petria Thomas, Karen Van Wirdum) 4:07.89, 2 England (Kathy Osher, Marie Hardiman, Alex Bennett, Karen Pickering) 4:12.83, 3 Canada (Beth Hazel, Lisa Flood, Jessica Amey, Marianne Limpert) 4:14.04.

Note: Stevenson nee Livingstone, Osher nee Read.

1998: 1 Australia (Giaan Rooney, Helen Denman, Petria Thomas, Susie O'Neill) 4:06.36, 2 Canada (Kelly Stefanyshyn, Lauren Van Oosten, Sara Albouraie, Laura Nicholls) 4:09.52, 3 England (Sarah Price, Jaime King, Caroline Foot, Sue Rolph) 4:13.96.

World records set at the Games

1930:
200 yards breaststroke (women) - 2:54.8 Celia Wolstenholme (Eng).

1958:
4 x 110 yards medley relay (men) - 4:14.2 Australia (John Monckton 1:01.9, Terry Gathercole 1:12.4, Brian Wilkinson 1:03.2, John Devitt 56.7).

110 yards freestyle (women) - 1:01.4 Dawn Fraser (Aus).

4 x 110 yards freestyle relay (women) - 4:17.4 Australia (Dawn Fraser 1:03.1, Sandra Morgan 1:03.2, Lorraine Crapp 1:05.9, Alva Colquhoun 1:05.2).

1962:
4 x 110 yards freestyle relay (men) - 3:43.9 Australia (Peter Phelps 56.4, Murray Rose 56.2, Peter Doak 55.8, David Dickson 55.5).

4 x 220 yards freestyle relay (men) - 8:13.4 Australia (Murray Rose 2:02.2, Allan Wood 2:04.2, Anthony Strahan 2:03.3, Bob Windle 2:03.7).

110 yards freestyle (women) - 59.5 Dawn Fraser (Aus).

110 yards backstroke (women) - 1:10.9 Linda Ludgrove (Eng). Note: set in heats.

110 yards backstroke (women) - 1:10.8 Pam Sergeant (Aus). Note: set in medley relay final.

220 yards backstroke (women) - 2:35.2 Linda Ludgrove (Eng). Note: set in both heats and final.

220 yards breaststroke (women) - 2:52.2 and 2:51.7 Anita Lonsbrough (Eng). Note: set in heats and final.

4 x 110 yards freestyle (women) - 4:11.0 Australia (Lynette Bell 1:04.3, Ruth Everuss 1:04.2, Robin Thorn 1:03.3, Dawn Fraser 59.2.)

4 x 110 yards medley relay (women) - 4:45.9 Australia (Pam Sergeant 1:10.8, Marguerite Ruygrok 1:24.2, Linda McGill 1:11.7, Dawn Fraser 59.2).

1966:

220 yards freestyle (men) - 1:57.3 Mike Wenden (Aus). Note: set in relay.

440 yards freestyle (men) - 4:15.0 Bob Windle (Aus).

220 yards backstroke (men) - 2:12.0 Peter Reynolds (Aus).

110 yards breaststroke - 1:08.5 and 1:08.2 Ian O'Brien (Aus). Note: set in heats and final.

220 yards breaststroke - 2:28.0 Ian O'Brien (Aus). Note: set in heats.

440 yards individual medley (men) - 4:50.8 Peter Reynolds (Aus).

4 x 110 yards freestyle relay (men) - 3:35.6 Australia (Mike Wenden 53.8, John Ryan 53.7, David Dickson 53.7, Bob Windle 54.4).

4 x 220 yards freestyle relay (men) - 7:59.5 Australia (Mike Wenden 1:57.3, Peter Reynolds 2:01.9, David Dickson 2:01.4, Bob Windle 1:58.9).

440 yards freestyle (women) - 4:39.6 and 4:38.8 Kathy Wainwright (Aus). Note: set in heats and final.

220 yards backstroke (women) - 2:28.5 Linda Ludgrove (Eng).

220yards butterfly (women) - 2:29.9 Elaine Tanner (Can).

4 x 110 yards freestyle relay (women) - 4:10.8 Canada (Elaine Tanner, Jane Hughes, Louise Kennedy, Marion Lay).

4 x 110 yards medley relay (women) - 4:40.6 England (Linda Ludgrove 1:09.3, Diana Harris 1:19.3, Judy Gegan 1:08.7, Paula Sillett 1:03.3).

1970:

4 x 200 metres freestyle relay (men) - 7:50.77 Australia (Greg Rogers 1:57.28, William Devenish 1:58.61, Graham White 1:59.12, Mike Wenden 1:55.76).

800 metres freestyle (women) - 9:02.45 Karen Moras (Aus).

1974:

800 metres freestyle (men) - 8:15.88 Steven Holland (Aus).

Note: set in 1500 metres freestyle final.

1978:

400 metres freestyle (women) - 4:08.45 Tracey Wickham (Aus).

800 metres freestyle (women) - 8:24.62 Tracey Wickham (Aus).

1990:

100 metres breaststroke (men) - 1:01.49 Adrian Moorhouse (Eng).

1994:

800 metres freestyle (men) - 7:46.00 Kieren Perkins (Aus).

Note: set in 1500 metres freestyle final.

1500 metres freestyle (men) - 14:41.66 Kieren Perkins (Aus).

1998:

4 x 200 metres freestyle (men) - 7:11.86 Australia (Ian Thorpe 1:47.48, Daniel Kowalski 1:47.81, Matt Dunn 1:49.15, Michael Klim 1:47.42).

AQUATICS - SYNCHRONISED SWIMMING

Clean sweep for Canada

Synchronised swimming made its Games debut in Edinburgh in 1986 and Canada maintained an unbeaten record in Kuala Lumpur in 1998, having now won all eight gold medals since the sport was introduced. Sylvie Fréchette, winner of the first solo gold medal, retained her title in 1990, and she was to go on to be World champion and then Olympic champion in the next two years. Lisa Alexander became a double gold-medallist in 1994 when partnering Erin Woodley in the Duet after winning the solo title.

Solo:
1986: 1 Sylvie Fréchette (Can) 199.50pts, 2 Jackie Dodd (Eng) 188.05, 3 Katie Stadlier (NZ) 175.08.
1990: 1 Sylvie Fréchette (Can) 196.68, 2 Kerry Shacklock (Eng) 184.79, 3 Semon Rohloff (Aus) 173.32.
1994: 1 Lisa Alexander (Can) 189.4835, 2 Kerry Shacklock (Eng) 183.9717, 3 Celeste Ferraris (Aus) 172.6626.
1998: 1 Valérie Hould-Marchand (Can) 93.640, 2 Naomi Young (Aus) 90.933, 3 Gayle Adamson (Eng) 87.564.

Duet:
1986: 1 Michelle Cameron & Carolyn Waldo (Can) 199.54, 2 Jackie Dodd & Nicola Shearn (Eng) 186.59, 3 Donna Rankin & Lisa Lieschke (Aus) 173.00.
1990: 1 Kathy Glen & Christine Larsen (Can) 191.23, 2 Kerry Shacklock & Sarah Northey (Eng) 185.435, 3 Lisa Lieschke & Semon Rohloff (Aus) 175.765.
1994: 1 Lisa Alexander & Erin Woodley (Can) 188.0894, 2 Kerry Shacklock & Laila Vakil (Eng) 182.6803, 3 Monique Downes & Celeste Ferraris (Aus) 167.1646.
1998: 1 Jacinthe Taillon & Kasia Kulesza (Can) 93.284, 2 Naomi Young & Irena Olevsky (Aus) 91.077, 3 Katherine Hooper & Adele Carlsen (Eng) 87.130.

AQUATICS - DIVING

Jenny makes it a Family Affair

Commonwealth divers have not enjoyed anything like the same measure of success in Olympic Games competition as have their swimming team-mates. There had been silver and bronze medals for English women in 1912 and 1920 but nothing comparable until Irene MacDonald, of Canada, won a springboard bronze in 1956.

In 1960 Brian Phelps, at the age of 16, and Liz Ferris each won bronze medals for Great Britain, and Phelps was to go on to become a quadruple Commonwealth champion. Much the most resounding achievement - and from an entirely unexpected source - came from Evan Stewart, of Zimbabwe, who won the World title at one-metre spring-board in 1994. The Canadian, Sylvie Bernier, had been Olympic spring-board champion in 1984, though this was a Games boycotted by many East European countries.

When the Australian Jenny Donnet won the springboard gold medal

Manchester 2002
THE XVII COMMONWEALTH GAMES

at the Brisbane Games of 1982, which she followed up again in 1986, it completed a family hat-trick which in many ways epitomised the family nature of The Commonwealth Games. Jenny was the daughter of Barbara McAuley, who had won at highboard in 1954. Barbara's sister, Irene Donnet, in turn had been champion at springboard in Sydney in 1938, thus making a family dynasty of champions lasting almost half a century.

The men's diving competition has been dominated by a host of double gold-medallists. Amongst these were English prodigy Phelps in 1962, who had come second four years previously at the age of just 14, Chris Snode of England in 1978 and Australia's Don Wagstaffe, who followed up his double in Edinburgh in 1970 with another four years later in Christchurch, New Zealand.

Beverley Boys of Canada is the most successful female competitor of all time, winning six medals from her debut as a 15-year old in 1966, including a double gold in 1970.

Evan Stewart of Zimbabwe won his country's first ever aquatics medals in 1994 with silver in the 3-metre springboard and bronze in the 1-metre and then went one better in 1998 in the 1-metre to take Zimbabwe's first gold.

DIVING MEDALLISTS

MEN

Springboard:
1930: 1 Alfred Phillips (Can) 147pts, 2 Cyril Kennett (Can) 138, 3 Arthur Stott (Can) 127.
1934: 1 J. Briscoe Ray (Eng) 117.12, 2 Doug Tomalin (Eng) 110.50, 3 Harry Class (Can) 106.57.
1938: 1 Ron Masters (Aus) 126.36, 2 Doug Tomalin (Eng) 124.78, 3 George Athans (Can) 117.90.
1950: 1 George Athans (Can) 169.21, 2 Peter Heatly (Sco) 168.80, 3 Jack Stewart (NZ) 168.17.
1954: 1 Peter Heatly (Sco) 146.76, 2 Tony Turner (Eng) 145.27, 3 Jack Stewart (NZ) 144.98.
1958: 1 Keith Collin (Eng) 126.78, 2 Bill Patrick (Can) 124.62, 3 David Tarsey (Eng) 118.81.
1962: 1 Brian Phelps (Eng) 154.14, 2 Thomas Dinsley (Can) 147.22, 3 Ernest Meissner (Can) 145.03.
1966: 1 Brian Phelps (Eng) 154.55, Don Wagstaff (Aus) 150.17, 3 Chris Robb (Aus) 136.52.
1970: 1 Don Wagstaff (Aus) 557.73, 2 Ken Sully (Can) 497.37, 3 Ronald Friesen (Can) 495.90.
1974: 1 Don Wagstaff (Aus) 531.54, 2 Scott Cranham (Can) 509.61, 3 Trevor

Simpson (Eng) 489.69.

1978: 1 Chris Snode (Eng) 643.83, 2 Scott Cranham (Can) 595.53, 3 Don Wagstaff (Aus) 572.16.

1982: 1 Chris Snode (Eng) 631.38, 2 Stephen Foley (Aus) 592.08, 3 Mark Graham (NZ) 551.46.

1986: 1 Shaun Panayi (Aus) 600.87, 2 John Nash (Can) 647.64, 3 Craig Rogerson (Aus) 620.43.

1990:

1-Metre: 1 Russell Butler (Aus) 583.65, 2 David Bedard (Can) 547.35, 3 Simon McCormack (Aus) 546.87.

3-Metre: 1 Craig Rogerson (Aus) 594.84, 2 Mark Rourke (Can) 569.97, 3 Larry Flewwelling (Can) 569.79.

1994:

1-Metre: 1 Jason Napper (Can) 364.08, 2 Michael Murphy (Aus) 363.18, 3 Evan Stewart (Zim) 357.78.

3-Metre: 1 Michael Murphy (Aus) 671.76, 2 Evan Stewart (Zim) 625.86, 3 Jason Napper (Aus) 572.85.

1998:

1-metre: 1 Evan Stewart (Zim) 384.66, 2 Dean Pullar (Aus) 381.66, 3 Robert Newbery (Aus) 369.15.

3-metre: 1 Shannon Roy (Aus) 608.37, 2 Dean Pullar (Aus) 598.14, 3 Tony Ali (Eng) 587.49.

Highboard:

1930: 1 Alfred Phillips (Can) 90.6, 2 Samuel Walker (Can) 83.3, 3 Terry Scott (Eng) 82.3.

1934: 1 Tommy Mather (Eng) 83.83, 2 Doug Tomalin (Eng) 83.63, 3 Louis Marchant (Eng) 70.64.

1938: 1 Doug Tomalin (Eng) 108.74, 2 Ron Masters (Aus) 102.87, 3 George Athans (Can) 98.93.

1950: 1 Peter Heatly (Sco) 156.07, 2 George Athans (Can) 145.36, 3 Frank Murphy (Aus) 129.40.

1954: 1 Bill Patrick (Can) 142.70, 2 Kevin Newell (Aus) 142.06, 3 Peter Heatly (Sco) 141.32.

1958: 1 Peter Heatly (Sco) 147.79, 2 Brian Phelps (Eng) 144.49, 3 Ray Cann (Eng) 138.50.

1962: 1 Brian Phelps (Eng) 168.35, 2 Graham Deuble (Aus) 151.00, 3 Tony Kitcher (Eng) 150.81.

1966: 1 Brian Phelps (Eng) 164.57, 2 Don Wagstaff (Aus) 148.44, 3 Chris Robb (Aus) 141.68.

1970: 1 Don Wagstaff (Aus) 485.73, 2 Philip Drew (Eng) 429.24, 3 Andy Gill (Eng) 421.47.

1974: 1 Don Wagstaff (Aus) 490.74, 2 Andrew Jackomos (Aus) 472.47, 3 Scott Cranham (Can) 460.98.

1978: 1 Chris Snode (Eng) 538.98, 2 Ken Armstrong (Can) 534.99, 3 Scott Cranham (Can) 512.37.

1982: 1 Chris Snode (Eng) 588.54, 2 Stephen Foley (Aus) 524.55, 3 John Nash (Can) 523.41.

1986: 1 Craig Rogerson (Aus) 600.87, 2 David Bedard (Can) 576.81, 3 Bobby Morgan (Wal) 561.54.

1990: 1 Bobby Morgan (Wal) 639.84, 2 David Bedard (Can) 555.54, 3 Bruno-Michel Fournier (Can) 544.50.

1994: 1 Michael Murphy (Aus) 614.70, 2 Bobby Morgan (Wal) 585.96, 3 Claude Villeneuve (Can) 581.22.

1998: 1 Alexandre Despatie (Can) 652.11, 2 Robert Newbery (Aus) 605.61, 3 Leon Taylor (Eng) 603.54.

WOMEN

Springboard:

1930: 1 Oonagh Whitsett (SA) 90.1, 2 Doris Ogilvie (Can) 89.7, 3 Mollie Bailey (Can) 88.7.

1934: 1 Judith Moss (Can) 62.27, 2 Lesley Thompson (Aus) 60.49, 3 Doris Ogilvie (Can) 57.00.

1938: 1 Irene Donnet (Aus) 91.18, 2 Lynda Adams (Can) 88.27, 3 Marie Sharkey (Can) 81.66.

1950: 1 Edna Child (Eng) 126.58, 2 Noeline MacLean (Aus) 124.59, 3 Lynda Hunt (Can) 115.38.

Note: Hunt nee Adams.

1954: 1 Ann Long (Eng) 128.26, 2 Barbara McAulay (Aus) 127.74, 3 Irene MacDonald (Can) 126.19.

1958: 1 Charmian Welsh (Eng) 118.81, 2 Irene MacDonald (Can) 117.01, 3 Liz Ferris (Eng) 113.30.

1962: 1 Susan Knight (Aus) 134.72, 2 Liz Ferris (Eng) 132.74, 3 Lorraine McArthur (Aus) 125.13.

1966: 1 Kathy Rowlatt (Eng) 147.10, 2 Beverley Boys (Can) 134.92, 3 Susan Knight (Aus) 134.90.

1970: 1 Beverley Boys (Can) 432.87, 2 Elizabeth Carruthers (Can) 391.20, 3 Gaye Morley (Aus) 389.04.

1974: 1 Cindy Shatto (Can) 430.88, 2 Beverley Boys (Can) 426.93, 3 Teri York (Can) 413.83.

1978: 1 Janet Nutter (Can) 477.33, 2 Beverley Boys (Can) 469.95, 3 Eniko Kiefer (Can) 447.42.

1982: 1 Jenny Donnet (Aus) 484.65, 2 Sylvie Bernier (Can) 478.83, 3 Valerie Beddoe (Aus) 446.63.

1986: 1 Debbie Fuller (Can) 513.09, 2 Jenny Donnet (Aus) 494.52, 3 Kathy Kelemen (Can) 484.65.

1990:

1-Metre: 1 Mary Depiero (Can) 443.28, 2 Tracy Cox (Zim) 423.93, 3 Peta Taylor (Aus) 418.71.

3-Metre: 1 Jenny Donnet (Aus) 491.79, 2 Barbara Bush (Can) 458.43, 3 Nicky Cooney (NZ) 457.29.

1994:

1-Metre: 1 Annie Pelletier (Can) 279.66, 2 Jodie Rogers (Aus) 252.72, 3 Mary Depiero (Can) 245.34.

3-Metre: 1 Annie Pelletier (Can) 529.86, 2 Paige Gordon (Can) 529.08, 3 Jodie

Rogers (Aus) 474.81.

1998:

1-metre: 1 Chantelle Mitchell (Aus) 271.56, 2 Blythe Hartley (Can) 248.28, 3 Eryn Bulmer (Can) 239.40.

3-metre: 1 Eryn Bulmer (Can) 515.88, 2 Chantelle Mitchell (Aus) 506.52, 3 Myriam Boileau (Can) 480.57.

Highboard:

1930: 1 Pearl Stoneham (Can) 39.3, 2 Helen McCormack (Can) 38.3.

Note: only two competitors.

1934: 1 Elizabeth Macready (Eng) 30.74, 2 Lesley Thompson (Aus) 27.64, 3 Cecily Cousens (Eng) 27.36.

1938: 1 Lurline Hook (Aus) 36.47, 2 Lynda Adams (Can) 36.39, 3 Irene Donnet (Aus) 34.57.

1950: 1 Edna Child (Eng) 70.89, 2 Gwen Fawcett (Aus) 65.64, 3 Noeline MacLean (Aus) 59.93.

1954: 1 Barbara McAulay (Aus) 86.55, 2 Eunice Miller (Eng) 79.86, 3 Ann Long (Eng) 79.53.

1958: 1 Charmian Welsh (Eng) 77.23, 2 Ann Long (Eng) 73.69, 3 Molly Wieland (Eng) 65.82.

1962: 1 Susan Knight (Aus) 101.15, 2 Margaret Austen (Eng) 98.93, 3 Patricia Plowman (Aus) 91.79.

1966: 1 Joy Newman (Eng) 98.87, 2 Robyn Bradshaw (Aus) 98.85, 3 Beverley Boys (Can) 97.21.

1970: 1 Beverley Boys (Can) 352.95, 2 Nancy Robertson (Can) 350.49, 3 Shelagh Burrow (Eng) 330.63.

1974: 1 Beverley Boys (Can) 361.95, 2 Beverley Williams (Eng) 352.14, 3 Madeleine Barnett (Aus) 339.30.

1978: 1 Linda Cuthbert (Can) 397.44, 2 Valerie McFarlane (Aus) 383.40, 3 Janet Nutter (Can) 374.67.

1982: 1 Valerie Beddoe (Aus) 404.16, 2 Jennifer McArton (Can) 390.21, 3 Kathy Kelemen (Can) 359.31.

Note: Beddoe nee McFarlane.

1986: 1 Debbie Fuller (Can) 431.61, 2 Valerie Beddoe (Aus) 414.78, 3 Julie Kent (Aus) 411.13.

1990: 1 Anna Dacyshyn (Can) 391.68, 2 April Adams (Aus) 380.49, 3 Paige Gordon (Can) 380.43.

1994: 1 Anne Montminy (Can) 428.58, 2 Paige Gordon (Can) 414.36, 3 Myriam Boileau (Can) 411.21.

1998: 1 Vyninka Arlow (Aus) 456.48, 2 Myriam Boileau (Can) 449.19, 3 Anne Montminy (Can) 443.46.

ATHLETICS

A cavalcade of great champions.
A host of marvellous moments.

Athletics has always remained the pre-eminent Games sport. More than 50 of the winners over the years have also been Olympic champions, and when the first Empire Games were held in 1930 it was two of the track gold-medallists from the Olympic Games of two years previously who were the most famous names among the 400 or so competitors who gathered in Hamilton, Ontario, to contest six different sports.

Percy Williams, of Canada, had won the Olympic 100 and 200 metres. Lord Burghley, of England, had won the Olympic 400 metres hurdles. In Hamilton Williams, hampered by injury, was restricted to a single victory in the 100 yards. Lord Burghley was the most successful athlete of the meeting, gathering gold medals in two hurdles races and a relay.

Over the years they have been emulated by a host of such icons of the sport as Jack Lovelock, Herb Elliott, Peter Snell, Lynn Davies, David Hemery, Kip Keino, Don Quarrie, Daley Thompson, Steve Cram,

THE COMMONWEALTH GAMES

Linford Christie, Colin Jackson, Steve Ovett and Donovan Bailey, and by Marjorie Jackson-Nelson, Yvette Williams, Betty Cuthbert, Mary Rand, Mary Peters, Merlene Ottey, Sally Gunnell, Liz McColgan, Cathy Freeman and Maria Mutola.

Between them, this elite reflects the marvellous diversity of the Games, representing 10 different countries and four continents, and yet there have been numerous other moments of glorious triumph and noble failure at the Games which remain steadfast even in the memory of those far too young to have been made aware of them at the time that they happened. Nothing symbolises more graphically the extremes of fortune than the Bannister-v-Landy mile and the marathon collapse of Jim Peters - and both these events occurred within an hour or so one afternoon almost half-a-century ago.

Other great athletes like Ron Clarke, Sebastian Coe and Jonathan Edwards do not figure at all in the list of winners. Clarke, who broke a multitude of distance-running records, came desperately close, as he had at the Olympics, with four silver medals, and his Scots conqueror at 10,000 metres in Edinburgh in 1970 was the first to apologise for inflicting yet another championship defeat on him. Coe, the most sublime middle-distance runner of his generation, missed the Games of 1978 and 1982, fell ill in the heats in 1986, and was a shadow of himself in 1990. Edwards has won World and Olympic titles and broken the World record but has twice lost the Commonwealth Games triple-jump by margins of three centimetres or less.

The virtues of youthful exuberance and dogged maturity have been served well. A Canadian, Sam Richardson, won the 1934 long jump at 16, while Cathy Freeman achieved her first major success for Australia at the same age as a relay runner at the 1990 Games. A stalwart 42-year-old Englishman, Jack Holden, threw away his rain-sodden shoes, fought off an attack by an excited dog, and won the 1950 marathon. Another English competitor, Judy Oakes, was 3rd in the shot in 1978 and kept coming back in between temporary retirements to win on three further occasions up to the age of 40.

As the cornerstone of the Games, athletics has manfully carried the burden of vital commercial success in more recent years. Despite the widespread boycott in 1986, the standard of performance was remarkably high. Then, when the fiscal attractions of the increasingly dominant Grand Prix circuit might have dictated otherwise, the big names rallied round - Ottey, McColgan, Christie, Fredericks, Boldon - to ensure that the successive Games of the 1990s satisfied the demands of a media more often enraptured by idolatry than by the simplistic ideal of competing for the sake of it.

So the Games survive, and that would have seemed unlikely in any form when they were last held in Britain in 1986 under leaden Edinburgh skies and with all the great Caribbean sprinters and Kenyan distance-men absent under political duress. Who, then, could possibly have imagined such a wondrous celebration of athletics as was to take place in Malaysia 12 years later ? Gold medals in athletics for 13 different countries, including three for the reinstated South Africa and the first ever for Barbados, Lesotho, Malaysia and Mozambique, and other medals for such as Cameroon, Mauritius, Zambia and Zimbabwe.

Leading countries:

England 158 gold medals; Australia 138; Canada 63; Kenya 37; New Zealand 30; Jamaica 24; South Africa 24; Scotland 17; Wales 13; Nigeria 10; Northern Ireland 7; Bahamas 4; Ghana 4; Trinidad & Tobago 4; Tanzania 3; Pakistan 2; Barbados, Bermuda, Cyprus, Fiji, Guyana (as British Guiana), India, Lesotho, Malaysia, Mozambique, Namibia, Sri Lanka (as Ceylon), Zambia, Zimbabwe (as Northern Rhodesia) 1 each.

Leading gold-medallists:

7 Marjorie Jackson-Nelson (Aus) 1950-54, Raelene Boyle (Aus) 1970-82
6 Don Quarrie (Jam) 1970-78
5 Decima Norman (Aus) 1938, Valerie Sloper-Young (NZ) 1958-74, Pam Kilborn-Ryan (Aus) 1962-70, Sally Gunnell (Eng) 1986-94
4 Hendrik "Harry" Hart (SA) 1930-34, Yvette Williams (NZ) 1950-54, Charles Asati (Ken) 1970-74, Allan Wells (Sco) 1978-82
3 Shirley Strickland-de la Hunty (Aus) 1950, Keith Gardner (Jam) 1954-58, Sonia Lannaman (Eng) 1974-82, Gael Mulhall-Martin (Aus) 1978-86, Judy Oakes (Eng) 1978-98, Kathy Smallwood-Cook (Eng) 1978-86, Debbie Flintoff-King (Aus) 1982-90, Merlene Ottey (Jam) 1982-90, Angela Taylor-Issajenko (Can) 1982-90.

A total of 15 women and five men have won three or more gold medals.

Leading medallists:
(G Gold, S Silver, B Bronze)

9 Boyle 7G 2S
8 Denise Robertson-Boyd (Aus) 2G 3S 3B 1974-1982
7 Jackson-Nelson 7G, Sloper-Young 5G 1S 1B, Smallwood-Cook 3G 3S 1B, Taylor-Issajenko 3G 2S 2B, Flintoff-King 3G 3S 1B
6 Hart 4G 1S 1B, Quarrie 6G, Mulhall-Martin 3G 3S, Oakes 3G 2S 1B,

Wells 4G 1S 1B, Gunnell 5G 1S
5 Aileen Meagher (Can) 1G 3S 1B 1934-38, Norman 5G, Strickland-de la Hunty 3G 2S, Williams 4G 1S, Gardner 3G 1S 1B, George Kerr (Jam) 2G 1S 2B 1958-66, Les Mills (NZ) 1G 3S 1B 1958-70, Kilborn-Ryan 5G, Jean Roberts (Aus) 3S 2B 1962-74, Ed Roberts (Tri) 1G 3S 1B 1966-70, Asati 4G 1B, Lannaman 3G 2S, Cameron Sharp (Sco) 1G 4B 1978-86, Ben Johnson (Can) 2G 2S 1B 1982-86, Ottey 3G 1S 1B, Paula Thomas-Dunn (Eng) 1G 2S 2B (1986-94).

A total of 19 women and 10 men have won five or more medals.

World records set at the Games

MEN:
440 yards hurdles - 49.73 Gert Potgieter (SA), Cardiff, 22 July 1958.
440 yards - 45.08 Wendell Mottley (Tri), Kingston, Jamaica, 11 August 1966.
Note: not officially ratified.
4 x 440 yards relay - 3:02.8 Trinidad & Tobago (Lennox Yearwood, Kent Bernard, Ed Roberts, Wendell Mottley), Kingston, Jamaica, 13 August 1966.
1500 metres - 3:32.16 Filbert Bayi (Tan), Christchurch, 2 February 1974.

WOMEN:
220 yards - 25.0 Eileen Hiscock (Eng), London, 7 August 1934.
220 yards - 24.9 Decima Norman (Aus), Sydney, 10 February 1938.
Note: set in the heats.
220 yards - 24.9 Aileen Meagher (Can), Sydney, 10 February 1938.
Note: set in the heats.
220 yards - 24.5 Decima Norman (Aus), Sydney, 10 February 1938.
100 yards - 10.8 Marjorie Jackson (Aus), Auckland, 4 February 1950.
Note: set in the heats.
100 yards - 10.8 Marjorie Jackson (Aus), Auckland, 6 February 1950.
220 yards - 24.3 Marjorie Jackson (Aus), Auckland, 9 February 1950.
220 yards - 24.0 Marjorie Nelson nee Jackson (Aus), Vancouver, 5 August 1954.
Javelin - 57.40 (188ft 4in) Anna Pazera (Aus), Cardiff, 24 July 1958.
4 x 110 yards relay - 45.37 England (Madeleine Weston, Dorothy Hyman, June Paul, Heather Young), Cardiff, 26 July 1958.
400 metres - 51.02 Marilyn Neufville (Jam), Edinburgh, 23 July 1970.

Highlights - Games by Games

1930: Bobby Robinson's dream becomes golden reality

The Civic Stadium in Hamilton, Ontario, was full to capacity with a crowd of 20,000 for the opening ceremony of the Games and the first of the athletics events. The Canadian sprint hero, Percy Williams, took the oath of allegiance on behalf of the athletes but subsequently ran only in the 100 yards, where he set a fast time of 9.6 in the heats but severely pulled a muscle when leading by a long way towards the finish of the final and limped home, still the winner, in 9.9. Williams had set a World record of 10.3 for 100 metres just before the Games and might have threatened the 100 yards record, had he been fit.

Lord Burghley won his speciality event, the 440 yards hurdles, ahead of three other Englishmen, and a week later added further gold medals in the 120 yards hurdles and the 4 x 440 yards relay. The mile title was also won for England - but by a Welshman, Reg Thomas, who had taken the silver medal two days earlier at 880 yards behind a future Olympic champion, Tom Hampson. Wales sent no athletes to Canada, but Thomas had happily accepted England's invitation instead.

The field events were generally modest by World standards - as they were to remain so at the Games for much of the next 70 years - but there were two winning performances of genuine merit by Vic Pickard, of Canada, in the pole vault and Stan Lay, of New Zealand, in the javelin. There was also an impressive demonstration of versatility by the South African, Hendrik "Harry" Hart, who won both the shot and the discus and was 3rd in the javelin. The hammer was notable for a win by the 1924 Olympic bronze-medallist, Malcolm Nokes, from Bill Britton, representing the Irish Free State in their one and only Games appearance, and a Canadian, Jack Cameron, who was 48 years of age and had competed in the 1920 Olympics.

The widely-acclaimed success of the Games in Hamilton, for which their creator, Bobby Robinson, had been the organising committee chairman, led to the formation of the British Empire Games Federation two years later, and after initially awarding the next Games to South Africa the Federation officials showed commendable concern for human rights by asking England to take them on instead.

1934: Lovelock lights up a grey summer's day in London

India, Jamaica, Rhodesia and Trinidad & Tobago made their first Games appearances at the White City Stadium, in North London, and a Jamaican-born medical student of British descent, Bernard Prendergast, won a bronze medal in the discus. For the most part, though, English athletes dominated - at least on the track - with nine wins for their men and four for their women, as the latter were making their athletics debut. The most impressive victories were those of Godfrey Rampling at 440 yards and New Zealand's Jack Lovelock in the mile.

Rampling set a British best performance - as yet, there was no official recognition for British records - with a time of 48.0sec for the quarter-mile which was remarkable running on the notoriously slow White City cinders, and his team-mate, Bill Roberts, took the silver medal after only a handful of races at the distance, having been nurtured on Northern handicap events. Lovelock, from New Zealand, was a Rhodes Scholar at Oxford University, and he had set a World record mile of 4:07.6 the previous year and was to win the Olympic 1500 metres in World-record time in 1936.

Another winner who later broke a World record was the Australian, Jack Metcalfe, in the triple jump (which was then described, more accurately as the hop step and jump). Metcalfe cleared 51ft 3½in (15.63m), and such was the calibre of the performance that his Games record was not beaten for 24 years. Metcalfe, truly one of the very finest of Empire-produced athletes in the prewar era, set a World record of 15.78m in 1935, then placed 3rd at the next year's Berlin Olympics and won the Empire title again in 1938.

The silver medal in the London triple jump went to a 16-year-old Canadian prodigy, Sam Richardson, who also won the long jump but never achieved such a level of performance again. Hendrik "Harry" Hart ensured himself a permanent place in Games history with another double in the shot and discus (and was also 2nd in the javelin).

England won six of the nine women's events, including double successes for Eileen Hiscock in the sprints and for Gladys Lunn in the unlikely pairing of the 880 yards and the javelin. The best of the women athletes, though, was Marjorie Clark, of South Africa, who had twice broken the World record for the high jump and won that event and the 80 metres hurdles.

ATHLETICS

1938: "Dashing Dessie" bowls the maidens over

Against all expectations the odd D-shaped track laid on the close-cropped grass of the Sydney Cricket Grounds turned out to be exceptionally fast, and there was a host of record-breaking performances. The women, having slipped in unobtrusively four years earlier, took centre stage this time in the person of the Australian sprinter, Decima Norman, who was joyfully dubbed by the local media as "Dashing Dessie" or "The Flying Handful". Young Dessie certainly had plenty in hand on the opposition because she won the 100, the 220 and the long jump by wide margins and then figured in two decisive sprint-relay wins.

England's Cyril Holmes also won both sprints in World-class times and his team-mate, Bill Roberts, narrowly took the 440 from the Canadian, Bill Fritz. There was no doubt about the 880 result as Pat Boot, of New Zealand, won by more than two seconds, but like so many others Boot's highly promising athletics career would be cut short when war broke out the following year. A few, like Roberts, managed to resume competition eight years after the Sydney Games, and South Africa's marathon winner, Johannes Coleman, was to finish 4th in the 1948 Olympics, while high-jump champion Dorothy Odam continued to compete at literally the highest level for another 16 years!

The outstanding performances came from the men's hurdles winners as Tom Lavery, of South Africa, ran 14.0sec for 120 yards hurdles, though this was declared to be wind-assisted in the opinion of the officials, and Canada's John Loaring, who had won the silver medal at the Berlin Olympics, took the 440 hurdles by the proverbial street in what appeared to be his first race in the event for almost 18 months. Another Canadian, Hal Brown, achieved an even more remarkable victory, having been sent to Sydney as a javelin-thrower and then beating his twin brother, among others, to win the long jump instead.

1950: Jack returns after 16 years to win barefoot in the rain

The projected 1942 Empire Games would have taken place in Montreal, but when the series was eventually resumed eight years later the chosen venue was Auckland. With a sea voyage entailing an absence of almost four months for competitors from the home countries, that inevitably meant that many of them were forced to decline their invitations. Leading Caribbean sprinters like Trinidad-born McDonald Bailey and the Jamaicans, Herb McKenley and Arthur Wint, also missed out when their countries did not enter teams.

Defying the years, Jack Holden won the marathon at the age of 42 despite not only having to throw away his sodden canvas shoes and run the last 10 miles barefoot and bleeding, but also having to fend off the unwelcome attentions of a pursuing Great Dane. Holden had competed in the 1934 Games at six miles and had been one of England's finest cross-country runners throughout the 1930s. Like his team-mate, John Parlett, at 880 yards, Holden was also to win a European Championships title later in 1950.

Don Finlay, now 40, and Tom Lavery, 38, had been the high hurdles champions in 1934 and 1938 respectively and appeared again, though beaten by two Australians on this occasion. Another Australian, Keith Pardon, repeated his hammer-throw silver medal of 12 years before. The 440 hurdles went to Ceylon's Olympic silver-medallist, Duncan White, who had run in the sprints in Sydney. Dorothy Tyler (nee Odam), still only 29, won her second Empire high-jump title and was by no means finished yet.

In World-class terms the most notable performances were achieved in women's events. Marjorie Jackson, who had beaten the legendary Fanny Blankers-Koen the previous year, won four gold medals in the sprints and relays, setting three World records in the process, and New Zealand's versatile Yvette Williams won the long jump and would have broken the World record in that event had her feet not slipped in the wet sand and caused her to fall backwards.

1954: Bannister and Landy run the "Mile Of The Century"

It was tough on Bill Parnell, defending his Empire mile title in front of his fellow-Canadians in Vancouver. Parnell had won in 4:11.0 in Auckland. In May of 1954 Roger Bannister ran his historic 3:59.4 on the Iffley Road track at Oxford. The following month John Landy, of Australia, reduced the World record to 3:57.9 in Finland.

World records had also been set by three other Empire athletes in the months leading up to the Empire Games. Hec Hogan, of Australia, had run 9.3sec for 100 yards. Jim Peters had run the fastest-ever marathon for the fourth time in two years. Yvette Williams, who was now also the Olympic champion, had beaten the long-jump record which had been held by Fanny Blankers-Koen for 10 years and had set Empire records in the shot and discus. Among other Empire records to fall in the field events, that for the pole vault had been improved after 23 years, and for the long jump after 48 years!

These Vancouver Games were the most significant of the 24-year-long series. There were 252 athletes from 23 countries. Among the men's

teams were the Bahamas, Gold Coast, India, Jamaica, Kenya, Nigeria, Pakistan, Trinidad & Tobago and Uganda. Women athletes were sent for the first time by Bermuda, Fiji and Northern Rhodesia. At long last the Games were truly reflecting the ethnic diversity of what was now called the British Empire & Commonwealth.

As important in the long term as the Worldwide-acclaimed "Mile Of The Century" was the fact that Africans took all three medals in the men's high jump, with the winner, Emmanuel Ifeajuna, setting the first ever Empire record by a black African athlete, and though Kenyan distance-runners made an auspicious debut at these Games it was understandably thought at the time that it would be in the high jump that African athletes would make their greatest impact in future Olympic competition. The pioneering Kenyans included Nyandika Maiyoro, 4th behind an English trio at three miles, and Lazaro Chepkwony, 7th at six miles.

Bannister beat Landy in the mile, and the critical moment was forever captured in one of the most famous of all sporting photographs, showing Landy looking to his left after leading for much of the race and Bannister sweeping past into the home straight on Landy's right. Almost simultaneously, Jim Peters was driving himself relentlessly on in the heatwave marathon despite leading by a quarter-of-an-hour or so and was then overcome by the conditions as he entered the stadium and gruesomely collapsed time and again before being lifted up and carried away to hospital. Almost forgotten now, the winner was Joe McGhee, of Scotland, who had himself stopped out on the course but got up again when he heard that Peters had failed to finish.

There was a first Caribbean win in the sprints for Mike Agostini, of Trinidad, at 100 yards and in the high hurdles for Keith Gardner, of Jamaica. Canada only just beat Nigeria for the 4 x 110 yards relay title, and Nigerians were also 2nd in the long jump and triple jump, where England's Ken Wilmshurst was the double winner. Pakistani athletes won the hammer and placed 2nd and 3rd in the javelin - though this was an enticing promise which was not to be fulfilled over the years.

Prolific medallists dominated the women's events. Marjorie Nelson (nee Jackson), who had won both sprints at the 1952 Olympics, added three more gold medals to her collection and set another World record in the 220. Yvette Williams won the long jump, shot and discus. Dorothy Tyler, at 34, took 2nd place in the high jump behind 18-year-old Thelma Hopkins, representing Northern Ireland. Tyler had set a World record in 1939; Hopkins would do so in 1956.

1958: Even three World records are put in the shade

On the newly-laid track at the Cardiff Arms Park rugby ground there were three Englishmen, three Australians, two New Zealanders and a Scotsman in the mile final - for the first half of the race. In the closing half-mile there was only one man in it. The winning time for Australia's Herb Elliott was actually a shade slower than Bannister's Games record, but the manner of the victory was imperious.

Two days later Elliott made the largest single improvement on the World mile record for 76 years when he ran 3:54.5 in Dublin. The following month, in Sweden, he beat the 1500 metres record by more than two seconds. At the 1960 Olympics he was to win the 1500 metres in a World-record time of 3:35.6. He never ran another international race after that year. Oh, and by the way, he also won the 880 in Cardiff. Unquestionably, he remains one of the greatest of all middle-distance runners … and many who saw him in action, this writer included, would say he was the greatest.

Even a marvellous World record at 440 hurdles by Gert Potgieter, of South Africa, was overshadowed by Elliott. Yet Potgieter's achievement was of the very highest order, as he coped with bizarre conditions which may even have produced a wind-assisted European record in the heats of the 440 yards flat for the third-ranked Englishman, Ted Sampson, who was subsequently eliminated in the semi-finals. That event was won, instead, by a gloriously fluent Indian runner, Milkha Singh.

Keith Gardner retained his high hurdles title from 1954 and also won the 100 yards, in which Caribbean-born athletes set a trend for the future by taking all three medals, but the distance events were yet to become an African preserve. Dave Power, of Australia, lived up to his name by winning the six miles in an enthralling finish with Welshman John Merriman and then taking the marathon in what was his first attempt (and, he assured everyone afterwards, his last) at the distance.

The men's field events caused rather less stir, but Australia's Polish-born Anna Pazera made up for that by setting a totally unexpected World record of 57.40m in the javelin. The women's programme still only consisted of nine events, and Marlene Willard succeeded Marjorie Jackson-Nelson as Australia's double sprint winner, but England surprisingly won the 4 x 110 yards in World-record time.

1962: Masterful Snell follows ably in Elliott's footsteps

Herb Elliott was now otherwise engaged, pursuing studies at Cambridge University, but a New Zealander, Peter Snell, proved to be the worthiest of successors. Snell, thriving on the radical marathon-style training

schedules devised by Arthur Lydiard, repeated Elliott's 880/mile double, and in the same masterful style. England's men failed to win a single individual track event in Perth, though they did take titles in the 4 x 110 relay and the marathon.

Snell already held the World records for 800 metres, 880 yards and the mile and was to set another mile record and win the 1964 Olympic 800 and 1500 metres. Australia's Dixie Willis was also a current World record-holder and she won the 880 for women, which had been introduced at long last. The field events were picking up in standard and Mike Ahey, of Ghana, was over eight metres in winning the long jump, though a capricious breeze aided him and the other two medallists but not Lynn Davies, of Wales, in 4th place. Valerie Young (nee Sloper) was another double winner for New Zealand, in the shot and discus.

Dave Power lost his six miles title to the youthful Bruce Kidd, of Canada, and also broke his promise not to run another marathon and was again 2nd to Brian Kilby, who had already won the European title earlier in the year. Murray Halberg, of New Zealand, retained the three miles ahead of Australia's Ron Clarke, who had been an outstanding junior miler and was starting a comeback. The sprints, uniquely, went to an Afro-Asian, Seraphino Antao, who had been born in the Portugese possession of Goa on the Indian sub-continent but now represented Kenya.

1966: Torrid track and field with a reggae beat

For the first time the Games moved outside the "old colonial" establishment, and 33 countries sent 305 men and 98 women to Kingston, Jamaica, to contest the athletics events. Among them were current World record-holders Harry Jerome (Canada), Kip Keino (Kenya) and Ron Clarke (Australia). Jerome had run 100 yards in 9.1 and Keino and Clarke had rewritten the records from 3000 to 10,000 metres. Also entered were the respective Olympic long-jump champions, Lynn Davies and Mary Rand.

Clarke, frustratingly, collected two more silver medals, beaten by Keino at three miles and by another Kenyan, Naftali Temu, at six miles. Keino also won the mile in 3:55.34 and had already broken Bannister's Games record with an extravagant 3:57.35 to win his heat by 50 yards or more. These, significantly, were the first major championship successes by Kenyan distance-men, and there were to be many more of these in the future.

Two former Olympic champions, Norman Read and Don Thompson, took part in the inaugural 20 miles walk and were beaten into 3rd and 4th places, but current Olympic title-holders Davies and Rand both won their events. Wendell Mottley was never given official credit for

a World record with his 45.08 in the 440 yards, which was the fastest ever automatic time, but made sure of his place in history by anchoring the Trinidad & Tobago quartet to an undisputed 4 x 440 relay record two days later.

Australian women won seven of their 11 events, including three golds for sprinter Dianne Burge, but it was a New Zealander, Valerie Young, who dominated the field events, winning the shot/discus double to bring her tally of titles to five.

1970: The Stewart "clan" lead the Scottish charge

An all-weather surface and automatic timing at last brought the Commonwealth Games into line with international convention, but the Edinburgh weather was typically unseasonal with wind speeds of up to 9.8 metres per second (almost 24 mph). Nevertheless, Scottish hearts were warmed from the very first day when Lachie Stewart beat the luckless Ron Clarke at 10,000 metres, and a week later Anglo-Scot Ian Stewart (no relation) completed a home double by winning the 5000 metres from team-mate Ian McCafferty and Kenya's Kip Keino.

Keino had won the 1500 metres three days earlier, and there were other Kenyan successes at 400 and 800 metres and in the 4 x 400 relay - but not in the distance events, where Ron Hill's crushing marathon triumph for England in the second fastest time ever run was the supreme achievement. Jamaica's Don Quarrie set the stage for an illustrious sprint career with his 100/200/4 x 100 treble.

The field events showed notable progress and husband-and-wife Howard Payne (hammer) and Rosemary Payne (discus) both won gold medals on the same day. At last there was a pentathlon for women and Liverpool-born (but Ulster resident) Mary Peters repeated her Olympic success of two years before. Yet even Mary and Australia's triple sprint gold-medallist, Raelene Boyle, were upstaged by 17-year-old Marilyn Neufville, who broke the World record for 400 metres with 51.02 but was never to match that brilliantly precocious form again.

1974: Jipcho and Thompson - contrasting cultures, same winning ways

Ian Thompson had only taken part in his first marathon the previous autumn to make up the numbers in his club team for the AAA championship. Astonishingly, he won that race. Then in January he went to Christchurch and won the Commonwealth title as well by more than two minutes in a European record time. Later in the year he was to be

European champion.

Filbert Bayi, from Tanzania, took 1500-metre running into a new era, running the first 400 metres in a breakneck 54.9sec and holding on to win narrowly from New Zealand's John Walker in a World-record 3:32.16. Ben Jipcho, of Kenya, was 3rd in that race and Brendan Foster 7th in a British record time, and they had earlier shared in a pulsating 5000 metres narrowly won by Jipcho. With another win in the steeplechase, Jipcho seemed scarcely ever off the track.

There were also Kenyan wins at 400, 800 and 4 x 400, as in 1970, and the underrated Charles Asati brought his total of gold medals to four. Don Quarrie again won the sprints. The field events were inevitably of a lesser calibre, but there were performances of the highest level from England's Geoff Capes in the shot and 18-year-old Charles Clover, who improved more than seven metres in the javelin with a Commonwealth record 84.92m.

Raelene Boyle again had a sprint treble, while Mary Peters retained her pentathlon title but only by 32pts from the Nigerian, Modupe Oshikoya, who six days later won the long jump to become the first black African woman champion in Games history.

1978: Gidemas? Gidamis? Is he 21 years old? Or 19? Or even 17?

No one seemed sure of the marathon winner's precise name or age, least of all himself, but it did not matter too much. The success of the unknown young Shahanga from Tanzania was yet another dramatic revelation in an event which so often produced the unexpected. Shahanga caught the favoured Canadian, Jerome Drayton, in the closing stages of an exciting but not particularly fast race.

The standard of performance in Edmonton was, in fact, generally moderate, though there was some fast wind-aided sprinting from Don Quarrie and Allan Wells and a highly competitive 1500 metres in which David Moorcroft beat the defending champion, Filbert Bayi. Henry Rono maintained Kenya's traditions with a 5000/steeplechase double, though not being unduly pressed.

The all-rounders also put on a good show: Commonwealth records in the pentathlon by Canada's Diane Konihowski and the decathlon by England's Daley Thompson. Keith Connor broke the British record in the triple jump with 16.76m and had further massive leaps of 17.21 and 17.17 with the wind just over the allowable limit. Tessa Sanderson beat the 20-year-old Games record in the javelin. Rumanian-born Carmen Ionesco was Australia's winner of the discus.

1982: Even modern technology cannot separate Wells and McFarlane

Allan Wells had already won the 100 metres for Scotland in a wind-assisted 10.02 and was then involved in a rare tie for the gold medal at 200 metres with England's Mike McFarlane. Even the automatic camera in use in Brisbane could not find a centimetre between them. Again, though, it was the distance events which caught rather more attention.

The Australian, Rob de Castella, who had a set a World's best time for the marathon the previous year, won that event on home territory after a titanic struggle with Juma Ikangaa, of Tanzania, as the defending champion, Gidamis Shahanga, finished 6th, having already won the 10,000 metres. There was the seemingly inevitable Kenyan victory in the steeplechase, while for the home countries Keith Connor kept his triple-jump title with another prodigious display and 21-year-old Bob Weir broke the British record in the hammer.

Again, standards were a shade subdued - maybe reflecting the timing of the Games in October, at the end of a long European season - but there was also some impressive women's sprinting and high hurdling, and a fine long-jump win for the Bahamas by Shonel Ferguson. The Bahamas sent six athletes to the Games and won two golds, two silvers and a bronze ! Both the high-jump winner, Canada's Milt Ottey, and the silver-medallist from the Bahamas, Steve Wray, attempted a World record 2.36.

1986: The anti-apartheid curtain rings down, but the shows goes on

There had been mutterings for some years about continued sporting relations with South Africa and these finally erupted into a full-scale boycott of the Edinburgh Games by 32 countries. So there were none of the great Caribbean sprinters or African distance-runners, and in hindsight it has to be said that if their absence helped to force change then it was a price worth paying.

Oddly, considering the absentees and the miserable weather, it was rather a good Games. Steve Cram ran one of the most glorious races of his career to win the 800 metres (and completed the double at 1500). Steve Ovett led an English clean-sweep at 5000 metres. Rob de Castella ran another swift marathon. Daley Thompson amassed yet one more big decathlon score for his third successive win.

Neither were the women outplayed. Kirsty Wade won both the 800 and 1500 for Wales. Lisa Martin ran a majestic solo marathon. Tessa Sanderson and Fatima Whitbread both threw the javelin a mighty long way. Judy Simpson, for England, and Jane Flemming, for Australia, finished only four points apart in the seven-event heptathlon. Above all, the Scots were enraptured by Dundee's own pencil-slim Liz Lynch winning an enthralling 10,000 metres race.

But would the Games survive?

1990: Farewell to the champions. Coe falls apart, Walker falls over

An out-of-season Commonwealth Games in faraway New Zealand would test the enthusiasm of many athletes, particularly from Britain, with the alternative attractions of an increasingly lucrative track and road racing circuit to tempt them. Happily, the likes of Linford Christie, Sebastian Coe, Colin Jackson and Merlene Ottey all made it their business to be in Auckland, and there was a record total of 672 athletes from 47 countries.

Christie, Jackson and Ottey duly won gold medals, but Coe was an uninspired 6th at 800 metres and another of the great middle-distance runners of his generation, John Walker, suffered an even more ignominious fate in front of his home crowd, getting knocked over in the 1500 final in which Peter Elliott won for England instead. Among a profusion of fine track performers no one outshone Angela Chalmers, who won the 1500 and 3000 double for Canada in the most graceful manner.

The men's high jump was as good a competition as any, with Nick Saunders, of Bermuda, winning at 2.36 from England's Dalton Grant, and there was an historic Cypriot success in the triple jump for Marios Hadjiandreou over Jonathan Edwards. The elegant Lisa Martin ran even faster in the marathon and won by almost eight minutes, while a French-speaking Canadian, Guillaume Leblanc, won the 30 kilometres walk.

1994: Sepeng sets the seal on South Africa's return

Drugs issues attracted too much attention for comfort. England's defending champion at 800 metres, Diane Modahl, was sent home before the Games began, though she later won a long and costly counter-action through the courts. Then a Sierra Leone sprinter named Horace Dove-Edwin seemed to have made miraculous improvement to take the 100 metres silver behind Linford Christie but was subsequently found to have dosed up on an anabolic steroid.

Otherwise, there was some spirited competition despite the absence of most of the leading Kenyans, in dispute with their officialdom, and the lack of spectators in the makeshift Victoria stadium. Christie ran a

marvellous 9.91 for the 100 and Frankie Fredericks won the 200 for Namibia in 19.97. The Kenyan "B Team" still took the 400, 800, 1500, 10,000 and steeplechase. South Africa's return after a 36-year absence was marked by a silver for Hezekiel Sepeng at 800 metres.

Again there was a great high-jump duel, as Australia's Tim Forsyth and England's Steve Smith both cleared 2.32, while the men's javelin curiously produced exactly the same first four as in the previous Games in Auckland. The women's heptathlon featured another close finish as Jane Flemming lost on this occasion by eight points to England's Denise Lewis, who made a colossal improvement in the javelin.

Cathy Freeman, who had won a 4 x 100 gold as a 16-year-old in Auckland, took the 200 and 400 in fine style, breaking Marilyn Neufville's 24-year-old Games record in the latter (as did the two other medallists). It was the first major championship success in an individual event for an Australian of Aboriginal origin. Angela Chalmers, of Sioux Indian descent, again ran superlatively to win the 3000 in her home town.

1998: The Games go Asian as Kuala Lumpur spends big money

There were eery overtones of the Vancouver Games of 1954. Craig Barrett, of New Zealand, was leading the 50 kilometres walk by a very long way with the finish almost in sight, but then he suddenly veered to the side of the road, overcome by the heat and humidity, and some minutes later a moustachioed little Malaysian named Govindaswamy Saravan trudged in as the totally unexpected winner to a delirious welcome.

It was misfortune for Barrett but some recompense for the Malaysian organisers of what was in every sense of the term, "The Friendly Games". The facilities were marvellous, centred round the Bukit Jalal National Stadium, and costing some £330 million in total - and the athletes responded with fine performances.

Ato Boldon took the 100 for Trinidad & Tobago in a scintillating 9.88, but neither he nor the silver-medallist, Frankie Fredericks, stayed for the 200 metres two days later, as they had by then rejoined the Grand Prix circuit. Iwan Thomas, for Wales, and Japheth Kimutai, for Kenya, won fast races at 400 and 800, and the distance events were eclipsed, though Thabiso Moqhali became Lesotho's first ever Games champion in any sport in winning the marathon. Two comparative veterans, Dalton Grant (high jump) and Bob Weir (discus), earned titles in the field events.

The women's events produced winners from the Bahamas, Barbados, Kenya and Mozambique, amongst other countries, though it has to be said that entries were thin in some events: seven in the 5000 metres, 400 metres hurdles and javelin and only six in the triple jump. It was Mozambique's first appearance in the Games and they took 1st and 2nd in the 800 metres through Maria Mutola and her cousin, Tina Paulino. Another intriguing double was that of Australia's 200 metres winner, Nova Peris-Kneebone, who had won hockey gold at the 1996 Atlanta Olympics.

Denise Lewis won the heptathlon for a second time as one of her England team-mates, Judy Oakes, took the shot for the third occasion on her sixth successive Games appearance, and another, Ashia Hansen, managed a triple-jump victory despite an injury-ruined preparation. The unheralded Francoise Mbango, of Cameroon, finished in 2nd place to Hansen.

ATHLETICS MEDALLISTS

MEN

Note: hand-timing to one-tenth of a second, automatic timing to one-hundredth of a second; - no time taken, e estimated time, w wind-assisted. All distances in field events converted to metric measurement.

100 metres:
100 yards (91.44 metres) 1930-1966
1930: 1 Percy Williams (Can) 9.9, 2 Ernie Page (Eng) 10.2, 3 Johnny Fitzpatrick (Can) -.
1934: 1 Arthur Sweeney (Eng) 10.0, 2 Marthinus Theunissen (SA) 10.0, 3 Ian Young (Sco) 10.1e.
1938: 1 Cyril Holmes (Eng) 9.7, 2 John Mumford (Aus) 9.8e, 3 Ted Best (Aus) 9.9e.
1950: 1 John Treloar (Aus) 9.7, 2 Bill de Gruchy (Aus) 9.8, 3 Don Pettie (Can) 9.9.
1954: 1 Mike Agostini (Tri) 9.6, 2 Don McFarlane (Can) 9.7, 3 Hec Hogan (Aus) 9.7.
1958: 1 Keith Gardner (Jam) 9.66, 2 Tom Robinson (Bah) 9.69, 3 Mike Agostini (Can) 9.79.
Note: Agostini competed for Trinidad & Tobago in 1954.
1962: 1 Seraphino Antao (Ken) 9.5, 2 Tom Robinson (Bah) 9.63, 3 Mike Cleary (Aus) 9.78.
Note: no automatic timing for 1st place.
1966: 1 Harry Jerome (Can) 9.41, 2 Tom Robinson (Bah) 9.44, 3 Ed Roberts (Tri) 9.52.
1970: 1 Don Quarrie (Jam) 10.24w (+ 3.6m), 2 Lennox Miller (Jam) 10.32, 3 Hasely Crawford (Tri) 10.33.
1974: 1 Don Quarrie (Jam) 10.38, 2 John Mwebi (Ken) 10.51, 3 Ohene Karikari (Gha) 10.51.
1978: 1 Don Quarrie (Jam) 10.03w (+ 7.5m), 2 Allan Wells (Sco) 10.07, 3 Hasely

Crawford (Tri) 10.09.

1982: 1 Allan Wells (Sco) 10.02w (+ 5.9m), 2 Ben Johnson (Can) 10.05, 3 Cameron Sharp (Sco) 10.07.

1986: 1 Ben Johnson (Can) 10.07, 2 Linford Christie (Eng) 10.28, 3 Mike McFarlane (Eng) 10.35.

1990: 1 Linford Christie (Eng) 9.93w (+ 3.9m), 2 Davidson Ezinwa (Nig) 10.05, 3 Bruny Surin (Can) 10.12.

1994: 1 Linford Christie (Eng) 9.91, 2 Michael Green (Jam) 10.05, 3 Frankie Fredericks (Nam) 10.06.

1998: 1 Ato Boldon (Tri) 9.88, 2 Frankie Fredericks (Nam) 9.96, 3 Obadele Thompson (Bar) 10.00.

200 metres:

220 yards (201.168 metres)1930-1966

1930: 1 Stanley Engelhart (Eng) 21.8, 2 Johnny Fitzpatrick (Can), 3 Bill Walters (SA) -.

1934: 1 Arthur Sweeney (Eng) 21.9, 2 Marthinus Theunissen (SA) 22.0e, 3 Walter Rangeley (Eng) 22.1e.

1938: 1 Cyril Holmes (Eng) 21.2, 2 John Mumford (Aus) 21.3e, 3 Ted Best (Aus) 21.4e.

1950: 1 John Treloar (Aus) 21.5, 2 David Johnson (Aus) 21.8, 3 Don Jowett (NZ) 21.8.

1954: 1 Don Jowett (NZ) 21.5, 2 Brian Shenton (Eng) 21.5, 3 Ken Jones (Wal) 21.9.

1958: 1 Tom Robinson (Bah) 21.08w, 2 Keith Gardner (Jam) 21.11, 3 Gordon Day (SA) 21.15.

Note: the wind was officially stated to be in excess of 2m per second, but no exact measurement was announced.

1962: 1 Seraphino Antao (Ken) 21.28, 2 David Jones (Eng) 21.59, 3 Johann du Preez (Rho) 21.70.

1966: 1 Stanley Allotey (Gha) 20.65, 2 Ed Roberts (Tri) 20.93, 3 David Ejoke (Nig) 20.95.

1970: 1 Don Quarrie (Jam) 20.56, 2 Ed Roberts (Tri) 20.63, 3 Charles Asati (Ken) 20.74.

1974: 1 Don Quarrie (Jam) 20.73, 2 George Daniels (Gha) 20.97, 3 Bevan Smith (NZ) 21.08.

1978: 1 Allan Wells (Sco) 20.12w (+ 4.3m), 2 James Gilkes (Guy) 20.18, 3 Colin Bradford (Jam) 20.43.

1982: 1= Mike McFarlane (Eng), Allan Wells (Sco) 20.43, 3 Cameron Sharp (Sco) 20.55.

1986: 1 Atlee Mahorn (Can) 20.31w (+ 2.15m), 2 Todd Bennett (Eng) 20.54, 3 Ben Johnson (Can) 20.64.

1990: 1 Marcus Adam (Eng) 20.10w (+ 2.4m), 2 John Regis (Eng) 20.16, 3 Ade Mafe (Eng) 20.26.

1994: 1 Frankie Fredericks (Nam) 19.97, 2 John Regis (Eng) 20.25, 3 Daniel Effiong (Nig) 20.40.

1998; 1 Julian Golding (Eng) 20.18, 2 Christian Malcolm (Wal) 20.29, 3 John Regis (Eng) 20.40.

400 metres:

440 yards (402.336 metres) 1930-1966

1930: 1 Alex Wilson (Can) 48.8, 2 Bill Walters (SA) 48.9, 3 George Golding (Aus) -.

1934: 1 Godfrey Rampling (Eng) 48.0, 2 Bill Roberts (Eng) 48.5e, 3 Crew Stoneley (Eng) 48.6e.

1938: 1 Bill Roberts (Eng) 47.9, 2 Bill Fritz (Can) 47.9e, 3 Dennis Shore (SA) 48.1e.

1950: 1 Edwin Carr (Aus) 47.9, 2 Les Lewis (Eng) 48.0, 3 David Batten (NZ) 48.8.

1954: 1 Kevan Gosper (Aus) 47.2, 2 Don Jowett (NZ) 47.4, 3 Terry Tobacco (Can) 47.8.

1958: 1 Milkha Singh (Ind) 46.71, 2 Malcolm Spence (SA) 46.90, 3 Terry Tobacco (Can) 47.05.

1962: 1 George Kerr (Jam) 46.74, 2 Robbie Brightwell (Eng) 46.86, 3 Amos Omolo (Uga) 46.88.

1966: 1 Wendell Mottley (Tri) 45.08, 2 Kent Bernard (Tri) 46.06, 3 Don Domansky (Can) 46.42.

1970: 1 Charles Asati (Ken) 45.01, 2 Ross Wilson (Aus) 45.61, 3 Saimoni Taimani (Fij) 45.82.

1974: 1 Charles Asati (Ken) 46.04, 2 Silver Ayoo (Uga) 46.07, 3 Claver Kamanya (Tan) 46.16.

1978: 1 Rick Mitchell (Aus) 46.34, 2 Joe Coombs (Tri) 46.54, 3 Glenn Bogue (Can) 46.63.

1982: 1 Bert Cameron (Jam) 45.89, 2 Rick Mitchell (Aus) 46.61, 3 Gary Minihan (Aus) 46.68.

1986: 1 Roger Black (Eng) 45.57, 2 Darren Clark (Aus) 45.98, 3 Phil Brown (Eng) 46.80.

1990: 1 Darren Clark (Aus) 44.60, 2 Samson Kitur (Ken) 44.88, 3 Simeon Kipkemboi (Ken) 44.93.

1994: 1 Charles Gitonga (Ken) 45.00, 2 Du'aine Ladejo (Eng) 45.11, 3 Sunday Bada (Nig) 45.45.

1998: 1 Iwan Thomas (Wal) 44.52, 2 Mark Richardson (Eng) 44.60, 3 Sugath Thilakaratne (SriL) 44.64.

800-metres:

880 yards (804.672 metres) 1930-1966.

1930: 1 Tom Hampson (Eng) 1:52.4, 2 Reg Thomas (Eng) 1:55.5e, 3 Alex Wilson (Can) 1:55.6e.

1934: 1 Phil Edwards (BG) 1:54.2, 2 Willie Botha (SA) 1:55.0, 3 Hamish Stothard (Sco) 1:55.1.

1938: 1 Pat Boot (NZ) 1:51.2, 2 Frank Handley (Eng) 1:53.5e, 3 Bill Dale (Can) 1:53.6e.

1950: 1 John Parlett (Eng) 1:53.1, 2 Jack Hutchins (Can) 1:53.4, 3 Bill Parnell (Can) 1:53.4.

1954: 1 Derek Johnson (Eng) 1:50.7, 2 Brian Hewson (Eng) 1:51.2, 3 Ian Boyd

(Eng) 1:51.9.

1958: 1 Herb Elliott (Aus) 1:49.32, 2 Brian Hewson (Eng) 1:49.47, 3 Mike Rawson (Eng) 1:50.94.

1962: 1 Peter Snell (NZ) 1:47.64, 2 George Kerr (Jam) 1:47.90, 3 Tony Blue (Aus) 1:48.99.

1966: 1 Noel Clough (Aus) 1:46.9, 2 Wilson Kiprugut (Ken) 1:47.2, 3 George Kerr (Jam) 1:47.2.

1970: 1 Robert Ouko (Ken) 1:46.89, 2 Ben Cayenne (Tri) 1:47.42, 3 Bill Smart (Can) 1:47.43.

1974: 1 John Kipkurgat (Ken) 1:43.91, 2 Mike Boit (Ken) 1:44.39, 3 John Walker (NZ) 1:44.92.

1978: 1 Mike Boit (Ken) 1:46.39, 2 Seymour Newman (Jam) 1:47.30, 3 Peter Lemashon (Ken) 1:47.57.

1982: 1 Peter Bourke (Aus) 1:45.18, 2 James Maina (Ken) 1:45.45, 3 Chris McGeorge (Eng) 1:45.60.

1986: 1 Steve Cram (Eng) 1:43.22, 2 Tom McKean (Sco) 1:44.80, 3 Peter Elliott (Eng) 1:45.42.

1990: 1 Sammy Tirop (Ken) 1:45.98, 2 Nixon Kiprotich (Ken) 1:46.00, 3 Matthew Yates (Eng) 1:46.62.

1994: 1 Patrick Konchellah (Ken) 1:45.18, 2 Hezekiel Sepeng (SA) 1:45.76, 3 Savieri Ngidhi (Zim) 1:46.06.

1998: 1 Japheth Kimutai (Ken) 1:43.82, 2 Hezekiel Sepeng (SA) 1:44.44, 3 Johan Botha (SA) 1:44.57.

1500 metres:

One mile (1609.344 metres) 1930-1966

1930: 1 Reg Thomas (Eng) 4:14.0, 2 William Whyte (Aus) 4:17.0e, 3 Jerry Cornes (Eng) -.

1934: 1 Jack Lovelock (NZ) 4:12.8, 2 Sydney Wooderson (Eng) 4:13.4e, 3 Jerry Cornes (Eng) 4:13.6e.

1938: 1 Jim Alford (Wal) 4:11.5, 2 Gerald Backhouse (Aus) 4:12.2, 3 Pat Boot (NZ) 4:12.6.

1950: 1 Bill Parnell (Can) 4:11.0, 2 Len Eyre (Eng) 4:11.8, 3 Maurice Marshall (NZ) 4:13.2.

1954: 1 Roger Bannister (Eng) 3:58.8, 2 John Landy (Aus) 3:59.6, 3 Rich Ferguson (Can) 4:04.6.

1958: 1 Herb Elliott (Aus) 3:59.03, 2 Merv Lincoln (Aus) 4:01.80, 3 Albie Thomas (Aus) 4:02.77.

1962: 1 Peter Snell (NZ) 4:04.58, 2 John Davies (NZ) 4:05.12, 3 Terry Sullivan (Rho) 4:06.61.

1966: 1 Kip Keino (Ken) 3:55.34, 2 Alan Simpson (Eng) 3:57.27, 3 Ian Studd (NZ) 3:58.61.

1970: 1 Kip Keino (Ken) 3:36.6, 2 Dick Quax (NZ) 3:38.1, 3 Brendan Foster (Eng) 3:40.6.

1974: 1 Filbert Bayi (Tan) 3:32.16, 2 John Walker (NZ) 3:32.52, 3 Ben Jipcho (Ken) 3:33.16.

1978: 1 David Moorcroft (Eng) 3:35.48, 2 Filbert Bayi (Tan) 3:35.59, 3 John Robson (Sco) 3:35.60.

1982: 1 Steve Cram (Eng) 3:42.37, 2 John Walker (NZ) 3:43.11, 3 Mike Boit (Ken) 3:43.33.

1986: 1 Steve Cram (Eng) 3:50.87, 2 John Gladwin (Eng) 3:52.17, 3 Dave Campbell (Can) 3:54.06.

1990: 1 Peter Elliott (Eng) 3:33.39, 2 Wilfred Kirochi (Ken) 3:34.41, 3 Peter O'Donoghue (NZ) 3:35.14.

1994: 1 Reuben Chesang (Ken) 3:36.70, 2 Kevin Sullivan (Can) 3:36.78, 3 John Mayock (Eng) 3:37.22.

1998: 1 Laban Rotich (Ken) 3:39.49, 2 John Mayock (Eng) 3:40.46, 3 Anthony Whiteman (Eng) 3:40.70. .

5000 metres:

Three miles (4828.032 metres) 1930-1966

1930: 1 Stan Tomlin (Eng) 14:27.4, 2 Alex Hillhouse (Aus) 14:27.6e, 3 Jack Winfield (Eng) 14:28.0e.

1934: 1 Walter Beavers (Eng) 14:32.6, 2 Cyril Allen (Eng) 14:37.8, 3 Alex Burns (Eng) 14:45.4.

1938: 1 Cecil Matthews (NZ) 13:59.6, 2 Peter Ward (Eng) 14:05.6, 3 Bob Rankine (Can) 14:24.0e.

1950: 1 Len Eyre (Eng) 14:23.6, 2 Harold Nelson (NZ) 14:27.8, 3 Anthony Chivers (Eng) 14:28.1.

1954: 1 Chris Chataway (Eng) 13:35.2, Freddie Green (Eng) 13:37.2, 3 Frank Sando (Eng) 13:37.4.

1958: 1 Murray Halberg (NZ) 13:14.75, 2 Albie Thomas (Aus) 13:24.37, 3 Neville Scott (NZ) 13:26.06.

1962: 1 Murray Halberg (NZ) 13:34.15, 2 Ron Clarke (Aus) 13:35.92, 3 Bruce Kidd (Can) 13:36.37.

1966: 1 Kip Keino (Ken) 12:57.4, 2 Ron Clarke (Aus) 12:59.2, 3 Allan Rushmer (Eng) 13:08.6.

1970: 1 Ian Stewart (Sco) 13:22.8, 2 Ian McCafferty (Sco) 13:23.4, 3 Kip Keino (Ken) 13:27.6.

1974: 1 Ben Jipcho (Ken) 13:14.3, 2 Brendan Foster (Eng) 13:14.6, 3 David Black (Eng) 13:23.52.

Note: no automatic times recorded for 1st and 2nd places.

1978: 1 Henry Rono (Ken) 13:23.04, 2 Mike Musyoki (Ken) 13:29.92, 3 Brendan Foster (Eng) 13:31.35.

1982: 1 David Moorcroft (Eng) 13:33.00, 2 Nick Rose (Eng) 13:35.97, 3 Peter Koech (Ken) 13:36.95.

1986: 1 Steve Ovett (Eng) 13:24.11, 2 Jack Buckner (Eng) 13:25.87, 3 Tim Hutchings (Eng) 13:26.84.

1990: 1 Andrew Lloyd (Aus) 13:24.86, 2 John Ngugi (Ken) 13:24.94, 3 Ian Hamer (Wal) 13:25.63.

1994: 1 Rob Denmark (Eng) 13:23.00, 2 Philemon Hanneck (Zim) 13:23.20, 3 John Nuttall (Eng) 13:23.54.

1998: 1 Daniel Komen (Ken) 13:22.57, 2 Tom Nyariki (Ken) 13:28.09, 3 Richard Limo (Ken) 13:37.42.

10,000 metres:

Six miles (9656.064 metres)1930-1966

1930: 1 Bill Savidan (NZ) 30:49.6, 2 Ernie Harper (Eng) 31:01.6e, 3 Tom Evenson (Eng) -.

1934: 1 Arthur Penny (Eng) 31:00.6, 2 Bob Rankine (Can) 31:03.0e, 3 Arthur Furze (Eng) 31:04.0e.

1938: 1 Cecil Matthews (NZ) 30:14.5, 2 Bob Rankine (Can) -, 3 Wally Hayward (SA) - .

1950: 1 Harold Nelson (NZ) 30:29.6, 2 Andrew Forbes (Sco) 30:31.9, 3 Noel Taylor (NZ) 30:31.9.

1954: 1 Peter Driver (Eng) 29:09.4, 2 Frank Sando (Eng) 29:10.0, 3 Jim Peters (Eng) 29:20.0.

1958: 1 Dave Power (Aus) 28:48.16, 2 John Merriman (Wal) 28:48.84, 3 Arere Anentia (Ken) 28:51.48.

1962: 1 Bruce Kidd (Can) 28:26.13, 2 Dave Power (Aus) 28:33.53, 3 John Merriman (Wal) 28:40.26

1966: 1 Naftali Temu (Ken) 27:14.21, 2 Ron Clarke (Aus) 27:39.42, 3 Jim Alder (Sco) 28:15.4.

1970: 1 Lachie Stewart (Sco) 28:11.8, 2 Ron Clarke (Aus) 28:13.4, 3 Dick Taylor (Eng) 28:15.4.

1974: 1 Dick Tayler (NZ) 27:46.40, 2 David Black (Eng) 27:48.49, 3 Richard Juma (Ken) 27:56.96.

1978: 1 Brendan Foster (Eng) 28:13.65, 2 Mike Musyoki (Ken) 28:19.14, 3 Mike McLeod (Eng) 28:34.30.

1982: 1 Gidamis Shahanga (Tan) 28:10.15, 2 Zacharia Barie (Tan) 28:10.55, 3 Julian Goater (Eng) 28:16.11.

1986: 1 Jon Solly (Eng) 27:57.42, 2 Steve Binns (Eng) 27:58.01, 3 Steve Jones (Wal) 28:02.48.

1990: 1 Eamonn Martin (Eng) 28:08.57, 2 Moses Tanui (Ken) 28:11.56, 3 Paul Williams (Can) 28:12.71.

1994: 1 Lameck Aguta (Ken) 28:38.22, 2 Tendai Chimusasa (Zim) 28:47.72, 3 Fackson Nkandu (Zam) 28:51.72.

1998: 1 Simon Maina (Ken) 28:10.00, 2 William Kalya (Ken) 29:01.6, 3 Steve Moneghetti (Aus) 29:02.76.

3000 metres steeplechase:

Approximately 1 mile 1660 yards (3127.248 metres) in 1930, Two miles (3218.688 metres) in 1934

1930: 1 George Bailey (Eng) 9:52.0, 2 Alex Hillhouse (Aus), 3 Vernon Morgan (Eng).

1934: 1 Stan Scarsbrook (Eng) 10:23.4, 2 Tom Evenson (Eng) 10:25.8e, 3 George Bailey (Eng).

1938-58: Not held.

1962: 1 Trevor Vincent (Aus) 8:43.4, 2 Maurice Herriott (Eng) 8:45.0, 3 Ron Blackney (Aus) 9:00.6.

1966: 1 Peter Welsh (NZ) 8:29.44, 2 Kerry O'Brien (Aus) 8:32.58, 3 Benjamin

Kogo (Ken) 8:32.81.

1970: 1 Tony Manning (Aus) 8:26.2, 2 Ben Jipcho (Ken) 8:29.6, 3 Amos Biwott (Ken) 8:30.8.

1974: 1 Ben Jipcho (Ken) 8:20.67, 2 John Davies (Wal) 8:24.8, 3 Evans Mogaka (Ken) 8:28.51.

Note: no automatic time recorded for 2nd place.

1978: 1 Henry Rono (Ken) 8:26.54, 2 James Munyala (Ken) 8:32.21, 3 Kiprotich Rono (Ken) 8:34.07.

1982: 1 Julius Korir (Ken) 8:23.94, 2 Graeme Fell (Eng) 8:26.64, 3 Greg Duhaime (Can) 8:29.14.

1986: 1 Graeme Fell (Can) 8:24.49, 2 Roger Hackney (Wal) 8:25.15, 3 Colin Reitz (Eng) 8:26.14.

Note: Fell competed for England in 1982.

1990: 1 Julius Kariuki (Ken) 8:20.64, Joshua Kipkemboi (Ken) 8:24.26, 3 Colin Walker (Eng) 8:26.50.

1994: 1 Johnstone Kipkoech (Ken) 8:14.72, 2 Gideon Chirchir (Ken) 8:15.25, 3 Graeme Fell (Can) 8:23.28.

1998: 1 John Kosgei (Ken) 8:15.34, 2 Bernard Barmasai (Ken) 8:15.37, 3 Kipkirui Misoi (Ken) 8:18.24.

Marathon

(26 miles 385 yards/42.195 kilometres):

1930: 1 Duncan McLeod Wright (Sco) 2:43:43, 2 Sam Ferris (Eng) 2:47:13e, 3 Johnny Miles (Can) -.

1934: 1 Harold Webster (Can) 2:40:36, 2 Donald McNab Robertson (Sco) 2:45.08, 3 Duncan McLeod Wright (Sco) 2:56:20.

1938: 1 Johannes Coleman (SA) 2:30:49.8, 2 Bert Norris (Eng) 2:37:57, 3 Jackie Gibson (SA) 2:38:20.

1950: 1 Jack Holden (Eng) 2:32:57.0, 2 Sid Luyt (SA) 2:37:02.2, 3 Jack Clarke (NZ) 2:39:26.4.

1954: 1 Joe McGhee (Sco) 2:39:36.0, 2 Jackie Mekler (SA) 2:40:57.0, 3 Jan Barnard (SA) 2:51:49.8.

1958: 1 Dave Power (Aus) 2:22:45.6, 2 Jan Barnard (SA) 2:22:57.4, 3 Peter Wilkinson (Eng) 2:24:42.0.

1962: 1 Brian Kilby (Eng) 2:21:17.0, 2 Dave Power (Aus) 2:22:15.4, 3 Rod Bonella (Aus) 2:24:07.0.

1966: 1 Jim Alder (Sco) 2:22:07.8, 2 Bill Adcocks (Eng) 2:22:13.0, 3 Mike Ryan (NZ) 2:27:59.0.

1970: 1 Ron Hill (Eng) 2:09:28, 2 Jim Alder (Sco) 2:12:04. 3 Don Faircloth (Eng) 2:12:19.

1974: 1 Ian Thompson (Eng) 2:09:12.0, 2 Jack Foster (NZ) 2:11:18.6, 3 Richard Mabuza (Swa) 2:12:54.4.

1978: 1 Gidamis Shahanga (Tan) 2:15:39.8, 2 Jerome Drayton (Can) 2:16:23.5, 3 Paul Bannon (Can) 2:16:51.6.

1982: 1 Rob de Castella (Aus) 2:09:18, 2 Juma Ikangaa (Tan) 2:09:30, 3 Mike Gratton (Eng) 2:12:06.

1986: 1 Rob de Castella (Aus) 2:10:15, 2 Dave Edge (Can) 2:11:08, 3 Steve Moneghetti (Aus) 2:11:18.

1990: 1 Douglas Wakiihuri (Ken) 2:10:27, 2 Steve Moneghetti (Aus) 2:10:34, 3 Simon Robert Naali (Tan) 2:10:38.

1994: 1 Steve Moneghetti (Aus) 2:11:49, 2 Sean Quilty (Aus) 2:14:57, 3 Mark Hudspith (Eng) 2:15:11.

1998: 1 Thabiso Moqhali (Les) 2:19:15, 2 Simon Bisiligitwa (Tan) 2:19:42, 3 Andea Geway Suja (Tan) 2:19:50.

110 metres hurdles:

120 yards hurdles (109.728 metres)1930-1966

1930: 1 Lord Burghley (Eng) 14.6, 2 Howard Davies (SA) 14.7e, 3 Fred Gaby (Eng) -.

1934: 1 Don Finlay (Eng) 15.2, 2 Jim Worrall (Can) 15.5e, 3 Ashleigh Pilbrow (Eng) 15.7e.

1938: 1 Tom Lavery (SA) 14.0w, 2 Larry O'Connor (Can) 14.2e, 3 Sid Stenner (Aus) 14.4e.

Note: officially stated to be wind-assisted.

1950: 1 Peter Gardner (Aus) 14.3, 2 Ray Weinberg (Aus) 14.4, 3 Tom Lavery (SA) 14.6.

1954: 1 Keith Gardner (Jam) 14.2, 2 Chris Higham (Eng) 14.9, 3 Norm Williams (Can) 14.9.

1958: 1 Keith Gardner (Jam) 14.20w (+ 3.5m), 2 Jacobus Swart (SA) 14.30, 3 Ghulam Raziq (Pak) 14.32.

1962: 1 Ghulam Raziq (Pak) 14.34, 2 David Prince (Aus) 14.48, 3 Laurie Taitt (Eng) 14.81.

1966: 1 David Hemery (Eng) 14.1, 2 Mike Parker (Eng) 14.2, 3 Ghulam Raziq (Pak) 14.3.

1970: 1 David Hemery (Eng) 13.60, 2 Mal Baird (Aus) 13.86, 3 Godfrey Murray (Jam) 14.2.

Note: no automatic time recorded for 3rd place.

1974: 1 Fatwell Kimaiyo (Ken) 13.69, 2 Berwyn Price (Wal) 13.84, 3 Max Binnington (Aus) 13.88.

1978: 1 Berwyn Price (Wal) 13.70w (+ 6.15m), 2 Max Binnington (Aus) 13.73, 3 Warren Parr (Aus) 13.73.

1982: 1 Mark McKoy (Can) 13.37, 2 Mark Holtom (Eng) 13.43, 3 Don Wright (Aus) 13.58.

1986: 1 Mark McKoy (Can) 13.31w (+ 4.46m), 2 Colin Jackson (Wal) 13.42, 3 Don Wright (Aus) 13.64.

1990: 1 Colin Jackson (Wal) 13.08, 2 Tony Jarrett (Eng) 13.34, 3 David Nelson (Eng) 13.54.

1994: 1 Colin Jackson (Wal) 13.08, 2 Tony Jarrett (Eng) 13.22, 3 Paul Gray (Wal) 13.54.

1998: 1 Tony Jarrett (Eng) 13.47, 2 Steve Brown (Tri) 13.48, 3 Shaun Bownes (SA) 13.53.

400 metres hurdles:

440 yards hurdles (402.336 metres)1930-1966

1930: 1 Lord Burghley (Eng) 54.4, 2 Roger Leigh-Wood (Eng) 55.9e, 3 Douglas

Neame (Eng) - .

1934: 1 Alan Hunter (Sco) 55.2, 2 Charles Reilly (Aus) 55.8e, 3 Ralph Brown (Eng) 56.0e.

1938: 1 John Loaring (Can) 52.9, 2 John Park (Aus) 54.6e, 3 Alan McDougall (Aus) 55.2e.

1950: 1 Duncan White (Cey) 52.5, 2 John Holland (NZ) 52.7, 3 Geoff Goodacre (Aus) 53.1.

1954: 1 David Lean (Aus) 52.4, 2 Harry Kane (Eng) 53.3, 3 Bob Shaw (Wal) 53.3.

1958: 1 Gert Potgieter (SA) 49.73, 2 David Lean (Aus) 50.59, 3 Bartonjo Rotich (Ken) 51.75.

1962: 1 Ken Roche (Aus) 51.5, 2 Kimaru Songok (Ken) 51.9, 3 Benson Ishiepai (Uga) 52.3.

1966: 1 Ken Roche (Aus) 50.95, 2 Kingsley Agbabokha (Nig) 51.46, 3 Peter Warden (Eng) 51.54.

1970: 1 John Sherwood (Eng) 50.03, 2 Bill Koskei (Uga) 50.15, 3 Charles Yego (Ken) 50.19.

1974: 1 Alan Pascoe (Eng) 48.83, 2 Bruce Field (Aus) 49.32, 3 Bill Koskei (Ken) 49.34.

Note Koskei competed for Uganda in 1970.

1978: 1 Daniel Kimaiyo (Ken) 49.48, 2 Garry Brown (Aus) 50.04, 3 Alan Pascoe (Eng) 50.09.

1982: 1 Garry Brown (Aus) 49.27, 2 Peter Rwamuhanda (Uga) 49.95, 3 Greg Rolle (Bah) 50.50.

1986: 1 Phil Beattie (NI) 49.60, 2 Max Robertson (Eng) 49.77, 3 John Graham (Can) 50.25.

1990: 1 Kriss Akabusi (Eng) 48.89, 2 Gideon Yego (Ken) 49.25, 3 John Graham (Can) 50.24.

1994: 1 Samuel Matete (Zam) 48.67, 2 Gideon Biwott (Ken) 49.43, 3 Barnabas Kinyor (Ken) 49.50.

1998: 1 Dinsdale Morgan (Jam) 48.28, 2 Rohan Robinson (Aus) 48.99, 3 Ken Harnden (Zim) 49.06.

20 kilometres walk

First held 1998

1998: 1 Nick A'Hern (Aus) 1:24:59, 2 Arturo Huerta (Can) 1:25:49, 3 Nathan Deakes (Aus) 1:26:06.

30 kilometres walk

20 miles (32.187 kilometres)1966-1974, replaced by 20 kilometres 1998.

1966: 1 Ron Wallwork (Eng) 2:44:42.8, 2 Ray Middleton (Eng) 2:45:19.0,
3 Norman Read (NZ) 2:46:28.2.

1970: 1 Noel Freeman (Aus) 2:33:33, 2 Bob Gardiner (Aus) 2:35:55; 3 Bill Sutherland (Sco) 2:37:24.

1974: 1 John Warhurst (Eng) 2:35:23.0, 2 Roy Thorpe (Eng) 2:39:02.2, 3 Peter Fullager (Aus) 2:42:08.2.

1978: 1 Olly Flynn (Eng) 2:22:03.7, 2 Willi Sawall (Aus) 2:22:58.6, 3 Tim Erickson (Aus) 2:26:34.0.

1982: 1 Steve Barry (Wal) 2:10:16, 2 Marcel Jobin (Can) 2:12:24, 3 Guillaume Leblanc (Can) 2:14:56.

1986: 1 Simon Baker (Aus) 2:07:47, 2 Guillaume Leblanc (Can) 2:08:38, 3 Ian McCombie (Eng) 2:10:36.

1990: 1 Guillaume Leblanc (Can) 2:08:28, 2 Andrew Jachno (Aus) 2:09:29, 3 Ian McCombie (Eng) 2:09:20.

1994: 1 Nick A'Hern (Aus) 2:07:53, 2 Tim Berrett (Can) 2:08:22, 3 Scott Nelson (NZ) 2:09:10.

50 kilometres walk
First held 1998

1998: 1 Govindaswamy Saravanan (Mal) 4:10:05, 2 Duane Cousins (Aus) 4:10:30, 3 Dominic McGrath (Aus) 4:12:50.

4 x 100 metres relay:
4 x 110 yards (100.584 metres)1930-1966

1930: 1 Canada (Jim "Buster" Brown, Leigh Miller, Ralph Adams, Johnny Fitzpatrick) 42.2, 2 England (John Hanlon, James Cohen, John Heap, Stanley Engelhart) 42.7e, 3 South Africa (Howard Davies, Werner Gerhardt, Billy Legg, Bill Walters) -.

1934: 1 England (Everard Davis, George Saunders, Walter Rangeley, Arthur Sweeney) 42.2, 2 Canada (Bert Pearson, Frank Nicks, Allan Poole, Bill Christie) 42.5e, 3 Scotland (Archie Turner, David Brownlee, Robin Murdoch, Ian Young) 43.0e.

1938: 1 Canada (Jack Brown, Pat Haley, John Loaring, Larry O'Connor) 41.6, 2 England (Ken Richardson, Sandy Duncan, Lawrence Wallace, Cyril Holmes) 41.8e, 3 Australia (Ted Best, Alf Watson, Teddy Hampson, Howard Yates) 41.9e.

1950: 1 Australia (Bill de Gruchy, David Johnson, Alastair Gordon, John Treloar) 42.2, 2 England (Les Lewis, Brian Shenton, Nick Stacey, Jack Archer) 42.5, 3 New Zealand (Clem Parker, Peter Henderson, Kevin Beardsley, Arthur Eustace) 42.6.

1954: 1 Canada (Don McFarlane, Don Stonehouse, Harry Nelson, Bruce Springbett) 41.3, 2 Nigeria (Edward Ajado, Karim Olowu, Abdul Karim Amu, Muslim Arogundade) 41.3, 3 Australia (Kevan Gosper, Brian Oliver, Hec Hogan, David Lean) 41.7.

1958: 1 England (Peter Radford, Roy Sandstrom, Dave Segal, Adrian Breacker) 40.72, 2 Nigeria (Smart Akraka, Thomas Obi, Victor Odofin, Jimmy Omagbemi) 41.05, 3 Australia (Terry Gale, Kevan Gosper, Jim McCann, Hec Hogan) 41.64.

1962: 1 England (Peter Radford, Len Carter, Alf Meakin, David Jones) 40.62, 2 Ghana (Mike Ahey, Bonner Mends, Bukari Bashiru, Mike Okantey) 40.74, 3 Wales (Dave England, Ron Jones, Berwyn Jones, Nick Whitehead) 40.80.

1966: 1 Ghana (Ebenezer Addy, Bonner Mends, James Addy, Stanley Allotey) 39.8, 2 Jamaica (Wellesley Clayton, Pablo McNeil, Lynn Headley, Mike Fray) 40.0, 3 Australia (Gary Eddy, Allan Crawley, Gary Holdsworth, Peter Norman) 40.0.

1970: 1 Jamaica (Errol Stewart, Lennox Miller, Carl Lawson, Don Quarrie) 39.46, 2 Ghana (Mike Ahey, James Addy, Edward Owusu, George Daniels) 39.82, 3 England (Ian Green, Martin Reynolds, Dave Dear, Brian Green) 40.05.

1974: 1 Australia (Greg Lewis, Lawrie D'Arcy, Andrew Ratcliffe, Graham Haskell)

39.31, 2 Ghana (Albert Lomotey, Ohene Karikari, Kofi Okyir, George Daniels) 39.61, 3 Nigeria (Timon Oyebami, Benedict Majekodunmi, Kola Abdulai, James Olakunle) 39.70.

1978: 1 Scotland (David Jenkins, Allan Wells, Cameron Sharp, Drew McMaster) 39.24, 2 Trinidad & Tobago (Eldwin Noel, Hasely Crawford, Chris Brathwaite, Ephraim Serrette) 39.29, 3 Jamaica (Errol Quarrie, Colin Bradford, Oliver Heywood, Floyd Brown) 39.33.

1982: 1 Nigeria (Lawrence Adegbeingbe, Iziak Adeyanju, Samson Olajidie Oyeledun, Ikpoto Eseme) 39.15, 2 Canada (Ben Johnson, Tony Sharpe, Desai Williams, Mark McKoy) 39.30, 3 Scotland (Gus McCuaig, Allan Wells, Cameron Sharp, Drew McMaster) 39.30.

1986: 1 Canada (Mark McKoy, Atlee Mahorn, Desai Williams, Ben Johnson) 39.15, 2 England (Lincoln Asquith, Daley Thompson, Mike McFarlane, Clarence Callender) 39.19, 3 Scotland (Jamie Henderson, George McCallum, Cameron Sharp, Elliot Bunney) 40.41.

1990: 1 England (Clarence Callender, John Regis, Marcus Adam, Linford Christie) 38.67, 2 Nigeria (Victor Nwankwo, Davidson Ezinwa, Osmond Ezinwa, Abdullahi Tetengi) 38.85, 3 Jamaica (Wayne Watson, John Mair, Clive Wright, Ray Stewart) 39.11.

1994: 1 Canada (Donovan Bailey, Carlton Chambers, Glenroy Gilbert, Bruny Surin) 38.39, 2 Australia (Shane Naylor, Tim Jackson, Paul Henderson, Damien Marsh) 38.88, 3 England (Jason John, Toby Box, Philip Goedluck, Terry Williams) 39.39.

Note: Mark Smith (Eng) ran in heats.

1998: 1 England (Dwain Chambers, Marlon Devonish, Julian Golding, Darren Campbell) 38.20, 2 Canada (Brad McCuaig, Glenroy Gilbert, O'Brian Gibbons, Trevino Betty) 38.46, 3 Australia (Gavin Hunter, Darryl Wohlsen, Steve Brimacombe, Matthew Shirvington) 38.69.

Note: Jason Gardener (Eng) and Rod Zuyderwyk (Aus) ran in heats..

4 x 400 metres relay:

4 x 440 yards (402.336 metres)1930-1966

1930: 1 England (Roger Leigh-Wood, Stuart Townend, Lord Burghley, Kenneth Brangwin) 3:19.4, 2 Canada (Art Scott, Stan Glover, Jimmy Ball, Alex Wilson) 3:19.8e, 3 South Africa (Billy Legg, Werner Gerhardt, John Chandler, Bill Walters).

1934: 1 England (Denis Rathbone, Geoff Blake, Crew Stoneley, Godfrey Rampling) 3:16.8, 2 Canada (Bill Fritz, Joe Addison, Art Scott, Ray Lewis) 3:17.4e, 3 Scotland (Ronnie Wallace, Ronald Wyld, Hamish Stothard, Alan Hunter) -.

1938: 1 Canada (Jack Orr, Bill Dale, Bill Fritz, John Loaring) 3:16.9, 2 England (Frank Handley, Harry Pack, Brian MacCabe, Bill Roberts) 3:19.2, 3 New Zealand (Arnold Anderson, Alan Sayers, Graham Quinn, Harold Tyrie) 3:22.0.

1950: 1 Australia (Ross Price, George Gedge, James Humphreys, Edwin Carr) 3:17.8, 2 England (Terry Higgins, Derek Pugh, John Parlett, Les Lewis) 3:19.3, 3 New Zealand (John Holland, David Batten, Derek Steward, Jack Sutherland) 3:20.0.

1954: 1 England (Peter Higgins, Alan Dick, Peter Fryer, Derek Johnson) 3:11.2, 2 Canada (Laird Sloan, Doug Clement, Joe Foreman, Terry Tobacco) 3:11.6,

3 Australia (Brian Oliver, Don Macmillan, David Lean, Kevan Gosper) 3:16.0.

1958: 1 South Africa (Gordon Day, Gerald Evans, Gert Potgieter, Malcolm Spence) 3:08.21, 2 England (Ted Sampson, Derek Johnson, John Wrighton, John Salisbury) 3:09.61, 3 Jamaica (Gerald James, Mal Spence, George Kerr, Keith Gardner) 3:10.08.

1962: 1 Jamaica (Laurie Kahn, Mal Spence, Mel Spence, George Kerr) 3:10.2, 2 England (Adrian Metcalfe, Bob Setti, Barry Jackson, Robbie Brightwell) 3:11.2, 3 Ghana (James Addy, Ebenezer Quartey, Fred Owusu, John Asare-Antwi) 3:12.3.

1966: 1 Trinidad & Tobago (Lennox Yearwood, Kent Bernard, Ed Roberts, Wendell Mottley) 3:02.8, 2 Canada (Ross MacKenzie, Brian McLaren, Don Domansky, Bill Crothers) 3:04.9, 3 England (Martin Winbolt Lewis, John Adey, Peter Warden, Tim Graham) 3:06.5.

1970: 1 Kenya (Hezekiah Nyamau, Julius Sang, Robert Ouko, Charles Asati) 3:03.63, 2 Trinidad & Tobago (Mel Wongshing, Ben Cayenne, Kent Bernard, Ed Roberts) 3:05.49, 3 England (Martin Bilham, Len Walters, Mike Hauck, John Sherwood) 3:05.53.

1974: 1 Kenya (Charles Asati, Francis Musyoki, Bill Koskei, Julius Sang) 3:04.43, 2 England (John Wilson, Andy Carter, Bill Hartley, Alan Pascoe) 3:06.66, 3 Uganda (Pius Olowo, William Dralu, Samuel Kakonge, Silver Ayoo) 3:07.45.

1978: 1 Kenya (Washington Njiri, Daniel Kimaiyo, Bill Koskei, Joel Ngetich) 3:03.54, 2 Jamaica (Clive Barriffe, Bert Cameron, Colin Bradford, Floyd Brown) 3:04.00, 3 Australia (John Higham, Chum Darvall, Garry Brown, Rick Mitchell) 3:04.23.

1982: 1 England (Steve Scutt, Garry Cook, Todd Bennett, Phil Brown) 3:05.45, 2 Australia (Gary Minihan, John Fleming, Greg Parker, Rick Mitchell) 3:05.82, 3 Kenya (Elisha Bitok, Juma Ndiwa, John Anzrah, James Maina) 3:06.33.

1986: 1 England (Kriss Akabusi, Roger Black, Todd Bennett, Phil Brown) 3:07.19, 2 Australia (Bruce Frayne, Miles Murphy, David Johnston, Darren Clark) 3:07.81, 3 Canada (Anton Skerritt, Andre Smith, John Graham, Atlee Mahorn) 3:08.69.

1990: 1 Kenya (Samson Kitur, Stephen Mwanzia, David Kitur, Simeon Kipkemboi) 3:02.48, 2 Scotland (Mark Davidson, Tom McKean, David Strang, Brian Whittle) 3:04.68, 3 Jamaica (Clive Wright, Devon Morris, Trevor Graham, Howard Burnett) 3:04.96.

1994: 1 England (David McKenzie, Peter Crampton, Adrian Patrick, Du'aine Ladejo) 3:02.14, 2 Jamaica (Orville Taylor, Dennis Blake, Linval Laird, Garth Robinson) 3:02.32, 3 Trinidad & Tobago (Patrick Delice, Neil De Silva, Hayden Stephen, Ian Morris) 3:02.78.

1998: 1 Jamaica (Michael McDonald, Roxbert Martin, Greg Haughton, Davian Clarke) 2:59.03, 2 England (Paul Slythe, Solomon Wariso, Mark Hylton, Mark Richardson) 3:00.82, 3 Wales (Paul Gray, Jamie Baulch, Doug Turner, Iwan Thomas) 3:01.86.

Note: Sean Baldock, Jared Deacon (both Eng) and Matthew Elias (Wal) ran in heats.

High Jump:

1930: 1 Johannes Viljoen (SA) 1.90, 2 Colin Gordon (BG) 1.88, 3 William Stargratt (Can) 1.85.

1934: 1 Edwin Thacker (SA) 1.90, 2 Joe Haley (Can) 1.90, 3 John Michie (Sco) 1.90.

1938: 1 Edwin Thacker (SA) 1.96, 2 Robert Heffernan (Aus) 1.88, 3 Doug Shetliffe (Aus) 1.88.

1950: 1 John Winter (Aus) 1.98, 2= Joshua Majekodunmi (Nig) & Alan Paterson (Sco) 1.95.

1954: 1 Emmanuel Ifeajuna (Nig) 2.03, 2 Patrick Etolu (Uga) 1.99, 3 Nafio Osagie (Nig) 1.99.

1958: 1 Ernle Haisley (Jam) 2.06, 2 Charles Porter (Aus) 2.03, 3 Robert Kotei (Gha) 2.01.

1962: 1 Percy Hobson (Aus) 2.11, 2 Charles Porter (Aus) 2.08, 3 Anton Norris (Bar) 2.03.

1966: 1 Lawrie Peckham (Aus) 2.08, 2 Samuel Igun (Nig) 2.03, 3 Anton Norris (Bar) 2.01.

1970: 1 Lawrie Peckham (Aus) 2.14, 2 John Hawkins (Can) 2.12, 3 Sheikh Tidiane Faye (Gam) 2.10.

1974: 1 Gordon Windeyer (Aus) 2.16, 2 Lawrie Peckham (Aus) 2.14, 3 Claude Ferragne (Can) 2.12.

1978: 1 Claude Ferragne (Can) 2.20, 2 Greg Joy (Can) 2.18, 3= Dean Bauck (Can), Brian Burgess (Sco) 2.15.

1982: 1 Milt Ottey (Can) 2.31, 2 Steve Wray (Bah) 2.31, 3 Nick Saunders (Ber) 2.19.

1986: 1 Milt Ottey (Can) 2.30, 2 Geoff Parsons (Sco) 2.28, 3= Alain Metellus (Can), Henderson Pierre (Eng) 2.14.

1990: 1 Nick Saunders (Ber) 2.36, 2 Dalton Grant (Eng) 2.34, 3= Milt Ottey (Can), Geoff Parsons (Sco) 2.23.

1994: 1 Tim Forsyth (Aus) 2.32, 2 Steve Smith (Eng) 2.32, 3 Geoff Parsons (Sco) 2.31.

1998: 1 Dalton Grant (Eng) 2.31, 2 Ben Challenger (Eng) 2.28, 3 Tim Forsyth (Aus) 2.28.

Pole Vault:

1930: 1 Vic Pickard (Can) 3.73, 2 Howard Ford (Eng) 3.73, 3 Robert Stoddard (Can) -.

1934: 1 Syl Apps (Can) 3.81 (3.88 in jump-off), 2 Alf Gilbert (Can) 3.81, 3 Fred Woodhouse (Aus) 3.66.

1938: 1 Andries du Plessis (SA) 4.11, 2 Les Fletcher (Aus) 3.97, 3 Stuart Frid (Can) 3.88.

1950: 1 Tim Anderson (Eng) 3.96, 2 Stan Egerton (Can) 3.96, 3 Peter Denton (Aus) 3.88.

1954: 1 Geoff Elliott (Eng) 4.27, 2 Ron Miller (Can) 4.20, 3 Andries Burger (SA) 4.13.

1958: 1 Geoff Elliott (Eng) 4.16, 2 Bob Reid (Can) 4.16, 3 Mervyn Richards (NZ) 4.16.

1962: 1 Trevor Bickle (Aus) 4.50, 2 Danie Burger (Rho) 4.42, 3 Ross Filshie (Aus)

4.42.

1966: 1 Trevor Bickle (Aus) 4.80, 2 Mike Bull (NI) 4.72, 3 Gerry Moro (Can) 4.65.

1970: 1 Mike Bull (NI) 5.10, 2 Allan Kane (Can) 4.90, 3 Bob Raftis (Can) 4.90.

1974: 1 Don Baird (Aus) 5.05, 2 Mike Bull (NI) 5.00, 3 Brian Hooper (Eng) 5.00.

1978: 1 Bruce Simpson (Can) 5.10, 2 Don Baird (Aus) 5.10, 3 Brian Hooper (Eng) 5.00.

1982: 1 Ray Boyd (Aus) 5.20, 2 Jeff Gutteridge (Eng) 5.20, 3 Graham Eggleton (Sco) 5.20.

1986: 1 Andy Ashurst (Eng) 5.30, 2 Bob Ferguson (Can) 5.20, 3 Neil Honey (Aus) 5.20.

1990: 1 Simon Arkell (Aus) 5.35, 2 Ian Tullett (Eng) 5.25, 3 Simon Poelman (NZ) 5.20.

1994: 1 Neil Winter (Wal) 5.40, 2 Curtis Heywood (Can) 5.30, 3 James Miller (Aus) 5.30.

1998: 1 Riaan Botha (SA) 5.60, 2 Paul Burgess (Aus) 5.50, 3 Kersley Gardenne (Mau) 5.35.

Note: Denis Petushinskiy (NZ) originally placed 2nd but subsequently disqualified for drugs offence.

Long Jump:

1930: 1 Len Hutton (Can) 7.20, 2 Reg Revans (Eng) 6.96, 3 Johannes Viljoen (SA) 6.96.

1934: 1 Sam Richardson (Can) 7.17, 2 Johann Luckhoff (SA) 7.10, 3 Jack Metcalfe (Aus) 6.93.

1938: 1 Hal Brown (Can) 7.43, 2 Jim Panton (Can) 7.25, 3 Basil Dickinson (Aus) 7.15.

1950: 1 Neville Price (SA) 7.31, 2 Bevan Hough (NZ) 7.20, 3 David Dephoff (NZ) 7.08.

1954: 1 Ken Wilmshurst (Eng) 7.54, 2 Karim Olowu (Nig) 7.39, 3 Sylvanus Williams (Nig) 7.22.

1958: 1 Paul Foreman (Jam) 7.47, 2 Deryck Taylor (Jam) 7.47, 3 Muhammad Ramzan Ali (Pak) 7.32.

1962: 1 Mike Ahey (Gha) 8.05w, 2 Dave Norris (NZ) 7.74w, 3 Wellesley Clayton (Jam) 7.73w.

1966: 1 Lynn Davies (Wal) 7.99, 2 John Morbey (Ber) 7.89, 3 Wellesley Clayton (Jam) 7.83.

1970: 1 Lynn Davies (Wal) 8.06w, 2 Phil May (Aus) 7.94, 3 Alan Lerwill (Eng) 7.94w.

1974: 1 Alan Lerwill (Eng) 7.94, 2 Chris Commons (Aus) 7.92, 3 Joshua Owusu (Gha) 7.75.

1978: 1 Roy Mitchell (Eng) 8.06w, 2 Chris Commons (Aus) 8.04w, 3 Suresh Babu (Ind) 7.94w.

1982: 1 Gary Honey (Aus) 8.13, 2 Steve Hanna (Bah) 7.79w, 3 Steve Walsh (NZ) 7.75.

1986: 1 Gary Honey (Aus) 8.08, 2 Fred Salle (Eng) 7.83, 3 Kyle McDuffie (Can) 7.79w.

1990: 1 Yussuf Ali (Nig) 8.39w, 2 David Culbert (Aus) 8.20w, 3 Festus Igbinoghene (Nig) 8.18w.

1994: 1 Obinna Eregbu (Nig) 8.05w, 2 David Culbert (Aus) 8.00, 3 Ian James (Can) 7.93w.

1998: 1 Peter Burge (Aus) 8.22, 2 Jai Taurima (Aus) 8.22, 3 Wendell Williams (Tri) 7.95.

Triple Jump:

Entitled Hop Step & Jump 1930-1958

1930: 1 Gordon Smallacombe (Can) 14.76, 2 Reg Revans (Eng) 14.29, 3 Len Hutton (Can) 13.90.

1934: 1 Jack Metcalfe (Aus) 15.63, 2 Sam Richardson (Can) 14.65, 3 Harold Brainsby (NZ) 14.62.

1938: 1 Jack Metcalfe (Aus) 15.49, 2 Lloyd Miller (Aus) 15.41, 3 Basil Dickinson (Aus) 15.28.

1950: 1 Brian Oliver (Aus) 15.61, 2 Les McKeand (Aus) 15.28, 3 Ian Polmear (Aus) 14.67.

1954: 1 Ken Wilmshurst (Eng) 15.27, 2 Paul Esiri (Nig) 15.25, 3 Brian Oliver (Aus) 15.14.

1958: 1 Ian Tomlinson (Aus) 15.74w, 2 Jack Smyth (Can) 15.69, 3 Dave Norris (NZ) 15.45.

1962: 1 Ian Tomlinson (Aus) 16.21, 2 John Baguley (Aus) 16.08, 3 Fred Alsop (Eng) 16.03.

1966: 1 Samuel Igun (Nig) 16.40w, 2 George Ogan (Nig) 16.08, 3 Fred Alsop (Eng) 15.96.

1970: 1 Phil May (Aus) 16.72, 2 Mick McGrath (Aus) 16.41, 3 Mohinder Singh (Ind) 15.90.

1974: 1 Joshua Owusu (Gha) 16.50, 2 Mohinder Singh (Ind) 16.44, 3 Moise Pomaney (Gha) 16.23.

1978: 1 Keith Connor (Eng) 17.21w, 2 Ian Campbell (Aus) 16.93w, 3 Aston Moore (Eng) 16.69.

1982: 1 Keith Connor (Eng) 17.81w, 2 Ken Lorraway (Aus) 17.54w, 3 Aston Moore (Eng) 16.76w.

1986: 1 John Herbert (Eng) 17.27, 2 Mike Makin (Eng) 16.87, 3 Peter Beames (Aus) 16.42.

1990: 1 Marios Hadjiandreou (Cyp) 16.95, 2 Jonathan Edwards (Eng) 16.93, 3 Edrick Floreal (Can) 16.89.

1994: 1 Julian Golley (Eng) 17.03, 2 Jonathan Edwards (Eng) 17.00, 3 Brian Wellman (Ber) 17.00.

1998; 1 Larry Achike (Eng) 17.10, 2 Andrew Owusu (Gha) 17.03, 3 Remmy Limo (Ken) 16.89.

Shot Putt:

1930: 1 Harry Hart (SA) 14.58, 2 Robert Howland (Eng) 13.46, 3 Charlie Herman (Can) 12.98.

1934: 1 Harry Hart (SA) 14.67, 2 Robert Howland (Eng) 13.53, 3 Kenneth Pridie (Eng) 13.43.

1938: 1 Louis Fouche (SA) 14.48, 2 Eric Coy (Can) 13.96, 3 Francis Drew (Aus) 13.80.

1950: 1 Mataika Tuicakau (Fij) 14.63, 2 Harold Moody (Eng) 13.92, 3 Leo Roininen (Can) 13.68.

1954: 1 John Savidge (Eng) 16.77, 2 John Pavelich (Can) 14.95, 3 Stephanus du Plessis (SA) 14.93.

1958: 1 Arthur Rowe (Eng) 17.57, 2 Martyn Lucking (Eng) 16.49, 3 Barry Donath (Aus) 15.79.

1962: 1 Martyn Lucking (Eng) 18.08, 2 Mike Lindsay (Sco) 18.05, 3 Dave Steen (Can) 17.90.

1966: 1 Dave Steen (Can) 18.79, 2 Les Mills (NZ) 18.37, 3 George Puce (Can) 17.14.

1970: 1 Dave Steen (Can) 19.21, 2 Jeff Teale (Eng) 18.43, 3 Les Mills (NZ) 18.40.

1974: 1 Geoff Capes (Eng) 20.74, 2 Mike Winch (Eng) 19.36, 3 Bruce Pirnie (Can) 18.68.

1978: 1 Geoff Capes (Eng) 19.77, 2 Bruno Pauletto (Can) 19.33, 3 Bishop Dolegiewicz (Can) 18.45.

1982: 1 Bruno Pauletto (Can) 19.55, 2 Mike Winch (Eng) 18.25, 3 Luby Chambul (Can) 17.46.

1986: 1 Billy Cole (Eng) 18.16, 2 Joe Quigley (Aus) 17.97, 3 Stuart Gyngell (Aus) 17.70.

1990: 1 Simon Williams (Eng) 18.54, 2 Adewale Olukoju (Nig) 18.48, 3 Paul Edwards (Wal) 18.17.

1994: 1 Matt Simson (Eng) 19.49, 2 Courtney Ireland (NZ) 19.38, 3 Chima Ugwu (Nig) 19.26.

1998: 1 Burger Lambrechts (SA) 20.01, 2 Michalis Louca (Cyp) 19.52, 3 Shaun Pickering (Wal) 19.33.

Discus:

1930: 1 Harry Hart (SA) 41.43, 2 Charlie Herman (Can) 41.22, 3 Abe Zvonkin (Can) 41.18.

1934: 1 Harry Hart (SA) 41.53, 2 Douglas Bell (Eng) 40.44, 3 Bernard Prendergast (Jam) 40.24.

1938: 1 Eric Coy (Can) 44.76, 2 David Young (Sco) 43.05, 3 George Sutherland (Can) 41.47.

1950: 1 Ian Reed (Aus) 47.72 (48.17 with extra throw), 2 Mataika Tuicakau (Fij) 43.96, 3 Svein Sigfusson (Can) 43.48.

1954: 1 Stephanus du Plessis (SA) 51.71, 2 Gino Roy Pella (Can) 49.54, 3 Mark Pharaoh (Eng) 47.85.

1958: 1 Stephanus du Plessis (SA) 55.94, 2 Les Mills (NZ) 51.72, 3 Gerry Carr (Eng) 51.62.

1962: 1 Warwick Selvey (Aus) 56.48, 2 Mike Lindsay (Sco) 52.58, 3 John Sheldrick (Eng) 50.67.

1966: 1 Les Mills (NZ) 56.19, 2 George Puce (Can) 55.93, 3 Robin Tait (NZ) 55.02.

1970: 1 George Puce (Can) 59.02, 2 Les Mills (NZ) 57.84, 3 Bill Tancred (Eng) 56.68.

1974: 1 Robin Tait (NZ) 63.08, 2 Bill Tancred (Eng) 59.48, 3 John Hillier (Eng) 57.22.

1978: 1 Borys Chambul (Can) 59.70, 2 Brad Cooper (Bah) 57.30, 3 Rob Gray

(Can) 55.48.

1982: 1 Brad Cooper (Bah) 64.04, 2 Rob Gray (Can) 60.66, 3 Bishop Dolegiewicz (Can) 60.34.

1986: 1 Ray Lazdins (Can) 58.86, 2 Paul Nandapi (Aus) 57.74, 3 Werner Reiterer (Aus) 57.34.

1990: 1 Adewale Olukoju (Nig) 62.62, 2 Werner Reiterer (Aus) 61.56, 3 Paul Nandapi (Aus) 59.94.

1994: 1 Werner Reiterer (Aus) 62.76, 2 Adewale Olukoju (Nig) 62.46, 3 Bob Weir (Eng) 60.86.

1998: 1 Bob Weir (Eng) 64.42, 2 Frantz Kruger (SA) 63.93, 3 Jason Tunks (Can) 62.22.

Hammer:

1930: 1 Malcolm Nokes (Eng) 47.13, 2 Bill Britton (Ire) 46.90, 3 Jack Cameron (Can) 44.46.

1934: 1 Malcolm Nokes (Eng) 48.25, 2 George Sutherland (Can) 46.25, 3 William Mackenzie (Sco) 42.50.

1938: 1 George Sutherland (Can) 48.71, 2 Keith Pardon (Aus) 45.13, 3 Jim Leckie (NZ) 44.34.

1950: 1 Duncan McDougall Clark (Sco) 49.94, 2 Keith Pardon (Aus) 48.84,
3 Herb Barker (Aus) 45.62.

1954: 1 Muhammad Iqbal (Pak) 55.38, 2 Vic Dreyer (SA) 54.75, 3 Ewan Douglas (Sco) 52.80.

1958: 1 Mike Ellis (Eng) 62.90, 2 Muhammad Iqbal (Pak) 61.70, 3 Peter Allday (Eng) 57.58.

1962: 1 Howard Payne (Eng) 61.64, 2 Dick Leffler (Aus) 59.83, 3 Bob Brown (Aus) 57.64.

1966: 1 Howard Payne (Eng) 61.98, 2 Praveen Kumar (Ind) 60.12, 3 Muhammad Iqbal (Pak) 59.56.

1970: 1 Howard Payne (Eng) 67.80, 2 Bruce Fraser (Eng) 62.90, 3 Barry Williams (Eng) 61.58.

1974: 1 Ian Chipchase (Eng) 69.56, 2 Howard Payne (Eng) 68.02, 3 Peter Farmer (Aus) 67.48.

1978: 1 Peter Farmer (Aus) 71.10, 2 Scott Neilson (Can) 69.92, 3 Chris Black (Sco) 68.14.

1982: 1 Bob Weir (Eng) 75.08, 2 Martin Girvan (NI) 73.62, 3 Chris Black (Sco) 69.84.

1986: 1 David Smith (Eng) 74.06, 2 Martin Girvan (NI) 70.48, 3 Phil Spivey (Aus) 70.30.

1990: 1 Sean Carlin (Aus) 75.66, 2 David Smith (Eng) 73.52, 3 Angus Cooper (NZ) 71.26.

1994: 1 Sean Carlin (Aus) 73.48, 2 Paul Head (Eng) 70.18, 3 Peter Vivian (Eng) 69.80.

1998: 1 Stuart Rendell (Aus) 74.71, 2 Michael Jones (Eng) 74.02, 3 Chris Harmse (SA) 72.83.

Javelin:

1930: 1 Stan Lay (NZ) 63.13, 2 Doral Pilling (Can) 55.94, 3 Harry Hart (SA) 53.22.

1934: 1 Bob Dixon (Can) 60.02, 2 Harry Hart (SA) 58.28, 3 Johann Luckhoff (SA) 56.50.

1938: 1 Jim Courtright (Can) 62.80, 2 Stan Lay (NZ) 62.21, 3 Jack Metcalfe (Aus) 55.53.

1950: 1 Leo Roininen (Can) 57.11, 2 Luke Tunabuna (Fij) 56.02, 3 Doug Robinson (Can) 55.60.

1954: 1 James Achurch (Aus) 68.51, 2 Muhammad Nawaz (Pak) 68.08, 3 Jalal Khan (Pak) 67.50.

1958: 1 Colin Smith (Eng) 71.28, 2 Jalal Khan (Pak) 70.82, 3 Hans Moks (Can) 70.40.

1962: 1 Alf Mitchell (Aus) 78.10, 2 Colin Smith (Eng) 77.89, 3 Nick Birks (Aus) 75.07.

1966: 1 John FitzSimons (Eng) 79.78, 2 Nick Birks (Aus) 76.15, 3 Muhammad Nawaz (Pak) 69.93.

1970: 1 David Travis (Eng) 79.50, 2 John McSorley (Eng) 76.74, 3 John FitzSimons (Eng) 73.20.

1974: 1 Charles Clover (Eng) 84.92, 2 David Travis (Eng) 79.92, 3 John Mayaka (Ken) 77.56.

1978: 1 Phil Olsen (Can) 84.00, 2 Mike O'Rourke (NZ) 83.18, 3 Peter Yates (Eng) 78.58.

1982: 1 Mike O'Rourke (NZ) 89.48, 2 Laslo Babits (Can) 84.88, 3 Zakayo Malekwa (Tan) 80.22.

1986: 1 David Ottley (Eng) 80.62, 2 Mick Hill (Eng) 78.56, 3 Gavin Lovegrove (NZ) 76.22.

1990: 1 Steve Backley (Eng) 86.02, 2 Mick Hill (Eng) 83.32, 3 Gavin Lovegrove (NZ) 81.66.

1994: 1 Steve Backley (Eng) 82.74, 2 Mick Hill (Eng) 81.84, 3 Gavin Lovegrove (NZ) 80.42.

1998: 1 Marius Corbett (SA) 88.75, 2 Steve Backley (Eng) 87.38, 3 Mick Hill (Eng) 83.80.

Decathlon:

First held 1966

Note: also given are the scores as revised according to the new tables introduced in 1984.

1966: 1 Roy Williams (NZ) 7270pts, 2 Clive Longe (Wal) 7123, 3 Gerry Moro (Can) 6983.

Note: 1984 tables - Williams 7133, Longe 6984, Moro 6867.

1970: 1 Geoff Smith (Aus) 7492, 2 Peter Gabbett (Eng) 7469, 3 Barry King (Eng) 7201.

Note: 1984 tables - Smith 7420, Gabbett 7400, King 7118.

1974: 1 Mike Bull (NI) 7417, 2 Barry King (Eng) 7277, 3 Rob Lethbridge (Aus) 7270.

Note: 1984 tables - Bull 7363, King 7179, Lethbridge 7236.

1978: 1 Daley Thompson (Eng) 8467, 2 Peter Hadfield (Aus) 7623, 3 Alan Drayton (Eng) 7484.

Note: 1984 tables - Thompson 8470, Hadfield 7561, Drayton 7431.

1982: 1 Daley Thompson (Eng) 8410, 2 Dave Steen (Can) 8004, 3 Fidelis Obikwu (Eng) 7726.

Note: 1984 tables - Thompson 8424, Steen 8003, Obikwu 7668. Steen is the nephew of Dave Steen, Shot Putt 1962-66-70.

1986: 1 Daley Thompson (Eng) 8663, 2 Dave Steen (Can) 8173, 3 Simon Poelman (NZ) 8015.

1990: 1 Michael Smith (Can) 8525, 2 Simon Poelman (NZ) 8207, 3 Eugene Gilkes (Eng) 7705.

1994: 1 Michael Smith (Can) 8326, 2 Peter Winter (Aus) 8074, 3 Simon Shirley (Eng) 7980.

1998: 1 Jagan Hames (Aus) 8490, 2 Scott Ferrier (Aus) 8307, 3 Michael Smith (Can) 8143.

WOMEN

100 metres:

100 yards (91.44 metres) 1934-1966

1934: 1 Eileen Hiscock (Eng) 11.3, 2 Hilda Strike (Can) 11.5e, 3 Lillian Chalmers (Eng) 11.6e.

1938: 1 Decima Norman (Aus) 11.1, 2 Joyce Walker (Aus) 11.3e, 3 Jeanette Dolson (Can) 11.4e.

1950: 1 Marjorie Jackson (Aus) 10.8, 2 Shirley Strickland (Aus) 11.0, 3 Verna Johnston (Aus) 11.1.

1954: 1 Marjorie Nelson (Aus) 10.7, 2 Winsome Cripps (Aus) 10.8, 3 Edna Maskell (NR) 10.8.

Note: Nelson nee Jackson.

1958: 1 Marlene Willard (Aus) 10.70, 2 Heather Young (Eng) 10.73, 3 Madeleine Weston (Eng) 10.81.

1962: 1 Dorothy Hyman (Eng) 11.2, 2 Doreen Porter (NZ) 11.3, 3 Brenda Cox (Aus) 11.4.

1966: 1 Dianne Burge (Aus) 10.6, 2 Irene Piotrowski (Can) 10.8, 3 Jill Hall (Eng) 10.8.

1970: 1 Raelene Boyle (Aus) 11.27w (+ 5.3m), 2 Alice Annum (Gha) 11.33,
3 Marion Hoffman (Aus) 11.36.

1974: 1 Raelene Boyle (Aus) 11.27, 2 Andrea Lynch (Eng) 11.31, 3 Denise Robertson (Aus) 11.50.

1978: 1 Sonia Lannaman (Eng) 11.27w (+ 2.81m), 2 Raelene Boyle (Aus) 11.35, 3 Denise Boyd (Aus) 11.37.

Note: Boyd nee Robertson.

1982: 1 Angella Taylor (Can) 11.00, 2 Merlene Ottey (Jam) 11.03, 3 Colleen Pekin (Aus) 11.24.

Note: Pekin nee Beazley.

1986: 1 Heather Oakes (Eng) 11.20w (+ 2.2m), 2 Paula Dunn (Eng) 11.21,
3 Angella Issajenko (Can) 11.21.

Note: Issajenko nee Taylor.

1990: 1 Merlene Ottey (Jam) 11.02, 2 Kerry Johnson (Aus) 11.17, 3 Pauline Davis (Bah) 11.20.

1994: 1 Mary Onyali (Nig) 11.06, 2 Christy Opara-Thompson (Nig) 11.22, 3 Paula Thomas (Eng) 11.23.

Note: Thomas nee Dunn.

1998: 1 Chandra Sturrup (Bah) 11.06, 2 Philomena Mensah (Can) 11.19, 3 Tania Van Heer (Aus) 11.29.

200 metres:

220 yards (201.168 metres)1934-1966

1934: 1 Eileen Hiscock (Eng) 25.0, 2 Aileen Meagher (Can) 25.4e, 3 Nellie Halstead (Eng) 25.6e.

1938: 1 Decima Norman (Aus) 24.7, 2 Jean Coleman (Aus) 25.1e, 3 Eileen Wearne (Aus) 25.3e.

1950: 1 Marjorie Jackson (Aus) 24.3, 2 Shirley Strickland (Aus) 24.5, 3 Daphne Robb (SA) 24.7.

1954: 1 Marjorie Nelson (Aus) 24.0, 2 Winsome Cripps (Aus) 24.5, 3 Shirley Hampton (Eng) 25.0.

Note: Nelson nee Jackson.

1958: 1 Marlene Willard (Aus) 23.65, 2 Betty Cuthbert (Aus) 23.77, 3 Heather Young (Eng) 23.90.

1962: 1 Dorothy Hyman (Eng) 24.00, 2 Joyce Bennett (Aus) 24.21, 3 Margaret Burvill (Aus) 24.42.

1966: 1 Dianne Burge (Aus) 23.73, 2 Jennifer Lamy (Aus) 23.86, 3 Irene Piotrowski (Can) 23.92.

1970: 1 Raelene Boyle (Aus) 22.75w (+ 4.0m), 2 Alice Annum (Gha) 22.86, 3 Margaret Critchley (Eng) 23.16.

1974: 1 Raelene Boyle (Aus) 22.50, 2 Denise Robertson (Aus) 22.73, 3 Alice Annum (Gha) 22.90.

1978: 1 Denise Boyd (Aus) 22.82w (+ 5.01m), 2 Sonia Lannaman (Eng) 22.89, 3 Colleen Beazley (Aus) 22.93.

Note: Boyd nee Robertson.

1982: 1 Merlene Ottey (Jam) 22.19w (+ 2.5m), 2 Kathy Smallwood (Eng) 22.21, 3 Angella Taylor (Can) 22.48.

1986: 1 Angella Issajenko (Can) 22.91w (+ 2.07m), 2 Kathy Cook (Eng) 23.18, 3 Sandra Whittaker (Sco) 23.46.

Note: Issajenko nee Taylor, Cook nee Smallwood.

1990: 1 Merlene Ottey (Jam) 22.76, 2 Kerry Johnson (Aus) 22.88, 3 Pauline Davis (Bah) 23.15.

1994: 1 Cathy Freeman (Aus) 22.25, 2 Mary Onyali (Nig) 22.35, 3 Melinda Gainsford (Aus) 22.86.

1998: 1 Nova Peris-Kneebone (Aus) 22.77, 2 Juliet Campbell (Jam) 22.79, 3 Lauren Hewitt (Aus) 22.83.

400 metres:

First held in 1966, 440 yards (402.336 metres)1966

1966: 1 Judy Pollock (Aus) 53.0, 2 Deirdre Watkinson (Eng) 54.1, 3 Una Morris (Jam) 54.2.

1970: 1 Marilyn Neufville (Jam) 51.02, 2 Sandra Brown (Aus) 53.66, 3 Judith Ayaa (Uga) 53.77.

1974: 1 Yvonne Saunders (Can) 51.67, 2 Verona Bernard (Eng) 51.94, 3 Charlene Rendina (Aus) 52.08.

1978: 1 Donna Hartley (Eng) 51.69, 2 Verona Elder (Eng) 52.94, 3 Beth Nail (Aus) 53.06.

Note: Elder nee Bernard.

1982: 1 Raelene Boyle (Aus) 51.26, 2 Michelle Scutt (Wal) 51.97, 3 Joslyn Hoyte-Smith (Eng) 52.53.

1986: 1 Debbie Flintoff (Aus) 51.29, 2 Jillian Richardson (Can) 51.62, 3 Kathy Cook (Eng) 51.88.

1990: 1 Fatima Yusuf (Nig) 51.08, 2 Linda Keough (Eng) 51.63, 3 Charity Opara (Nig) 52.01.

1994: 1 Cathy Freeman (Aus) 50.38, 2 Fatima Yusuf (Nig) 50.53, 3 Sandie Richards (Jam) 50.59.

1998: 1 Sandie Richards (Jam) 50.18, 2 Allison Curbishley (Sco) 50.71, 3 Donna Fraser (Eng) 51.01.

800 metres:

880 yards (804.672 metres)1934-1966

1934: 1 Gladys Lunn (Eng) 2:19.4, 2 Ida Jones (Eng) 2:21.0e, 3 Dorothy Butterfield (Eng) 2:21.4e.

1938-1958: Not held

1962: 1 Dixie Willis (Aus) 2:03.85, 2 Marise Chamberlain (NZ) 2:05.66, 3 Joy Jordan (Eng) 2:05.96.

1966: 1 Abby Hoffman (Can) 2:04.3, 2 Judy Pollock (Aus) 2:04.5, 3 Anne Smith (Eng) 2:05.0.

1970: 1 Rosemary Stirling (Sco) 2:06.24, 2 Pat Lowe (Eng) 2:06.27, 3 Cheryl Peasley (Aus) 2:06.33.

1974: 1 Charlene Rendina (Aus) 2:01.11, 2 Sue Haden (NZ) 2:02.04, 3 Sabina Chebichi (Ken) 2:02.61.

1978: 1 Judy Peckham (Aus) 2:02.82, 2 Tekla Chemabwai (Ken) 2:02.87, 3 Jane Colebrook (Eng) 2:03.10.

1982: 1 Kirsty McDermott (Wal) 2:01.31, 2 Anne Clarkson (Sco) 2:01.52,
3 Heather Barralet (Aus) 2:01.70.

1986: 1 Kirsty Wade (Wal) 2:00.94, 2 Diane Edwards (Eng) 2:01.12, 3 Lorraine Baker (Eng) 2:01.79.

Note: Wade nee McDermott.

1990: 1 Diane Edwards (Eng) 2:00.25, 2 Ann Williams (Eng) 2:00.40, 3 Sharon Stewart (Aus) 2:00.87.

1994: 1 Inez Turner (Jam) 2:01.74, 2 Charmaine Crooks (Can) 2:02.35, 3 Gladys Wamuyu (Ken) 2:03.12.

1998: 1 Maria Mutola (Moz) 1:57.60, 2 Tina Paulino (Moz) 1:58.39, 3 Diane Modahl (Eng) 1:58.81.
Note: Modahl nee Edwards.

1500 metres:
First held in 1970
1970: 1 Rita Ridley (Eng) 4:18.8, 2 Joan Page (Eng) 4:19.0, 3 Thelma Fynn (Can) 4:19.1.
1974: 1 Glenda Reiser (Can) 4:07.78, 2 Joan Allison (Eng) 4:10.66, 3 Thelma Wright (Can) 4:12.26.
Note: Allison nee Page, Wright nee Fynn.
1978: 1 Mary Stewart (Eng) 4:06.34, 2 Chris Benning (Eng) 4:07.53, 3 Penny Werthner (Can) 4:08.14.
1982: 1 Chris Boxer (Eng) 4:08.28, 2 Gillian Dainty (Eng) 4:10.80, 3 Lorraine Moller (NZ) 4:12.67.
1986: 1 Kirsty Wade (Wal) 4:10.91, 2 Debbie Bowker (Can) 4:11.94, 3 Lynn Williams (Can) 4:12.66.
1990: 1 Angela Chalmers (Can) 4:08.41, 2 Chris Cahill (Eng) 4:08.75, 3 Bev Nicholson (Eng) 4:09.00. Note: Cahill nee Boxer.
1994: 1 Kelly Holmes (Eng) 4:08.86, 2 Paula Schnurr (Can) 4:09.65, 3 Gwen Griffiths (SA) 4:10.16.
1998: 1 Jackline Maranga (Ken) 4:05.27, 2 Kelly Holmes (Eng) 4:06.10, 3 Julia Sakara (Zim) 4:07.82.

3000 metres/5000 metres:
First held in 1978, 3000 metres 1978-1994
1978: 1 Paula Fudge (Eng) 9:12.95, 2 Heather Thomson (NZ) 9:20.69, 3 Ann Ford (Eng) 9:24.05.
1982: 1 Anne Audain (NZ) 8:45.53, 2 Wendy Smith (Eng) 8:48.47, 3 Lorraine Moller (NZ) 8:55.76.
1986: 1 Lynn Williams (Can) 8:54.29, 2 Debbie Bowker (Can) 8:54.83, 3 Yvonne Murray (Sco) 8:55.32.
1990: 1 Angela Chalmers (Can) 8:38.38, 2 Yvonne Murray (Sco) 8:39.46, 3 Liz McColgan (Sco) 8:47.66.
1994: 1 Angela Chalmers (Can) 8:32.17, 2 Robyn Meagher (Can) 8:44.59, 3 Alison Wyeth (Eng) 8:47.98.
1998: 1 Kate Anderson (Aus) 15:52.74, 2 Andrea Whitcombe (Eng) 15:56.85, 3 Samukeliso Moyo (Zam) 15:57.57.

10,000 metres:
First held in 1986
1986: 1 Liz Lynch (Sco) 31:41.42, 2 Anne Audain (NZ) 31:53.31, 3 Angela Tooby (Wal) 32:25.38.
1990: 1 Liz McColgan (Sco) 32:23.56, 2 Jill Hunter (Eng) 32:33.21, 3 Barbara Moore (NZ) 32:44.73. Note: McColgan nee Lynch.
1994: 1 Yvonne Murray (Sco) 31:56.97, 2 Elana Meyer (SA) 32:06.02, 3 Jane Omoro (Ken) 32:13.01.

ATHLETICS

1998: 1 Esther Wanjiru (Ken) 33:40.13, 2 Kylie Risk (Aus) 33:42.11, 3 Clare Fearnley (Aus) 33:52.13.

Marathon

(26 miles 385 yards/42.195 kilometres):

First held in 1986

1986: 1 Lisa Martin (Aus) 2:26:07, 2 Lorraine Moller (NZ) 2:28:17, 3 Odette Lapierre (Can) 2:31:48.

1990: 1 Lisa Martin (Aus) 2:25:28, 2 Tani Ruckle (Aus) 2:33:15, 3 Angie Pain (Eng) 2:36:35.

1994: 1 Carole Rouillard (Can) 2:30:41, 2 Lizanne Bussières (Can) 2:31:07, 3 Yvonne Danson (Eng) 2:32:24.

1998: 1 Heather Turland (Aus) 2:41:24, 2 Lisa Dick (Aus) 2:41:48, 3 Elizabeth Mongudhi (Nam) 2:43:28.

80 metres hurdles/100 metres hurdles:

80 metres hurdles 1934-1966

1934: 1 Marjorie Clark (SA) 11.8, 2 Betty Taylor (Can) 11.9e, 3 Elsie Green (Eng) 12.2e.

1938: 1 Barbara Burke (SA) 11.7, 2 Isobel Grant (Aus) 11.7, 3 Rona Tong (NZ) 11.8e.

1950: 1 Shirley Strickland (Aus) 11.6, 2 June Schoch (NZ) 11.6, 3 Joan Shackleton (NZ) 11.7.

1954: 1 Edna Maskell (NR) 10.9w, 2 Gwen Hobbins (Can) 11.2, 3 Jean Desforges (Eng) 11.2.

Note: officially stated to be wind-assisted.

1958: 1 Norma Thrower (Aus) 10.72w (+ 4.89m), 2 Carole Quinton (Eng) 10.77, 3 Gloria Wigney (Aus) 10.94.

1962: 1 Pam Kilborn (Aus) 11.07, 2 Betty Moore (Eng) 11.40, 3 Avis McIntosh (NZ) 11.47.

1966: 1 Pam Kilborn (Aus) 10.9, 2 Carmen Smith (Jam) 11.0, 3 Jenny Wingerson (Can) 11.0.

1970: 1 Pam Kilborn (Aus) 13.27, 2 Maureen Caird (Aus) 13.73, 3 Christine Bell (Eng) 13.82.

1974: 1 Judy Vernon (Eng) 13.45, 2 Gaye Dell (Aus) 13.54, 3 Modupe Oshikoya (Nig) 13.69.

1978: 1 Lorna Boothe (Eng) 12.98w (+ 3.56m), 2 Shirley Strong (Eng) 13.08, 3 Sharon Colyear (Eng) 13.17.

1982: 1 Shirley Strong (Eng) 12.78w (+ 4.5m), 2 Lorna Boothe (Eng) 12.90, 3 Sue Kameli (Can) 13.10.

1986: 1 Sally Gunnell (Eng) 13.29, 2 Wendy Jeal (Eng) 13.41, 3 Glynis Nunn (Aus) 13.44.

1990: 1 Kay Morley (Wal) 12.91, 2 Sally Gunnell (Eng) 13.12, 3 Lesley-Ann Skeete (Eng) 13.31.

1994: 1 Michelle Freeman (Jam) 13.12, 2 Jackie Agyepong (Eng) 13.14, 3 Samantha Farquharson (Eng) 13.38.

1998: 1 Gillian Russell (Jam) 12.70, 2 Sriyani Kulawansa (SriL) 12.95, 3 Katie

Anderson (Can) 13.04.

400 metres hurdles:
First held in 1982

1982: 1 Debbie Flintoff (Aus) 55.89, 2 Ruth Kyalisima (Uga) 57.10, 3 Yvette Wray (Eng) 57.17.

1986: 1 Debbie Flintoff-King (Aus) 54.94, 2 Donalda Duprey (Can) 56.55, 3 Jenny Laurendet (Aus) 56.57.

Note: Flintoff-King nee Flintoff.

1990: 1 Sally Gunnell (Eng) 55.38, 2 Debbie Flintoff-King (Aus) 56.00, 3 Jenny Laurendet (Aus) 56.74.

1994: 1 Sally Gunnell (Eng) 54.51, 2 Deon Hemmings (Jam) 55.11, 3 Debbie Ann Parris (Jam) 55.25.

1998: 1 Andrea Blackett (Bar) 53.91, 2 Gowry Retchakan (Eng) 55.25, 3 Karlene Haughton (Can) 55.53.

10 kilometres walk:
First held in 1990

1990: 1 Kerry Saxby (Aus) 45:03, 2 Anne Judkins (NZ) 47:03, 3 Lisa Langford (Eng) 47.23.

1994: 1 Kerry Saxby-Junna (Aus) 44:25; 2 Anne Manning (Aus) 44:37, 3 Janice McCaffrey (Can) 44:54.

Note: Saxby-Junna nee Saxby.

1998: 1 Jane Saville (Aus) 43:57, 2 Kerry Saxby-Junna (Aus) 44:27, 3 Lisa Kehler (Eng) 45:03. Note: Kehler nee Langford.

4 x 100 metres relay
440 yards relay (220x110x110) and 660 yards relay (220x220x110x110) 1934-1950, 4 x 110 yards (100.584 metres) 1954-1966.

1934: 440 yards relay - 1 England (Nellie Halstead, Eileen Hiscock, Elsie Maguire) 49.4, 2 Canada (Aileen Meagher, Audrey Dearnley, Hilda Strike) -, 3 Rhodesia (Dorothy Ballantyne, Cynthia Keay, Mollie Bragge) -.

660 yards relay - 1 Canada (Lillian Palmer, Betty White, Aileen Meagher, Audrey Dearnley) 1:14.4, 2 England (Nellie Halstead, Eileen Hiscock, Ethel Johnson, Ivy Walker), 3 Scotland (Joan Cunningham, Sheila Dobbie, Cathie Jackson, Margaret Mackenzie) -.

1938: 440 yards relay -1 Australia (Jean Coleman, Eileen Wearne, Decima Norman) 49.1, 2 Canada (Aileen Meagher, Jeanette Dolson,. Barbara Howard) 49.5, 3 England (Kathleen Stokes, Dorothy Saunders, Winifred Jeffrey) 51.3.

660 yards relay - 1 Australia (Jean Coleman, Decima Norman, Thelma Peake, Joan Woodland) 1:15.2, 2 England (Kathleen Stokes, Ethel Raby, Dorothy Saunders, Winifred Jeffrey) 1:17.2e, 3 Canada (Violet Montgomery, Barbara Howard, Aileen Meagher, Jeanette Dolson) 1:19.0e.

1950: 440 yards relay - 1 Australia (Marjorie Jackson, Shirley Strickland, Verna Johnston) 47.9, 2 New Zealand (Lesley Rowe, Shirley Hardman, Doris Parker) 48.7, 3 England (Sylvia Cheeseman, Margaret Walker, Dorothy Hall) 50.0.

660 yards relay - 1 Australia (Shirley Strickland, Verna Johnston, Marjorie Jackson,

Ann Shanley) 1:13.4, 2 England (Sylvia Cheeseman, Margaret Walker, Doris Batten, Dorothy Hall) 1:17.5, 3 Canada (Eleanor McKenzie, Gerry Bemister, Pat Jones, Elaine Silburn) -.

1954: 1 Australia (Gwen Wallace, Nancy Fogarty, Winsome Cripps, Marjorie Nelson) 46.8, 2 England (Shirley Hampton, Shirley Burgess, Heather Armitage, Ann Pashley) 46.9, 3 Canada (Margery Squires, Dorothy Kozak, Annabelle Murray, Gerry Bemister) 47.8.

Note: Nelson nee Jackson.

1958: 1 England (Madeleine Weston, Dorothy Hyman, June Paul, Heather Young) 45.37, 2 Australia (Betty Cuthbert, Kay Johnson, Wendy Hayes, Marlene Willard) 46.12, 3 Canada (Diane Matheson, Eleanor Haslam, Maureen Reever, Freyda Berman) 47.21.

Note: Young nee Armitage.

1962: 1 Australia (Joyce Bennett, Glenys Beasley, Brenda Cox, Betty Cuthbert) 46.71, 2 England (Ann Packer, Dorothy Hyman, Daphne Arden, Betty Moore) 46.81, 3 New Zealand (Nola Bond, Avis McIntosh, Yvonne Cowan, Doreen Porter) 46.93.

1966: 1 Australia (Jennifer Lamy, Pam Kilborn, Joyce Bennett, Dianne Burge) 45.3, 2 England (Maureen Tranter, Janet Simpson, Daphne Slater, Jill Hall) 45.6, 3 Jamaica (Adlin Mair, Una Morris, Vilma Charlton, Carmen Smith) 45.6.

Note: Slater nee Arden.

1970: 1 Australia (Maureen Caird, Jennifer Lamy, Marion Hoffman, Raelene Boyle) 44.14, 2 England (Anita Neil, Margaret Critchley, Madeleine Cobb, Val Peat) 44.28, 3 Canada (Joan Hendry, Joyce Sadowick, Patti Loverock, Stephanie Berto) 44.68.

Note: Cobb nee Weston.

1974: 1 Australia (Jennifer Lamy, Denise Robertson, Robyn Boak, Ralene Boyle) 43.51, 2 England (Sonia Lannaman, Barbara Martin, Judy Vernon, Andrea Lynch) 44.30, 3 Ghana (Rose Assiedua, Josephine Ocran, Hannah Afriye, Alice Annum) 44.35.

1978: 1 England (Bev Goddard, Kathy Smallwood, Sharon Colyear, Sonia Lannaman) 43.70, 2 Canada (Angela Bailey, Patti Loverock, Margaret Howe, Marjorie Bailey) 44.26, 3 Australia (Roxanne Gelle, Denise Boyd, Colleen Beazley, Lyn Jacenko) 44.78.

Note: Boyd nee Robertson.

1982: 1 England (Wendy Hoyte, Kathy Smallwood, Bev Callender, Sonia Lannaman) 43.15, 2 Canada (Angela Bailey, Marita Payne, Angella Taylor, Molly Killingbeck) 43.66, 3 Jamaica (Lelieth Hodges, Merlene Ottey, Cathy Rattray, Grace Jackson) 43.69.

Note: Callender nee Goddard.

1986: 1 England (Paula Dunn, Kathy Cook, Joan Baptiste, Heather Oakes) 43.39, 2 Canada (Angela Bailey, Esmie Lawrence, Angela Phipps, Angella Issajenko) 43.83, 3 Wales (Helen Miles, Sian Morris, Sallyanne Short, Carmen Smart) 45.37.

Note: Cook nee Smallwood, Issajenko nee Taylor.

1990: 1 Australia (Cathy Freeman, Monique Dunstan, Kathy Sambell, Kerry Johnson) 43.87, 2 England (Stephanie Douglas, Jennifer Stoute, Simmone Jacobs, Paula Dunn) 44.15, 3 Nigeria (Beatrice Otondu, Fatima Yusuf, Charity Opara, Chioma Ajunwa) 44.67.

1994: 1 Nigeria (Faith Idehen, Mary Tombiri, Christy Opara-Thompson, Mary Onyali) 43.29, 2 Australia (Monique Miers, Cathy Freeman, Melinda Gainsford, Kathy Sambell) 43.43, 3 England (Stephanie Douglas, Geraldine McLeod, Simmone Jacobs, Paula Thomas) 43.46.

Note: Miers nee Dunstan, Thomas nee Dunn.

1998: 1 Australia (Tania Van Heer, Lauren Hewitt, Nova Peris-Kneebone, Sharon Cripps) 43.39, 2 Jamaica (Donette Brown, Juliet Campbell, Gillian Russell, Bridgette Foster) 43.49, 3 England (Marcia Richardson, Donna Fraser, Simmone Jacobs, Joice Maduaka) 43.69.

4 x 400 metres relay:

First held in 1974

1974: 1 England (Sue Pettett, Ruth Kennedy, Jannette Roscoe, Verona Bernard) 3:29.23, 2 Australia (Margaret Ramsay, Judy Canty, Terri-Anne Wangman, Charlene Rendina) 3:30.72, 3 Canada (Margaret MacGowan, Maureen Crowley, Brenda Walsh, Yvonne Saunders) 3:33.92.

1978: 1 England (Ruth Kennedy, Joslyn Hoyte, Verona Elder, Donna Hartley) 3:27.19, 2 Australia (Judy Peckham, Denise Boyd, Maxine Corcoran, Beth Nail) 3:28.65, 3 Canada (Margaret Stride, Debbie Campbell, Anne Mackie-Morelli, Rachelle Campbell) 3:35.83.

Note: Elder nee Bernard, Peckham nee Canty, Stride nee MacGowan.

1982: 1 Canada (Charmaine Crooks, Jillian Richardson, Molly Killingbeck, Angella Taylor) 3:27.70, 2 Australia (Leanne Evans, Denise Boyd, Debbie Flintoff, Raelene Boyle) 3:27.72, 3 Scotland (Sandra Whittaker, Anne Clarkson, Angela Bridgeman, Linsey Macdonald) 3:32.92.

1986: 1 Canada (Charmaine Crooks, Marita Payne, Molly Killingbeck, Jillian Richardson) 3:28.92, 2 England (Jane Parry, Linda Keough, Angela Piggford, Kathy Cook) 3:32.82, 3 Australia (Maree Chapman, Sharon Stewart, Julie Schwass, Debbie Flintoff) 3:32.86.

1990: 1 England (Angela Piggford, Jennifer Stoute, Sally Gunnell, Linda Keough) 3:28.08, 2 Australia (Maree Holland, Sharon Stewart, Sue Andrews, Debbie Flintoff-King) 3:30.74, 3 Canada (Rosey Edeh, France Gareau, Cheryl Allen, Gail Harris) 3:33.26.

Note: Holland nee Chapman, Flintoff-King nee Flintoff.

1994: 1 England (Phyllis Smith, Tracy Goddard, Linda Keough, Sally Gunnell) 3:27.06, 2 Jamaica (Revoli Campbell, Deon Hemmings, Inez Turner, Sandie Richards) 3:27.63, 3 Canada (Alana Yawichuk, Stacy Bowen, Donalda Duprey, Charmaine Crooks) 3:32.52.

1998: 1 Australia (Sue Andrews, Tamsyn Lewis, Lee Naylor, Tania Van Heer) 3:27.28, 2 England (Michelle Thomas, Michelle Pierre, Vicky Day, Donna Fraser) 3:29.28, 3 Canada (Karlene Haughton, Diane Cummins, Ladonna Antoine, Foy Williams) 3:29.97.

High jump:

1934: 1 Marjorie Clark (SA) 1.60, 2 Eva Dawes (Can) 1.57, 3 Margaret Bell (Can) 1.52.

1938: 1 Dorothy Odam (Eng) 1.60, 2 Dora Gardner (Eng) 1.57, 3 Betty Forbes (NZ) 1.57.

1950: 1 Dorothy Tyler (Eng) 1.60, 2 Bertha Crowther (Eng) 1.60, 3 Noeline Swinton (NZ) 1.55.

1954: 1 Thelma Hopkins (NI) 1.68, 2 Dorothy Tyler (Eng) 1.60, 3 Alice Whitty (Can) 1.60.

1958: 1 Michele Mason (Aus) 1.70, 2 Mary Donaghy (NZ) 1.70, 3 Helen Frith (Aus) 1.65.

1962: 1 Robyn Woodhouse (Aus) 1.78, 2 Helen Frith (Aus) 1.73, 3 Michele Mason (Aus) 1.73.

1966: 1 Michele Brown (Aus) 1.73, 2 Dorothy Shirley (Eng) 1.70, 3 Robyn Woodhouse (Aus) 1.70.

Note: Brown nee Mason.

1970: 1 Debbie Brill (Can) 1.78, 2 Ann Wilson (Eng) 1.70, 3 Moira Walls (Sco) 1.70.

1974: 1 Barbara Lawton (Eng) 1.84, 2 Louise Hanna (Can) 1.82, 3 Brigitte Bittner (Can) 1.80.

1978: 1 Katrina Gibbs (Aus) 1.93, 2 Debbie Brill (Can) 1.90, 3 Julie White (Can) 1.83.

1982: 1 Debbie Brill (Can) 1.88, 2 Chris Stanton (Aus) 1.88, 3 Barbara Simmonds (Eng) 1.83.

1986: 1 Chris Stanton (Aus) 1.92, 2 Sharon McPeake (NI) 1.90, 3 Janet Boyle (NI) 1.90.

1990: 1 Tania Murray (NZ) 1.88, 2 Janet Boyle (NI) 1.88, 3 Tracy Phillips (NZ) 1.88.

1994: 1 Alison Inverarity (Aus) 1.94, 2 Charmaine Weavers (SA) 1.94, 3 Debbie Marti (Eng) 1.91.

1998: 1 Hestrie Storbeck (SA) 1.91, 2 Jo Jennings (Eng) 1.91, 3 Alison Inverarity (Aus) 1.88.

Pole vault:

First held in 1998

1998: 1 Emma George (Aus) 4.20, 2 Elmarie Gerryts (SA) 4.15, 3 Trisha Bernier (Can) 4.15.

Long jump:

1934: 1 Phyllis Bartholomew (Eng) 5.47, 2 Evelyn Goshawk (Can) 5.41, 3 Violet Webb (Eng) 5.23.

1938: 1 Decima Norman (Aus) 5.80, 2 Ethel Raby (Eng) 5.66, 3 Thelma Peake (Aus) 5.55.

1950: 1 Yvette Williams (NZ) 5.91, 2 Judy Canty (Aus) 5.77, 3 Ruth Dowman (NZ) 5.74.

1954: 1 Yvette Williams (NZ) 6.08, 2 Thelma Hopkins (NI) 5.84, 3 Jean Desforges (Eng) 5.84.

1958: 1 Sheila Hoskin (Eng) 6.02, 2 Mary Bignal (Eng) 5.97, 3 Beverley Watson (Aus) 5.97.

1962: 1 Pam Kilborn (Aus) 6.27w, 2 Helen Frith (Aus) 6.24w, 3 Janet Knee (Aus) 6.13w.

1966: 1 Mary Rand (Eng) 6.36, 2 Sheila Parkin (Eng) 6.30, 3 Violet Odogwu (Nig) 6.15.

Note: Rand nee Bignal.

1970: 1 Sheila Sherwood (Eng) 6.73, 2 Ann Wilson (Eng) 6.50, 3 Joan Hendry (Can) 6.28.

Note: Sherwood nee Parkin.

1974: 1 Modupe Oshikoya (Nig) 6.46, 2 Brenda Eisler (Can) 6.38, 3 Ruth Martin-Jones (Wal) 6.38.

1978: 1 Sue Reeve (Eng) 6.59, 2 Erica Hooker (Aus) 6.58, 3 June Griffith (Guy) 6.52.

1982: 1 Shonel Ferguson (Bah) 6.91w, 2 Robyn Strong (Aus) 6.88w, 3 Bev Kinch (Eng) 6.78w.

1986: 1 Joyce Oladapo (Eng) 6.42w, 2 Mary Berkeley (Eng) 6.40, 3 Robyn Lorraway (Aus) 6.35.

Note: Lorraway nee Strong.

1990: 1 Jane Flemming (Aus) 6.78, 2 Beatrice Otondu (Nig) 6.65w, 3 Fiona May (Eng) 6.55.

1994: 1 Nicole Boegman (Aus) 6.82w, 2 Yinka Idowu (Nig) 6.73, 3 Christy Opara-Thompson (Nig) 6.72.

1998: 1 Jo Wise (Eng) 6.63, 2 Jackie Edwards (Bah) 6.59, 3 Nicole Boegman (Aus) 6.58.

Triple jump:

First held in 1998

1998: 1 Ashia Hansen (Eng) 14.32, 2 Francoise Mbango (Cam) 13.95, 3 Connie Henry (Eng) 13.94.

Shot putt:

First held in 1954

1954: 1 Yvette Williams (NZ) 13.96, 2 Jackie McDonald (Can) 12.98, 3 Magdalena Swanepoel (SA) 12.81.

1958: 1 Valerie Sloper (NZ) 15.54, 2 Suzanne Allday (Eng) 14.44, 3 Jackie Gelling (Can) 14.03.

Note: Gelling nee McDonald.

1962: 1 Valerie Young (NZ) 15.23, 2 Jean Roberts (Aus) 14.51, 3 Suzanne Allday (Eng) 13.56.

Note: Young nee Sloper.

1966: 1 Valerie Young (NZ) 16.50, 2 Mary Peters (NI) 16.29, 3 Nancy McCredie (Can) 15.34.

1970: 1 Mary Peters (NI) 15.93, 2 Barbara Poulsen (NZ) 15.87, 3 Jean Roberts (Aus) 15.32.

1974: 1 Jane Haist (Can) 16.12, 2 Valerie Young (NZ) 15.29, 3 Jean Roberts (Aus) 15.24.

1978: 1 Gael Mulhall (Aus) 17.31, 2 Carmen Ionesco (Can) 16.45, 3 Judy Oakes (Eng) 16.14.

1982: 1 Judy Oakes (Eng) 17.92, 2 Gael Mulhall (Aus) 17.68, 3 Rose Hauch (Can) 16.71.

1986: 1 Gael Martin (Aus) 19.00, 2 Judy Oakes (Eng) 18.75, 3 Myrtle Augee (Eng) 17.52.

Note: Martin nee Mulhall.

1990: 1 Myrtle Augee (Eng) 18.48, 2 Judy Oakes (Eng) 18.43, 3 Yvonne Hanson-Nortey (Eng) 16.00.

1994: 1 Judy Oakes (Eng) 18.16, 2 Myrtle Augee (Eng) 17.64, 3 Lisa-Marie Vizaniari (Aus) 16.61.

1998: 1 Judy Oakes (Eng) 18.82, 2 Myrtle Augee (Eng) 17.16, 3 Veronica Abrahamse (SA) 16.52.

Discus:

First held in 1954

1954: 1 Yvette Williams (NZ) 45.02, 2 Suzanne Allday (Eng) 40.02, 3 Marie Anne Depree (Can) 38.66.

1958: 1 Suzanne Allday (Eng) 45.90, 2 Jennifer Thompson (NZ) 45.30, 3 Valerie Sloper (NZ) 44.94.

1962: 1 Valerie Young (NZ) 50.20, 2 Rosslyn Williams (Aus) 46.66, 3 Mary McDonald (Aus) 46.24.

Note: Young nee Sloper.

1966: 1 Valerie Young (NZ) 49.78, 2 Jean Roberts (Aus) 49.20, 3 Carol Martin (Can) 48.70.

1970: 1 Rosemary Payne (Sco) 54.46, 2 Jean Roberts (Aus) 51.02, 3 Carol Martin (Can) 48.42.

1974: 1 Jane Haist (Can) 55.52, 2 Rosemary Payne (Sco) 53.94, 3 Carol Martin (Can) 53.16.

1978: 1 Carmen Ionesco (Can) 62.16, 2 Gael Mulhall (Aus) 57.60, 3 Lucette Moreau (Can) 56.64.

1982: 1 Meg Ritchie (Sco) 62.98, 2 Gael Mulhall (Aus) 58.64, 3 Lynda Whiteley (Eng) 54.78.

1986: 1 Gael Martin (Aus) 56.42, 2 Venissa Head (Wal) 56.20, 3 Karen Pugh (Eng) 54.72.

Note: Martin nee Mulhall.

1990: 1 Lisa-Marie Vizaniari (Aus) 56.38, 2 Jackie McKernan (NI) 54.86, 3 Astra Vitols (Aus) 53.84.

1994: 1 Daniela Costian (Aus) 63.72, 2 Beatrice Faumuina (NZ) 57.12, 3 Lizette Etsebeth (SA) 55.74.

1998: 1 Beatrice Faumuina (NZ) 65.92, 2 Lisa-Marie Vizaniari (Aus) 62.14, 3 Alison Lever (Aus) 59.90.

Hammer:

First held in 1998

1998: 1 Debbie Sosimenko (Aus) 66.56, 2 Lorraine Shaw (Eng) 62.66, 3 Caroline Wittrin (Can) 61.77.

Javelin:

1934: 1 Gladys Lunn (Eng) 32.18, 2 Edith Halstead (Eng) 30.94, 3 Margaret Cox (Eng) 30.08.

Note: Edith Halstead was later pronounced to have been male from birth and as Eddie Halstead became a father; 4th place was taken by the only other competi-

tor, Louise Fawcett (Eng), 29.28.

1938: 1 Robina Higgins (Can) 38.28, 2 Toni Robertson (SA) 36.98, 3 Gladys Lunn (Eng) 36.40.

1950: 1 Charlotte MacGibbon (Aus) 38.84, 2 Yvette Williams (NZ) 37.96, 3 Cleo Rivett-Carnac (NZ) 34.42.

1954: 1 Magdalena Swanepoel (SA) 43.82, 2 Terry Thornhill-Fisher (NR) 41.96, 3 Shirley Couzins (Can) 38.98.

1958: 1 Anna Pazera (Aus) 57.40, 2 Magdalena Swanepoel (SA) 48.72, 3 Averil Williams (Eng) 46.76.

1962: 1 Sue Platt (Eng) 50.24, 2 Rosemary Morgan (Eng) 49.62, 3 Anna Pazera (Aus) 48.68.

1966: 1 Margaret Parker (Aus) 51.38, 2 Anna Bocson (Aus) 47.80, 3 Jay Dahlgren (Can) 47.68.

Note: Bocson formerly Pazera.

1970: 1 Petra Rivers (Aus) 52.00, 2 Anne Farquhar (Eng) 50.82, 3 Jay Dahlgren (Can) 49.54.

1974: 1 Petra Rivers (Aus) 55.48, 2 Jenny Symon (Aus) 52.14, 3 Sharon Corbett (Eng) 50.26.

1978: 1 Tessa Sanderson (Eng) 61.34, 2 Alison Hayward (Can) 54.52, 3 Laurie Kern (Can) 53.60.

1982: 1 Sue Howland (Aus) 64.46, 2 Petra Rivers (Aus) 62.28, 3 Fatima Whitbread (Eng) 58.86.

1986: 1 Tessa Sanderson (Eng) 69.80, 2 Fatima Whitbread (Eng) 68.54, 3 Sue Howland (Aus) 64.74.

1990: 1 Tessa Sanderson (Eng) 65.72, 2 Sue Howland (Aus) 61.18, 3 Kate Farrow (Aus) 58.98.

1994: 1 Louise McPaul (Aus) 63.76, 2 Kirsten Hellier (NZ) 60.40, 3 Sharon Gibson (Eng) 58.20.

1998: 1 Louise McPaul (Aus) 66.96, 2 Karen Martin (Eng) 57.82, 3 Kirsty Morrison (Eng) 56.34.

Heptathlon:

First held in 1970, Pentathlon (100 metres hurdles, Shot putt, High jump, Long jump, 200 metres) 1970-1978, Heptathlon since (Javelin throw and 800 metres added)

Note: also given are the scores revised according to the new tables introduced in 1971.

1970: 1 Mary Peters (NI) 5148pts, 2 Ann Wilson (Eng) 5037, 3 Jenny Meldrum (Can) 4736.

Note: 1971 tables - Peters 4515, Wilson 4416, Meldrum 4120.

1974: 1 Mary Peters (NI) 4455, 2 Modupe Oshikoya (Nig) 4423, 3 Ann Wilson (Eng) 4236.

1978: 1 Diane Konihowski (Can) 4768, 2 Sue Mapstone (Eng) 4222, 3 Yvette Wray (Eng) 4211.

1982: 1 Glynis Nunn (Aus) 6282, 2 Judy Livermore (Eng) 6214, 3 Jill Ross-Giffen (Can) 5981.

1986: 1 Judy Simpson (Eng) 6282, 2 Jane Flemming (Aus) 6278, 3 Kim Hagger

ATHLETICS

(Eng) 5823.

Note: Simpson nee Livermore.

1990: 1 Jane Flemming (Aus) 6695, 2 Sharon Jaklofsky-Smith (Aus) 6115, 3 Judy Simpson (Eng) 6085

1994: 1 Denise Lewis (Eng) 6325. 2 Jane Flemming (Aus) 6317, 3 Catherine Bond-Mills (Can) 6193.

1998: 1 Denise Lewis (Eng) 6513, 2 Jane Jamieson (Aus) 6354, 3 Joanne Henry (NZ) 6096.

BADMINTON

Gillian, and Gillian, lead the way for England

If the thought of badminton conjures up an image of energetic chaps named Simon or Peter and strapping young women called Gillian or Fiona bounding around the white-lined floor of a village church hall every Tuesday evening, then it has to be said that there is just a glimmer of truth in the fable.

As it happens, there has been a Simon and a Peter, and more than one Gillian, and a Fiona, who have contributed to England's dominance of Commonwealth Games badminton since it was first held in 1966. Yet anyone who has ever seen Gillian Gilks play will know that badminton is a game which demands an abundance of speed, strength and agility, and that there is no place for faint-hearts with the shuttlecock speed estimated to reach 180 miles (300km) per hour.

The roots of the game can be traced back 2000 years to China, but its modern development stems from a children's pastime which was developed at the Duke of Beaufort's ancestral home of Badminton

Manchester 2002
THE XVII COMMONWEALTH GAMES

BADMINTON

House and then by British Army officers in India in the 19th Century. England's Badminton Association was founded in 1893, and the International Badminton Federation was set up in 1934, with 133 nations now affiliated. The All-England Championships remain an event of major importance and Mrs Gilks - born in prime badminton country at Epsom, in Surrey - won 11 titles at singles and doubles between 1969 and 1984. She made her international debut at 16, played on 111 occasions for England, won a dozen European titles, and was twice named Britain's Sportswoman of the Year.

She is also the only player to have won all three available titles at the Commonwealth Games - singles, doubles and mixed doubles - in the same year. Six of the nine women's singles titles at the Games have gone to English players, as have all but one at women's doubles, all but two at mixed doubles, and all but one in the team events. England's total of 81 medals is far ahead of the next most successful country, which is Malaysia, with 34, and then follows Canada, with 18. Uncommonly, this is not a sport in which Australians excel and they have won only 11 medals.

Yet at World level the initiative has long since passed elsewhere. Malaysia won the Thomas Cup - the Worldwide team competition for men - for the first time in 1949 and Indonesia is now the most successful country in the event. The Uber Cup for women has been shared by China, Japan, the USA and Malaysia, and the only British successes in the World Championships, instituted in 1977, have come from Nora Perry and Jane Webster in the women's doubles in 1980 and from a share which Nora Perry had in the mixed doubles three years later.

The most successful badminton dynasty at the Commonwealth Games is that of the Sidek family from Malaysia. Rashid has twice been men's singles champion and his brother, Razif, has twice figured in men's doubles wins, including a partnership with a third brother, Jalani. Their sister, Zamaliah, was a member of the silver-medal winning team in 1994.

Another Gillian, from England - Gillian Clark - is the most successful Games medallist with 12 between 1982 and 1994: one in singles, five in women's doubles, two in mixed doubles, and four in team events, including two doubles golds in 1986 and four team golds. Helen Troke, also of England, is the only player to win the women's singles twice, and did so on the first occasion in 1982 at the age of 17. She went on to represent England on 115 occasions.

Leading countries:

England 30 gold medals; Malaysia 13; Australia, Canada, India 2 each; Hong Kong, Scotland, Wales 1 each.

Leading gold-medallists:

6 Gillian Clark (Eng) 1982-94; 5 Helen Troke (Eng) 1982-86, Joanne Wright-Goode (Eng) 1994-98; 4 Derek Talbot (Eng) 1970-74, Steve Baddeley (Eng) 1982-90, Fiona Elliott-Smith (Eng) 1986-90.

Highlights - Games by Games

1966: Badminton made its debut at the Games on four portable plastic courts imported from England and - predictably - it was Malaysian men and English women who were dominant. Tan Aik Huang, who had won the All-England title earlier in the year, took the men's singles from Yew Cheng Hoe, and the men's doubles was another all-Malaysian final in which Ng Boon Bee & Tan Yee Khan, who had twice been All-England champions, lost to the two singles finalists, though the latter had only just managed to beat a Canadian pair 17-14, 18-15 in the first round. Also represented in the competition were Canada, India, Jamaica, New Zealand, Scotland, Singapore and Wales - and of these countries Canada, India and Scotland also won medals. One of the Jamaican women competitors managed to reach the second round - on a bye - and then had the misfortune to meet the eventual champion, Angela Bairstow, and lost 11-0, 11-0.

1970: The hall at Edinburgh's Meadowbank indoor complex was packed for the finals, and the Malaysians - apparently suffering from the cold weather - appeared in only one of them. England won three of the five events and Maggie Boxall took home two gold medals and a bronze, including the women's doubles title with Sue Whetnall, who had also been her partner in two All-England victories. Consolation for Malaysia was that they provided both pairs again for a men's doubles final which was described as "a lesson in reflexes ... and the best entertainment of the evening". Ng Boon Bee was on the winning side on this occasion. It was a Canadian, Jamie Paulson, who was the unexpected men's singles champion with no Malaysian among the medals, and the Scots, on their home ground, won a welcome bronze in the mixed doubles.

1974: England 4 Malaysia 1 - that was the gold-medal tally, and between them these two countries won 14 of the 15 medals. Punch Gunalan, of Malaysia, beat the Canadian defending champion in the men's singles final, but the outstanding player of the Games was the prolific Gillian

BADMINTON

Gilks, who won the women's singles and added further golds in the women's doubles and mixed doubles. In each event she went one better than she had done when she had taken three silvers four years earlier under her maiden name of Perrin. Derek Talbot, bronze-medallist in the singles, also won three medals for England by adding gold in the men's doubles and mixed doubles finals.

1978: With defending champion Punch Gunalan now the national team coach, the best the Malaysians could do in the men's singles was only 4th place, as Prakash Padukone, of India, upset the major powers and won the gold. At least Malaysia did provide both women's singles finalists with Sylvia Meow Eng Ng tearfully beating her room-mate, Katherine Swee Phek Teh. India also won bronze in the women's doubles and other medals went to Canada (in the women's singles and women's doubles), New Zealand and Scotland. A team event was introduced - providing a rare opportunity at any level in international sport for mixed participation - and in England's winning team Derek Talbot won his sixth Games medal. His team-mates, Mike Tredgett and Nora Perry, both won three golds.

1982: Another Indian, Syed Modi, was the men's singles champion and Canada took the women's doubles. Helen Troke won the women's singles for England at the age of only 17 and was also in England's winning team, with the other medals going to Canada and Australia - and Malaysia getting nothing at all. During the course of the badminton matches more than 9,000 shuttlecocks were hammered into submission.

1986: With Malaysia and India among the many nations to boycott the Games the way was left open for the Home Countries to sweep all the medals, but it did not quite happen like that. English players duly took the men's singles, women's singles (Helen Troke again), women's doubles and the team event, and the Scottish pair of Billy Gilliland and Don Travers became men's doubles champions to the excitement of their home crowd. However, the sequence was unexpectedly broken when the Australians, Mike Scandolera and Audrey Tuckey, won their country's first ever badminton gold.

1990: Rashid Sidek, from the immensely successful extended family of Malaysian badminton, became his country's first men's singles champion at the Games for 16 years. Then between them the Sidek brothers provided three of the four participants in the men's doubles final, and Razif and Jalani emerged successful from the exercise in fratricide. England won the women's singles and doubles and the team event (three golds for

Fiona Smith), but there was another surprise in the mixed doubles when the Hong Kong pairing of Chan Chi Choi and Amy Chan beat their English opponents in the final.

1994: Rashid Sidek became the first man to twice win the men's singles and was joined by his sister, Zamaliah, in the silver-medal-winning Malaysian team. The women's singles, which had always previously been won by England or Malaysia, this time went to the Australian, Lisa Campbell - and there was not one English or Malaysian player even in the semi-finals. For these Games the play-offs for 3rd place were dispensed with and both losing semi-finalists received bronze medals.

1998: For the first time at the Games England and Malaysia shared the same number of gold medals, with three each. Separate team events were introduced for men and women, with entries from 19 countries in the former and 16 in the latter, and Malaysia won the men's from India. England still had the most successful player in the person of Joanne Goode, with gold medals in both doubles finals and the team event. The Malaysians had appointed five coaches from China back in 1993 to prepare their teams from an elite group of 126 players and had brought in the Danish former World champion, Morten Frost, as team director. Wong Choon Hann, the men's singles winner, was aged 21 and the successful women's doubles players were both only 18. Kelly Morgan, the highest-ranked Commonwealth player at 26th in the World, won the women's singles to gain the first ever Welsh medal of any kind in Games badminton.

BADMINTON MEDALLISTS

Note: both semi-finalists were awarded bronze medals from 1994.

Men's Singles:
1966: 1 Tan Aik Huang (Mal), 2 Yew Cheng Hoe (Mal), 3 Dinesk Khanna (Ind).
1970: 1 Jamie Paulson (Can), 2 Paul Whetnall (Eng), 3 Ray Sharp (Eng).
1974: 1 Punch Gunalan (Mal), 2 Jamie Paulson (Can), 3 Derek Talbot (Eng).
1978: 1 Prakash Padukone (Ind), 2 Derek Talbot (Eng), 3 Ray Stevens (Eng).
1982: 1 Syed Modi (Ind), 2 Nick Yates (Eng), 3 Razif Sidek (Mal).
1986: 1 Steve Baddeley (Eng), 2 Sze Yu (Aus), 3 Nick Yates (Eng).
1990: 1 Rashid Sidek (Mal), 2 Foo Koo Keong (Mal), 3 Darren Hall (Eng).
1994: 1 Rashid Sidek (Mal), 2 Ong Ewe Hock (Mal), 3 Nick Hall (NZ), Anders Nielsen (Eng).
1998: 1 Wong Choon Hann (Mal), 2 Yong Hock Kin (Mal), 3 Gopi Chand Pullela (Ind), Darren Hall (Eng).

BADMINTON

Men's Doubles:

1966: 1 Tan Aik Huang &Yew Cheng Hoe (Mal), 2 Ng Boon Bee & Tan Yee Khan (Mal), 3 Roger Mills & David Horton (Eng).

1970: 1 Ng Boon Bee & Punch Gunalan (Mal), 2 Tan Soon Hooi & Ng Tat Wai (Mal), 3 Jamie Paulson & Yves Paré (Can).

1974: 1 Derek Talbot & Elliot Stuart (Eng), 2 Ray Stevens & Mike Tredgett (Eng), 3 Punch Gunalan & Dominic Soong Chok Soong (Mal).

1978: 1 Ray Stevens & Mike Tredgett (Eng), 2 Moo Foot Lian & Beng Teong Ong (Mal), 3 Richard Purser & Bryan Purser (NZ).

1982: 1 Razif Sidek & Beng Teong Ong (Mal), 2 Martin Drew & Nick Yates (Eng), 3 Pat Tryon & Paul Johnson (Can).

1986: 1 Billy Gilliland & Don Travers (Sco), 2 Andy Goode & Nigel Tier (Eng), 3 Kerrin Harrison & Glenn Stewart (NZ).

1990: 1 Razif Sidek & Jalani Sidek (Mal), 2 Rashid Sidek & Cheah Soon Kit (Mal), 3 Bryan Blanshard & Mike Bitten (Can).

1994: 1 Cheah Soon Kit & Soo Beng Kiang (Mal), 2 Simon Archer & Chris Hunt (Eng), 3 Peter Blackburn & Mark Nichols (Aus), Tan Kim Her & Ong Ewe Hock (Mal).

1998: 1 Choong Tan Fook & Lee Wan Wah (Mal), 2 Cheah Soon Kit & Yap Kim Hock (Mal), 3 Simon Archer & Chris Hunt (Eng), Nathan Robertson & Julian Robertson (Eng).

Women's Singles:

1966: 1 Angela Bairstow (Eng), 2 Sharon Whittaker (Can), 3 Ursula Smith (Eng).

1970: 1 Maggie Beck (Eng), 2 Gillian Perrin (Eng), 3 Maggie Boxall (Eng).

1974: 1 Gillian Gilks (Eng), 2 Maggie Beck (Eng), 3 Sylvia Meow Eng Ng (Mal). Note: Gilks nee Perrin.

1978: 1 Sylvia Meow Eng Ng (Mal), 2 Katherine Swee Phek Teh (Mal), 3 Wendy Clarkson (Can).

1982: 1 Helen Troke (Eng), 2 Sally Podger (Eng), 3 Gillian Clark (Eng).

1986: 1 Helen Troke (Eng), 2 Fiona Elliott (Eng), 3 Gillian Clark (Eng).

1990: 1 Fiona Smith (Eng), 2 Denyse Julien (Can), 3 Helen Troke (Eng).

1994: 1 Lisa Campbell (Aus), 2 Deng Si-An (Can), 3 Song Yang (Aus), Rhona Robertson (NZ).

1998: 1 Kelly Morgan (Wal), 2 Aparna Popot (Ind), 3 Tracey Hallam (Eng), Julia Mann (Eng).

Women's Doubles:

1966: 1 Helen Horton & Ursula Smith (Eng), 2 Angela Bairstow & Iris Rogers (Eng), 3 Rosalind Ang & Teoh Siew Yong (Mal).

1970: 1 Maggie Boxall & Sue Whetnall (Eng), 2 Gillian Perrin & Julie Rickard (Eng), 3 Rosalind Ang & Teoh Siew Yong (Mal).

1974: 1 Maggie Beck & Gillian Gilks (Eng), 2 Maggie Boxall & Sue Whetnall (Eng), 3 Rosalind Ang & Sylvia Meow Eng Ng (Mal). Note: Gilks nee Perrin.

1978: 1 Nora Perry & Ann Statt (Eng), 2 Jane Youngberg & Claire Backhouse (Can), 3 Ami Ghia & Kanwal Singh (Ind).

1982: 1 Claire Backhouse & Johanne Falardeau (Can), 2 Gillian Clark & Karen

Beckman (Eng), 3 Karen Chapman & Sally Podger (Eng).

1986: 1 Gillian Clark & Gillian Gowers (Eng), 2 Johanne Falardeau & Denyse Julien (Can), 3 Helen Troke & Fiona Elliott (Eng).

1990: 1 Fiona Smith & Sara Sankey (Eng), 2 Gillian Clark & Gillian Gowers (Eng), 3 Johanne Falardeau & Denyse Julien (Can).

Note: Smith nee Elliott.

1994: 1 Joanne Muggeridge & Joanne Wright (Eng), 2 Gillian Clark & Julie Bradbury (Eng), 3 Denyse Julien & Deng Si-An (Can), Leng Lee Wai & Tan Lee Wai (Mal).

1998: 1 Joanne Goode & Donna Kellogg (Eng), 2 Choi Hooi Yee & Lim Pek Siah (Mal), 3 Rhona Robertson & Tammy Jenkins (NZ), Sandra Watt & Elinor Middlemiss (Sco).

Note: Goode nee Wright.

Mixed Doubles:

1966: 1 Roger Mills & Angela Bairstow (Eng), 2 Tony Jordan & Helen Horton (Eng), 3 Robert McCoig & Muriel Ferguson (Sco).

1970: 1 Derek Talbot & Maggie Boxall (Eng), 2 Roger Mills & Gillian Perrin (Eng), 3 David Eddy & Sue Whetnall (Eng).

1974: 1 Derek Talbot & Gillian Gilks (Eng), 2 Paul Whetnall & Nora Gardner (Eng), 3 Elliot Stuart & Sue Whetnall (Eng).

Note: Gilks nee Perrin.

1978: 1 Mike Tredgett & Nora Perry (Eng), 2 Billy Gilliland & Joanna Flockhart (Sco), 3 Derek Talbot & Barbara Sutton (Eng).

Note: Perry nee Gardner.

1982: 1 Martin Drew & Karen Chapman (Eng), 2 Duncan Bridge & Karen Beckman (Eng), 3 Steve Wilson & Robin Denton (NZ).

1986: 1 Mike Scandolera & Audrey Tuckey (Aus), 2 Andy Goode & Fiona Elliott (Eng), 3 Billy Gilliland & Christine Heatly (Sco).

1990: 1 Chan Chi Choi & Amy Chan (HK), 2 Miles Johnson & Sara Sankey (Eng), 3 Andy Goode & Gillian Clark (Eng).

1994: 1 Chris Hunt & Gillian Clark (Eng), 2 Simon Archer & Julie Bradbury (Eng), 3 Nick Ponting & Joanne Wright (Eng), Peter Blackburn & Rhona Cator (Aus).

1998: 1 Simon Archer & Joanne Goode (Eng), 2 Nathan Robertson & Joanne Davies (Eng), 3 Peter Blackburn & Rhona Cator (Aus), Chris Hunt & Donna Kellogg (Eng).

Note: Goode nee Wright.

Teams:

First held 1978, Mixed 1978-1994, Men & Women separate since

1978: 1 England (Karen Bridge, David Eddy, Kevin Jolly, Nora Perry, Ann Statt, Ray Stevens, Barbara Sutton, Derek Talbot, Mike Tredgett, Jane Webster), 2 Canada (Claire Backhouse, Greg Carter, Wendy Clarkson, Sharon Crawford, John Czich, Lucio Fabris, Johanne Falardeau, Jamie McKee, Ken Priestman, Jane Youngberg), 3 Malaysia (Abu Bakar Sufran, Beng Teong Ong, Geok Whee Chee, Sylvia Meow Eng Ng, Moo Foot Lian, James Selvaraj, Swee Leong Sew, Katherine Swee Phek Teh).

BADMINTON

1982: 1 England (Steve Baddeley, Karen Beckman, Duncan Bridge, Karen Chapman, Gillian Clark, Martin Drew, Sally Podger, Dipak Tailor, Helen Troke, Nick Yates), 2 Canada (Claire Backhouse, Johanne Falardeau, Mark Freitag, Paul Johnson, Denyse Julien, Bob MacDougall, Keith Priestman, Sandra Skillings, Pat Tryon, Jane Youngberg), 3 Australia (Jennifer Cunningham, Maxine Evans, Jane Forrest, Mark Harry, Trevor James, Darren McDonald, Julie McDonald, Paul Morgan, Mike Scandolera, Audrey Swabey).

Note: Keith Priestman (Can) was a brother of Ken Priestman (1978).

1986: 1 England (Steve Baddeley, Gillian Clark, Fiona Elliott, Andy Goode, Gillian Gowers, Nigel Tier, Helen Troke), 2 Canada (Mike Bitten, Mike Butler, Linda Cloutier, Michael de Belle, Johanne Falardeau, John Goss, Denyse Julien, Ken Poole, Sandra Skillings), 3 Australia (Paul Bee Kong, Rhonda Cator, Karen Jupp, Gordon Lang, Darren McDonald, Julie McDonald, Mike Scandolera, Tracey Small, Sze Yu, Audrey Tuckey),

Note: Sharpe nee Backhouse, Tuckey nee Swabey.

1990: 1 England (Steve Baddeley, Steve Butler, Gillian Clark, Andy Goode, Gillian Gowers, Darren Hall, Miles Johnson, Sara Sankey, Fiona Smith, Helen Troke), 2 Canada (Mike Bitten, Bryan Blanshard, Mike Butler, Linda Cloutier, Johanne Falardeau, David Humble, Denyse Julien, Anil Kaul, Doris Piché, Claire Sharpe), 3 Hong Kong (Amy Chan, Chan Chi Choi, Chan Sui Kwong, Cheng Yin Sat, Chung Hoi Yuk, Kin Ngai Chan, Man Wa Chan, Mei Yun Chui, Pak Kum Ng, Yik Kei Yeung).

Note: Sharpe nee Backhouse.

1994: 1 England (Simon Archer, Julie Bradbury, Gillian Clark, Chris Hunt, Peter Knowles, Suzanne Louis Lane, Joanne Muggeridge, Anders Nielsen, Nick Ponting, Joanne Wright), 2 Malaysia (Cheah Soon Kit, Kuak Sieok Choon, Leng Lee Wai, Leong Yeng Cheng, Ong Ewe Hock, Rashid Sidek, Soo Beng Kiang, Tan Kim Her, Tan Lee Wai, Zamaliah Sidek), 3 Australia (Peter Blackburn, Lisa Campbell, Rhonda Cator, Amanda Hardy, Murray Hocking, Stuart Metcalfe, Mark Nichols, Wendy Shinners, Paul Stevenson, Song Yang), Hong Kong (Chan Oi Ni, Cheng Yin Sat, Chung Hoi Yuk, Kwong Chan Siu, Ma Che Kong, Tam Kai Chuen, Man Tung Chau, Wong Chun Fan, Wong Wai Lap).

1998:

Men -1 Malaysia (Cheah Soon Kit, Choong Tan Fook. Lee Wan Wah, Ong Ewe Hock, Wong Choon Hann, Yap Kim Hock, Yong Hock Kin), 2 India (Abhinshyam Gupta, Markose Bristow, Gopi Chand Pullela, Ismail Jaseel, Vincent Lobo, Nikhil Karnetkar, George Thomas), 3 England (Simon Archer, Mark Constable, Darren Hall, Chris Hunt, Peter Knowles, Julian Robertson, Nathan Robertson), New Zealand (Geoffrey Bellingham, Chris Blair, Dean Galt, Anthony Garguilo, Nick Hall, Jarrod King, Daniel Shirley).

Women - 1 England (Joanne Davies, Joanne Goode, Tracey Hallam, Donna Kellogg, Julia Mann, Sara Sankey, Tanya Woodward), 2 Malaysia (Choi Hooi Yee, Joanne Quay, Law Pei Pei, Lim Pek Siah, Ng Mee Fen, Norashikin Amin, Woon Sze Mei), 3 Australia (Rhonda Cator, Amanda Hardy, Rayoui Head, Sarah Hicks, Kellie Lucas, Michaela Smith, Kate Wilson-Smith), India (Aparna Popat, Archana Deodhar, P. Lakshmi, Madhumita Bisht, Manjusha Kanwar, Neelima Choudary).

BOWLS

David the Goliath makes it a foursome

Lawn bowls - that quintessential old Empire game - is one of the most durable of Games survivors. It was held at the inaugural meeting of 1930 and has been omitted only once since, when the 1966 Games went to Jamaica where there were no greens. From its beginnings as something of a preserve for the Home Countries, Australasia and South Africa, bowls has expanded exhilaratingly so that in 1998, for instance, the men's singles was won by Zimbabwe (not their first such success) and Malaysia had three medal-winning appearances.

The trend for "non-establishment" countries to break in was set by Hong Kong in 1970 when they won the men's fours, including in their team players named Delgado, Da Silva and Souza, who were assuredly the first Commonwealth gold-medallists whose original native tongue was Portuguese. When women appeared in 1982 the triples (since replaced by the fours) went to Zimbabwe, and medals have also been won by women from Botswana, Papua New Guinea, the Norfolk Islands and

Manchester 2002
THE XVII COMMONWEALTH GAMES

Malaysia in the singles, from Guernsey in the pairs, and from Hong Kong, Papua New Guinea and Malaysia in the fours.

In any evaluation of bowls, the name of David Bryant soon comes to the fore. Bryant won the inaugural World singles title in 1966 and was champion again in 1980 and 1988. At the Commonwealth Games he was the gold-medallist in 1962, 1970, 1974 and 1978 - on the last occasion at the age of 46 - and the likelihood is that he would also have won in 1966 had he had the chance. An additional fours win in 1962 gives Bryant five Games golds, and his only remote challenger is the Scotsman, Willie Wood, with four medals (including two golds) from 1974 to 1990 - and eight more in World Championship competition.

Pre-eminent among women bowlers is Margaret Johnston, of Northern Ireland, who won the Commonwealth Games singles in 1994, having been bronze-medallist in the previous Games. A nurse by profession, she was also World singles champion in 1992 and pairs champion on three occasions from 1988 to 1996.

Bowls, by its very nature, lends itself to longevity, and the Games have provided numerous examples. England's Percy Baker - another legendary figure of the game - was aged 63 when he won singles silver in 1958. Percy Watson, of Northern Ireland, won silver in 1934 and gold 20 years later, and he went on to compete in the Games of 1958 and 1962. Andrew Harvey was a bronze-medallist for South Africa in 1934; his son, Horace, won gold in 1938; and Horace's son, Tom, was a World champion in 1972. Thomas Skoglund won bronze for New Zealand in the 1950 fours; his nephew, Phil Skoglund, won pairs' bronze in 1974; and Phil's son, Philip jnr, competed in the 1994 Games.

Bowls has an ancient history with references traced back to 5200 BC, while the first greens in England were laid possibly in Chesterfield in 1294 and certainly in Southampton in 1299. The English Bowling Association was formed in 1903 - with the great cricketer, Dr W.G. Grace, as its first President - and the World Bowls Board was set up within two years.

Altogether, 15 countries have won medals in men's bowls at the Commonwealth Games, and there are 14 countries which have shared the 45 women's medals awarded in only four celebrations of the Games.

Leading countries:

England 13 gold medals; New Zealand, Scotland 9 each; South Africa 8; Australia 6; Northern Ireland 4; Hong Kong, Zimbabwe (including 1 as Southern Rhodesia) 3 each; Wales 2; Papua New Guinea 1.

Leading gold-medallists:

5 David Bryant (Eng) 1962-78; 2 Tommy Hills (Eng) 1930-34, George Wright (Eng) 1930-34, Ernest Gudgeon (Eng) 1930-34, Norman King (Eng) 1958-70, Clementi Delgado (HK) 1970-78, Bob Da Silva (HK) 1970-78, Willie Wood (Sco) 1982-90, George Adrain (Sco) 1986-90, Margaret Johnston (NI) 1986-94, Lorna Trigwell (SA) 1994-98.

Highlights Games-by-Games

1930: England won all three titles, but there were also medals for Canada, New Zealand, Scotland and South Africa. A New Zealander, William Fielding, was a medallist in both the singles and pairs, while a Canadian, Tom Chambers, won a bronze medal in the fours - but for Scotland after stepping in as a generous replacement by the hosts after the death of one of the Scottish team.

1934: Three English bowlers won gold for the second time: Tommy Hills and George Wright in the pairs and Ernest Gudgeon in the fours. Northern Ireland and Wales took medals for the first time, and the first non-English winner was a Scotsman, Robert Sprot, in the singles.

1938: England sent a team of six to Sydney, including double champion Tommy Hills, but they failed to win any medals, with Hills placing 4th in the singles. The winner of that event was Horace Harvey, of South Africa, while New Zealand took both the pairs and the fours. One of the winners in the pairs, William Denison, had the unusual distinction of having his son row in the New Zealand eight at the same Games. Despite the distance to travel to the Games there were nine countries represented in bowls, including also Australia, Canada, Fiji, Northern Ireland, Rhodesia and Scotland.

1950: England sent no bowlers at all to Auckland, and there were only five competitors in the singles and four each in the pairs and fours, but there was a singles bronze for a Fijian, Lionel Garnett. The host country won two of the titles, with Jim Pirret in the singles and the partnership of Bob Henry and Phil Exelby in the pairs. Henry and Exelby were a formidable team, according to the subsequent account in "The New Zealand Sportsman" magazine, and "from the first head of the first game carried all before them and were always prospective winners". The skip of the winning South African four, Norman "Snowy" Walker, had also won silver at the previous Games of 12 years earlier.

1954: A record-breaking entry of 61 bowlers from 11 countries guaranteed the future of bowls as a Games sport, and Northern Ireland and Southern Rhodesia both took titles. The Rhodesian, Ralph Hodges, won eight of his nine matches to earn the singles gold ahead of the defending champion, Jim Pirret, while South Africa retained the fours gold with eight wins and a tie. Intriguingly, a Hong Kong quartet including two players of Portuguese origin took the silver, and one of them was imposingly named Raoul Francisco Eustaquio da Luz. Edwin Bateman, a competitor for England in the pairs, can lay claim to being the oldest games competitor ever in any sport, taking part at the age of 74 !

1958: Norman "Snowy" Walker reappeared in the South African team and won his third medal in 20 years at the Games. One of his teammates, Phineas "Pinky" Danilowitz, won the singles from the 63-year-old Englishman, Percy Baker, while New Zealand took the pairs and England the fours.

1962: David Bryant was at the start of a remarkable Games career at the age of 31 and was already being described in the authoritative British magazine, "World Sports", as "David the Goliath". He duly won golds in the singles and the fours in conditions which he described as "a bowler's paradise", while Rhodesian bowlers - as in Cardiff in 1958 - collected medals in all three events and in every instance were involved in a play-off to do so. The Australian hosts surprisingly won no medals and one local observer darkly remarked that "there will be many long talks in clubhouses about this".

1970: Perhaps most at ease of all of the teams was the four from Hong Kong, playing in familiar conditions beneath an airport flypath at the Balgreen rinks, and they duly won 11 of their 12 matches and the gold medals. Indicative of the changing ethnic makeup of the Commonwealth, three of the players were of Portugese descent and the fourth, Abdul Kitchell, was originally from Malaysia. Their only loss was to the unplaced veteran Australian quartet in the gathering dusk of a typically cold Scottish summer's evening. Curiously, the length of the bowls programme, with 14 entrants in each of the events, meant that Hong Kong were already champions three days before the Games opening ceremony even took place. David Bryant, who had compensated for the absence of bowls at the 1966 Games in Jamaica by winning the inaugural World Championship instead that same year, became the first man to retain a Commonwealth singles title.

1974: David Bryant made it three in a row in the singles and a perennial rival, Willie Wood, took the bronze for Scotland. The Scottish pair of John Christie and Alex McIntosh won the first bowls gold medals for their country in 40 years.

1978: Hong Kong returned to form in the fours, with only Bob Da Silva surviving from the 1970 team, and won gold with 12 wins and two losses. Hong Kong also took the pairs title through Eric Liddell and Clementi Delgado, who had together been World champions in 1972. Delgado had figured in the winning four at the 1970 Commonwealth Games, and Liddell was taking part in his sixth Commonwealth Games at the age of 54. David Bryant, almost inevitably, won a fourth consecutive singles gold, though he did actually lose two of his 15 encounters. Having been in Scotland's bronze-medal four at the previous Games, Morgan Moffatt went one better for his adopted country, New Zealand, with a silver medal.

1982: Willie Wood finally brought the Bryant saga to a close by succeeding him as singles champion and Scotland also took the pairs. In the fours Morgan Moffatt earned another silver for New Zealand as Australia won their first ever gold medals in bowls. Women bowlers appeared for the first time in a triples event, and the experiment proved its value as Zimbabwe won the gold from New Zealand and an England trio which included the previous year's World singles champion, Norma Shaw.

1986: Not quite so hard hit as other sports by the boycott, the bowls events produced a singles win for New Zealand, a first win in any event for Wales in the fours - and for the hosts, Scotland, a third win in four Games in the pairs. Of particular significance, Edinburgh welcomed women bowlers to a full programme for the first time and although all three titles went to the Home Countries there was a bronze for Botswana in the singles and a silver for Guernsey in the pairs.

1990: Mixed fortunes for the big names of bowls. Willie Wood, competing in the fours, won his second gold medal for Scotland and one of his partners, George Adrain, had been a World pairs champion in 1984. Rowan "Radar" Brassey, of New Zealand, who had shared a pairs World championship with Peter Belliss in 1988, was 3rd in this event. David Bryant, bidding for a fifth singles gold at the age of 58, was beaten into 4th place. Australia won two gold medals at the Games, which was something of a transformation of their fortunes as they had only ever won one title previously, and even more of a revelation was the women's singles winner, Geua Tau, from Papua New Guinea, where there were only

200 competitive women bowlers.

1994: Richard Corsie became the next Scot after Willie Wood to win the Commonwealth singles title and in the process beat the reigning World champion, England's Tony Allcock, into 2nd place. The Australian defending champion, Rob Parella, shared bronze as play-offs for 3rd place were done away with. The women's singles title went to Northern Ireland's reigning World champion, Margaret Johnston, who had been 3rd in 1990 and who had already won two other World titles in pairs. Sarah Gourlay won gold for Scotland in the pairs 12 years after husband David had achieved the same feat. South Africa, back in the Games after a 36-year absence, took the women's fours.

1998: The Malaysians, who had never previously figured at all prominently in Games bowls, caused much of a stir by winning medals in three of the six events. Saedah Abdul Rahim reached the women's singles final before losing to the immensely experienced South African, Lesly Hartwell, and if anything the Malaysians were disappointed at their overall results. Before 1992 there had been only one green in Malaysia, built by the Royal Australian Air Force in the 1970s, and the first major open tournament did not take place until 1993. Extensive technical aid from Australian officials speeded up the ambitious development programme, and the national coach was Robbie Dobbins, a Games gold-medallist for Australia in 1982.

BOWLS MEDALLISTS

Note: from 1994 onwards all losing semi-finalists received bronze medals.

Men's Singles:
1930: 1 Robert Colquhoun (Eng), 2 J.G. Thomas (SA), 3 William Fielding (NZ).
1934: 1 Robert Sprot (Sco), 2 W.S. MacDonald (Can), 3 Andrew Harvey (SA).
1938: 1 Horace Harvey (SA), 2 Frank Livingstone (NZ), 3 Jack Low (Aus).
1950: 1 Jim Pirret (NZ), 2 Albert Newton (Aus), 3 Lionel Garnett (Fij).
1954: 1 Ralph Hodges (SRho), 2 Jim Pirret (NZ), 3 Arthur Saunders (SA).
1958: 1 Phineas Danilowitz (SA), 2 Percy Baker (Eng), 3 William Jackson (SRho).
1962: 1 David Bryant (Eng), 2 Joseph Watson Black (Sco), 3 Alan Bradley (SRho).
1966: Not held
1970: 1 David Bryant (Eng), 2 Neal Bryce (Zam), 3 Roy Fulton (NI).
1974: 1 David Bryant (Eng), 2 Clive White (Aus), 3 Willie Wood (Sco).
1978: 1 David Bryant (Eng), 2 John Snell (Aus), 3 John Russell Evans (Wal).
1982: 1 Willie Wood (Sco), 2 Rob Parrella (Aus), 3 Peter Belliss (NZ).
1986: 1 Ian Dickison (NZ), 2 Ian Schuback (Aus), 3 Richard Corsie (Sco).
1990: 1 Rob Parrella (Aus), 2 Mark McMahon (HK), 3 Richard Corsie (Sco).

1994: 1 Richard Corsie (Sco), 2 Tony Allcock (Eng), 3 Rob Parrella (Aus), Ken Wallis (HK).

1998: 1 Roy Garden (Zim), 2 John Price (Wal), 3 Gerald Baker (SA), Jeremy Henry (NI).

Men's Pairs:

1930: 1 Tommy Hills & George Wright (Eng), 2 Peter McWhannell & William Fielding (NZ), 3 Arthur Reid & W.H. Moore (Can).

1934: 1 Tommy Hills & George Wright (Eng), 2 W.G. Hutchinson & A.A. Langford (Can), 3 Thomas Davies & Stan Weaver (Wal).

1938: 1 Lance Macey & Walter Denison (NZ), 2 Percy Hutton & Howard Mildren (Aus), 3 D. A. Adamson & J.R. Appleford (SA).

1950: 1 Bob Henry & Phil Exelby (NZ), 2 W. Gibb & H.J. van Zyl (SA), 3 James Poulton & Leslie Brown (Fij).

1954: 1 William Rosbotham & Percy Watson (NI), 2 Sam Gardiner & Richard Williams (Can), 3 George Budge & John Carswell (Sco).

1958: 1 John Morris & Richard Pilkington (NZ), 2 John Myrdal & Rudolph van Vuuren (SA), 3 William Yuill & Hector Philp (SRho).

1962: 1 Bob McDonald & Hugh Robson (NZ), 2 Michael Purdon & Thomas Hamill (Sco), 3 Charles Bradley & William Jackson (SRho).

1966: 1 Not held

1970: 1 Norman King & Peter Line (Eng), 2 Bob McDonald & Hugh Robson (NZ), 3 Jimmy Donnelly & Syd Thompson (NI).

1974: 1 John Christie & Alex McIntosh (Sco), 2 John Evans & Peter Line (Eng), 3 Phil Skoglund & Bob McDonald (NZ).

1978: 1 Eric Liddell & Clementi Delgado (HK), 2 Alex McIntosh & Willie Wood (Sco), 3 James Morgan & Ray Williams (Wal).

1982: 1 John Watson & David Gourlay (Sco), 2 Lyn Perkins & Spencer Wilshire (Wal), 3 Denis Dalton & Peter Rheuben (Aus).

1986: 1 George Adrain & Grant Knox (Sco), 2 Bill Boettger & Ronnie Jones (Can), 3 Chris Ward & David Ward (Eng).

1990: 1 Trevor Morris & Ian Schuback (Aus), 2 George Boxwell & Alf Wallace (Can), 3 Rowan Brassey & Maurice Symes (NZ).

1994: 1 Rex Johnston & Cameron Curtis (Aus), 2 Robert Weale & John Price (Wal), 3 Andy Thomson & Gary Smith (Eng), Sammy Allen & Stephen Adamson (NI).

1998: 1 Brett Duprez & Mark Jacobsen (Aus), 2 William Thomas & Robert Weale (Wal), 3 Mohamed Aziz Maswadi & Mohamed Tazman Jahir (Mal), Theunis Fraser & Rudi Jacobs (SA).

Men's Fours:

1930: 1 England (Ernest Gudgeon, James Edney, F. Hough, Jack Frith), 2 Canada (Jimmy Campbell, Mitch Thomas, Billy Rae, Harry Allen), 3 Scotland (David Fraser, Tom Chambers, William Campbell, John Orr).

Note: Chambers was a Canadian who was brought in as a substitute.

1934: 1 England (Robert Slater, Percy Tomlinson, Ernest Gudgeon, Fred Biggin), 2 Northern Ireland (Cecil Curran, George Watson, Charlie Clawson, Percy Watson), 3 Scotland (James Brown, James Morrison, Charles Tait, William Low).

1938: 1 New Zealand (Bill Whittaker, Alec Robertson, Ernie Jury, Bill Bremner), 2 South Africa (Norman Walker, F. Stevenson, T.H. Samson, J.G. Donaldson), 3 Australia (Frank Murray, Aubrey Murray, Charlie McNeil, Tom Kinder).

1950: 1 South Africa (Harry Atkinson, H. Currer, Alfred Blumberg, Norman Walker), 2 Australia (John Cobley, Leonard Knight, Charles Cordaiy, James Cobley), 3 New Zealand (Noel Jolly, Fred Russell, John Engbretsen, Thomas Skoglund)

1954: 1 South Africa (George Wilson, John Anderson, Frank Mitchell, Wilf Randall), 2 Hong Kong (José da Luz, Alfred Coates, Robert Gourlay, Raoul da Luz), 3 Southern Rhodesia (Alan Bradley, Fred Hockin, Alex Pascoe, Ronald Turner).

1958: 1 England (John Bettles, Norman King, Walter Phillips, George Scadgell), 2 South Africa (Wilf Randall, Edward Stuart, Norman Walker, Edward Williams), 3 Northern Rhodesia (Charles Bradley, Alex Pascoe, Ronald Turner, Basil Wells).

1962: 1 England (David Bryant, George Fleming, John Watson, Sid Drysdale), 2 Scotland (Michael Purdon, Thomas Hamill, Joseph Watson Black, Willy Moore), 3 Rhodesia & Nyasaland (Malcolm Bibb, Victor Blyth, John Milligan, Ronald Turner).

1966: Not held

1970: 1 Hong Kong (Clementi Delgado, Abdul Kitchell, Bob Da Silva, George Souza), 2 Scotland (John Slight, Norman Pryde, David Pearson, Alex McIntosh), 3 Northern Ireland (John Higgins, Edward Gordon, Harold Stevenson, William Tate).

1974: 1 New Zealand (Dave Baldwin, Kerry Clark, Gordon Jolly, John Somerville), 2 Australia (Robert King, Errol Bungey, Errol Stewart, Keith Poole), 3 Scotland (Morgan Moffatt, John Marshall, William Scott, John McRae).

1978: 1 Hong Kong (Kim Fun Chok, Majid Hassan, Bob Da Silva, Omar Kachong Dallah), 2 New Zealand (Dave Baldwin, John Malcolm, Morgan Moffatt, Phil Skoglund), 3 Wales (Ellis Stanbury, Ian Sutherland, John Thomson, Gwyn Evans).

Note: Moffatt competed for Scotland in 1974.

1982: 1 Australia (Robbie Dobbins, Keith Poole, Bert Sharp, Don Sherman), 2 New Zealand (Rowan Brassey, Morgan Moffatt, Danny O'Connor, Jim Scott), 3 Northern Ireland (Sammy Allen, John McCloydhin, Frank Campbell, Willie Watson).

1986: 1 Wales (Robert Weale, William Thomas, Haford Thomas, Jim Morgan), 2 Canada (Dave Brown, Dave Duncalf, Dave Houtby, Dan Milligan), 3 Northern Ireland (Billy Montgomery, Roy McCune, Ernie Parkinson, Willie Watson).

1990: 1 Scotland (Willie Wood, Denis Love, Ian Bruce, George Adrain), 2 Northern Ireland (Rodney McCutcheon, John McCloughlin, Sammy Allen, Jim Baker), 3 New Zealand (Peter Shaw, Stewart McConnell, Kevin Darling, Phil Skoglund).

1994: 1 South Africa (Neil Burkett, Robbie Rayfield, Alan Lofthouse, Donald Piketh), 2 Australia (Stephen Anderson, Steve Srhoy, Robert Ball, Ian Taylor), 3 Northern Ireland (Noel Graham, Ian McClure, John McCloughlin, Victor Dallas), New Zealand (Peter Belliss, Rowan Brassey, Stewart Buttar, Bruce McNish).

1998: 1 Northern Ireland (Martin McHugh, Ian McClure, Neil Booth, Gary

McCloy), 2 Australia (Adam Jeffrey, Kevin Walsh, Stewart Davies, Rex Johnston), 3 South Africa (Neil Burkett, Robbie Rayfield, Bruce Makkink, Mike Redshaw), Wales (Mark Anstey, Neil Rees, Ian Slade, David Wilkins).

Women's Singles:

First held 1986

1986: 1 Wendy Line (Eng), 2 Senga McCrone (Sco), 3 Flora Anderson (Bot).

1990: 1 Geua Tau (PNG), 2 Millie Khan (NZ), 3 Margaret Johnston (NI).

1994: 1 Margaret Johnston (NI), 2 Rita Jones (Wal), 3 Carmelia Anderson (NorI), Norma Shaw (Eng).

1998: 1 Lesly Hartwell (SA), 2 Saedah Abdul Rahim (Mal), 3 Jean Baker (Eng), Millie Khan (NZ).

Women's Pairs:

First held 1986

1986: 1 Freda Elliott & Margaret Johnston (NI), 2 Janet Nicolle & Marie Smith (Gue), 3 Jean Valls & Betty Stubbings (Eng).

1990: 1 Judy Howart & Marie Watson (NZ), 2 Edda Bonutto & Maureen Hobbs (Aus), 3 Mary Price & Jayne Roylance (Eng).

1994: 1 Frances Whyte & Sarah Gourlay (Sco), 2 Jo Peacock & Lyn Dwyer (SA), 3 Brenda Atherton & Mary Price (Eng), Ann Dainton & Janet Ackland (Wal).

1998: 1 Margaret Letham & Joyce Linores (Sco), 2 Lynne Lindsay-Payne & Cathelean du Plessis (Nam), 3 Gordana Baric & Willow Fong (Aus), Ann Sutherland & Rita Jones (Wal).

Women's Fours:

Triples 1982.

1982: 1 Zimbabwe (Florence Kennedy, Anna Bates, Margaret Mills), 2 New Zealand (Pearl Dymond, Joyce Osborne, Jennifer Simpson), 3 England (Mavis Steele, Betty Stubbings, Norma Shaw).

1986: 1 Wales (Linda Evans, Joan Ricketts, Rita Jones, Linda Parker), 2 Australia (Audrey Hefford, Hilda Pochon, Clarice Power, Barbara Schenke), 3 England (Brenda Atherton, Margaret Allan, Mary Price, Barbara Fuller).

1990: 1 Australia (Marion Stevens, Daphne Shaw, Andrea Rutherford, Dorothy Roche), 2 New Zealand (Rhoda Ryan, Lyn McLean, Adrienne Lambert, Marlene Castle), 3 Hong Kong (Jenny Wallis, Natividad Rozario, Yee Lai Lee, Sau Ling Chau).

1994: 1 South Africa (Colleen Grondein, Hester Bekker, Lorna Trigwell, Anna Pretorius), 2 Papua New Guinea (Linda Ahmat, Elizabeth Bure, Cunera Monalua, Wena Piande), 3 New Zealand (Adrienne Lambert, Ann Muir, Colleen Ferrick, Marlene Castle), Scotland (Janice Maxwell, Elizabeth Forsyth, Elizabeth Dickson, Dorothy Barr).

1998: 1 South Africa (Trish Steyn, Lorraine Victor, Lorna Trigwell, Hester Bekker), 2 Australia (Marilyn Peddall, Lee Poletti, Karen Murphy, Margaret Sumner), 3 England (Samanda Jacklin, Shirley Page, Norma Shaw, Jean Baker), Malaysia (Siti Zalina Ahmad, Haslah Hj Hassan, Nor Hashimah Ismail, Nor Azwa Mohamed Di).

BOXING

It's the spread of the medals that counts

The usual yardstick by which any amateur boxing tournament is meas-
ured is the number of its contestants who went on to become World professional champions. Any list which includes the likes of Howard
Winstone, John Conteh, Barry McGuigan, Azumah Nelson, Lennox
Lewis, Jeff Harding, Richie Woodhall and Wayne McCullough is bound
to impress, though whether that select group fairly reflects the calibre of
Commonwealth Games competition over the years is not the significant
point.

The fact is that whatever extremes of opinion the sport of boxing
might arouse - and there is no shortage of its detractors - it offers in
some of the less developed countries one of the very few disciplined out-
lets for youngsters. The 611 medals which have been awarded at 12 different weights in Commonwealth Games boxing since 1930 have been
shared among 37 countries, and no other Games sport can match that
universality of opportunity across such relatively few events.

In 1998 alone gold medals were won by Cameroon, Canada, England, Ghana, Malaysia, Mauritius and the Seychelles, and other medals by Australia, Cyprus, India, Kenya, New Zealand, Northern Ireland, Pakistan, Papua New Guinea, Scotland, South Africa, Tanzania, Uganda, Wales and Zambia. That amounts to 48 medals spread among 21 countries in Europe, Asia, Africa, North America and Oceania. Together with athletics and swimming, boxing is the only sport to have been contested at every Games since 1930.

Eight weight divisions were fought at the inaugural Games, and England won five of them, South Africa two and Scotland one. In London four years later English boxers won six titles and even the patrician efforts of Lord David Douglas-Hamilton, of Scotland, were sufficient for no more than the bronze medal at heavyweight. A featherweight from Ceylon (now Sri Lanka) named Ansdale Henricus deserves recognition as the first successful boxer from the Third World, winning the gold in Sydney in 1938.

Ceylonese boxers took three more medals in 1950, and when the African nations began to enter in force in 1954 Abubakar Idi Garuba, of Nigeria, won an historic bronze at bantamweight. Since then African boxers have provided all but one of the six double gold medallists at the Games, with Stephen Muchoki (Kenya) at light-flyweight in 1970-74, Sulley Shittu (Ghana) at flyweight and bantamweight in 1966-70, Philip Waruinge (Kenya) at featherweight in 1966-70, Eddie Blay (Ghana) at lightweight and welterweight in 1962-66, and Muhammad Muruli (Uganda) at light-welterweight and welterweight in 1970-74. Waruinge had also been a flyweight bronze-medallist in 1962.

The only other double champion is Tony Madigan, of Australia, winner at light-heavyweight in 1958 and 1962 and who at the 1960 Olympic Games had the dubious privilege of being the losing semi-finalist to the eventual champion, Cassius Clay (later Muhammad Ali). Madigan, like Waruinge, won three Commonwealth medals in all, and yet the only boxers to have won both Olympic and Commonwealth titles have been the Scotsman, Dick McTaggart, at lightweight in 1956 and 1958 and the Canadian, Lennox Lewis, at super-heavyweight in 1986 and 1988. Lewis later became a World professional champion for Britain.

Leading countries:

England 41 gold medals; Canada 21; South Africa 14; Scotland 13; Kenya, Nigeria 12 each; Ghana 9; Australia, Northern Ireland, Uganda 8 each; New Zealand 5; Jamaica, Wales 2 each; Fiji, Guyana, Malaysia, Mauritius, St Vincent, Sri Lanka (as Ceylon), Tanzania, Zambia, Zimbabwe (as Southern Rhodesia) 1 each.

BOXING

Leading gold-medallists:

2 Tony Madigan (Aus) 1958-62, Eddie Blay (Gha) 192-66, Sulley Shittu (Gha) 1966-70, Philip Waruinge (Ken) 1966-70, Stephen Muchoki (Ken) 1970-74, Muhammad Muruli (Uga) 1970-74.

Highlights - Games by Games

1930: Competition was held in eight weight divisions, and England won five titles, South Africa two and Scotland one. The heavyweight final was fought out by the only two contestants, both guaranteed medals unless either of them was disqualified.

1934: England's domination was even more marked with six wins to one each for Australia and South Africa. There were also medals for Canada, Northern Ireland, Rhodesia, Scotland and Wales.

1938: There were no more than six entries in any of the eight weight divisions, but nine countries took part and six of them won gold medals. The same number of countries won gold in the 28-event athletics programme. Ceylon (now Sri Lanka) sent two boxers and one of them, Ansdale Henricus, was an historic winner at featherweight. Wales, whose entire team for all sports numbered only six, selected one boxer, Dennis Reardon, and he won the middleweight title.

1950: Four boxers lost their only fights but still won medals. There were only two entries at heavyweight and three each at light-heavyweight and middleweight. Then at welterweight the bronze medal was awarded to Alex Obeyesekere, of Ceylon, though he lost his one bout, while Jim McIvor, of New Zealand, got nothing despite winning one of his two bouts. This curious state of affairs arose because the Ceylonese received a bye to the semi-finals and McIvor was unable to appear for the bronze medal match after being beaten in the other semi-final. England won three titles and the heavyweight champion, Frank Creagh, had immigrated from England to New Zealand two years before. In any case, it was generally reckoned that England's light-heavyweight winner, Don Scott (an Olympic silver-medallist in 1948), had the class to have won the heavyweight division as well.

1954: More than 7000 spectators, including the Duke of Edinburgh, crowded into the 6650-capacity stadium for finals night. Again, as in

1938, there had been no more than six competitors at any one weight, and there was something for almost everyone with five countries winning gold and nine winning medals of any kind. The official report of the Games cheerfully summed up matters with the comment that "for a crowd spectacle and for sportsmanship the boxing competitions were excellent; as for boxing itself, the general overall standard was not so hot". Of longer-term significance, Nigeria, Pakistan and Trinidad each had one representative, and the Nigerian at bantamweight, Abubakar Idi Garuba, won a trend-setting bronze medal.

1958: Howard Winstone, at bantamweight, gave promise to his fans in Cardiff of a highly successful professional career by winning Wales's second boxing gold, and other titles went to two of the finest of all amateur fighters - Dick McTaggart, of Scotland, who had already won Olympic gold two years previously, and Tony Madigan, of Australia. At welterweight Thomas Kawere, of Uganda, notably became the first African finalist who was not either South African or Rhodesian by birth.

1962: Two gold medals for Ghana and one for Uganda marked this out as the most significant Games boxing tournament so far. Ghana also won four other medals, Uganda three and Kenya two, and there was a first ever boxing gold for Jamaica. Ghana's winners were Eddie Blay, beating Kesi Odongo, of Uganda, for the lightweight title, and Clement Quartey, controversially awarded the light-welterweight title over Blay's predecessor as champion, Dick McTaggart. In all, African boxers provided 10 of the 20 finalists. At light-heavyweight Tony Madigan became the first boxer to successfully defend a Commonwealth Games title, and Scotland - with two gold medals (one of them their fourth in succession at flyweight), a silver and a bronze from a team of five - did rather better than England, whose only finalist was John Pritchett at welterweight, who later became British professional champion.

1966: Africa Advance ! Ghana won three golds, Nigeria two and Kenya one, leaving England, New Zealand and Northern Ireland to share the remaining four titles. Eddie Blay took gold again for Ghana, moving up to welterweight, and Sulley Shittu won at bantamweight. Philip Waruinge, who had been the flyweight bronze-medallist in 1962, moved two divisions to featherweight and became champion. Jim McCourt was Northern Ireland's first boxing gold-medallist, having won bronze for Ireland in the 1964 Olympics, and at heavyweight Bill Kini was only New Zealand's second champion in the sport at the Games, defeating the splendidly-named Adonis Ray, of Ghana, in the final.

BOXING

1970: Two outstanding boxers among the 135 contestants won their second gold medals - Sulley Shittu at bantamweight and Philip Waruinge at featherweight - but it was another African nation, Uganda, which won more golds than anyone else. With a new division, light-flyweight, brought on to the schedule, there were 11 titles at stake and Uganda won three of them, Ghana and Nigeria two each and Kenya one. England had two title-winners, including 19-year-old John Conteh at middleweight, and the light-middleweight gold went to Tom Imrie, in his home town of Edinburgh, after winning silver four years earlier. The officiating again caused aggravation throughout and in Imrie's victory over Julius Luipa, of Zambia, one judge scored the fight 60-56 to the Scot and another 60-56 for the Zambian!

1974: African boxers won six titles - two each for Nigeria and Uganda, one each for Kenya and Zambia - and there was a rare Caribbean success, but England actually accumulated the most gold medals through Pat Cowdell, Billy Knight and Neville Meade. The Kenyan success came at light-flyweight for a 16-year-old, Stephen Muchoki, while Muhammad Muruli won the welterweight title for Uganda to add to his light-welterweight success four years earlier. There were also a pleasing spread of medals for Canada, India, Jamaica, New Zealand, Northern Ireland (including gold at flyweight for David Larmour), Scotland, Singapore and Western Samoa, while Frankie Lucas from the West Indies island of St Vincent (population 100,000 or so) won the middleweight final from Zambia's Julius Luipa, who was thus a silver-medallist for the second successive Games.

1978: Eight different countries won titles: Canada, Kenya and Northern Ireland two each; Australia, England, Ghana, Guyana and Jamaica one each. Stephen Muchoki, the teenage sensation in Chistchurch four years before, became only the third boxer in Commonwealth Games history to retain a title at the same weight, and another talented youngster took the bantamweight gold for Northern Ireland - 17-year-old Finbarr ("Barry") McGuigan. England's lone winner was the heavyweight, Julius Awome, but Delroy Parkes managed to win a silver despite being counted out. He was knocked down by the Canadian, Roddy MacDonald, who then unwisely hit Parkes again when he was on the floor and was rightly disqualified - but was still given a bronze medal. Kelly Perlette, fighting for Canada in his home province of Alberta, had his nose broken in his opening light-middleweight bout but courageously battled on to take gold.

1982: Kenyans and Nigerians between them won all six lighter weight divisions up to light-welterweight. England and Canada each won two golds, and the remaining title - at light-heavyweight - went to Fiji, who thus became the 19th country to win Games boxing gold. Zambia, frustratingly, came away with five bronzes and a silver, and there were also bronze medals for the Bahamas, India and Swaziland. England's winners were Chris Pyatt at welterweight and Jimmy Price at middleweight.

1986: The boycott kept the Africans away, and so Canada and England almost swept the board between them. The Canadians, who had previously won eight golds in 12 celebrations of the Games, took six titles and England took five. With the super-heavyweight division added, and won for Canada by another big name of the future, Lennox Lewis, the one other title on offer at heavyweight went to a New Zealander, Jimmy Peau. Two of the handful of African nations which came to Edinburgh were suitably rewarded in the ring as Swaziland won a silver and Malawi two bronzes. At bantamweight John Sollitoe received a bronze medal for Jersey.

1990: Back in action Kenya, Nigeria and Uganda each won two golds, but the Home Countries rose to the challenge manfully - and no wonder because two future World professional champions were among their winners. Wayne McCullough took the flyweight title for Northern Ireland and Richie Woodhall the light-middleweight for England. Canada, New Zealand and Scotland also had winners, but this was a Games which featured names which were much more exotic than Irwin, Johnson, Kane or Kenny. Among the medallists were Geronimo Bie, Wesley Christmas, Nicodemus Odore and Duke Chinyadza.

1994: Such was the widespread Commonwealth support for boxing that there were 38 nations taking part. Canada enjoyed its most successful Games on home territory, winning four titles, to two for Kenya and Northern Ireland and one each for Australia, England, Nigeria and Scotland. The Seychelles won a medal for the first time, but in a roundabout fashion. Rival Cadeau failed to appear for his light-middleweight semi-final against the eventual champion but as it was due to a lapse in communication the organisers gave Cadeau a bronze medal anyway.

1998: Malaysia, Mauritius, Tanzania, Scotland, Ghana, Canada: the list of nations which won in order the six lighter divisions could scarcely have been more varied. Canada took a second gold at welterweight, but after that it was all one-way traffic to England - five gold medals in five finals, including the charismatic Audley Harrison at super-heavyweight. For

Malaysia and Mauritius it was their first Games boxing golds and Mauritius also got a silver and both countries got a bronze apiece. Also figuring for the first time was Cameroon - the latter having only recently joined the Commonwealth. Unfortunately, average attendances were no more than 200 or so until home hero Sapok Biki reached the light-flyweight final and 8000 spectators turned up to see him win.

BOXING MEDALLISTS

Note: from 1958 onwards both losing semi-finalists received bronze medals.

Light-Flyweight (48kg):
First held 1970
1970: 1 James Odwori (Uga), 2 Anthony Davies (Wal), 3 Michael Abrams (Eng), Peter Butterfield (Aus).
1974: 1 Stephen Muchoki (Ken), 2 James Odwori (Uga), 3 John Bambrick (Sco), Syed Kedir (Sin).
1978: 1 Stephen Muchoki (Ken), 2 Francis Musankabala (Zam), 3 Birender Thapa (Ind), Kid Sumalia (Gha).
1982: 1 Abraham Wachire (Ken), 2 John Lyon (Eng), 3 Leonard Makhanya (Swa), Lucky Siame (Zam).
1986: 1 Scott Olson (Can), 2 Mark Epton (Eng), 3 Wilson Docherty (Sco), Johnston Todd (NI).
1990: 1 Justin Juko (Uga), 2 Abdurahman Ramadhani (Ken), 3 Domenic Filane (Can), Michael Chantwell (Eng).
1994: 1 Abdurahman Ramadhani (Ken), 2 Victor Kasote (Zam), 3 Birju Sah (Ind), Domenic Figliomeni (Can).
Note: Figliomeni formerly Filane.
1998: 1 Sapok Biki (Mal), 2 Moses Kinyua (Ken), 3 Gary Jones (Eng), Roudik Kazanijan (Cyp).

Flyweight (51kg):
1930: 1 Jacob Smith (SA), 2 Thomas Pardoe (Eng), 3 Ross Galloway (Can).
1934: 1 Patrick Palmer (Eng), 2 Maxie Berger (Can), 3 Jackie Pottinger (Wal).
1938: 1 Johannes Joubert (SA), 2 Joseph Gagnon (Can), 3 Hugh Cameron (Sco).
1950: 1 Hugh Riley (Sco), 2 K. Edwin (Cey), 3 Marcus Temple (SA).
1954: 1 Dick Currie (Sco), 2 Abe Bekker (NRho), 3 Warren Batchelor (Aus).
1958: 1 Jackie Brown (Sco), 2 Tommy Bache (Eng), 3 Donald Braithwaite (Wal), Peter Lavery (NI).
1962: 1 Robert Mallon (Sco), 2 Cassis Aryee (Gha), 3 Mike Pye (Eng), Philip Waruinge (Ken).
1966: 1 Sulley Shittu (Gha), 2 Kenneth Campbell (Jam), 3 John Rakowski (Aus), Frank Scott (Can).
1970: 1 Dave Needham (Eng), 2 Leo Rwabogo (Uga), 3 David Larmour (NI), Alex McHugh (Sco).

1974: 1 David Larmour (NI), 2 Chandra Narayanan (Ind), 3 John Byaruhanga (Uga), Saliu Ishola (Nig).

1978: 1 Michael Irungu (Ken), 2 Ian Clyde (Can), 3 Hugh Russell (NI), Peter Wighton (Aus).

1982: 1 Michael Mutua (Ken), 2 Joseph Kelly (Sco), 3 Albert Musankabala (Zam), Grant Richards (Aus).

1986: 1 John Lyon (Eng), 2 Leonard Makhanya (Swa), 3 Steve Beaupré (Can), Kerry Webber (Wal).

1990: 1 Wayne McCullough (NI), 2 Nokuthula Tshabangu (Zim), 3 Maurice Maina (Ken), Born Siwakwi (Zam).

1994: 1 Paul Shepherd (Sco), 2 Duncan Karanja (Ken), 3 Danny Costello (Eng), Boniface Mukuka (Zam).

1998: 1 Richard Sunee (Mau), 2 Liam Cunningham (NI), 3 Jackson Asiku (Uga), Phumzile Matyhila (SA).

Bantamweight (54kg):

1930: 1 Hyman Mizler (Eng), 2 Tommy Holt (Sco), 3 John Keller (Can).

1934: 1 Freddy Ryan (Eng), 2 Albert Barnes (Wal), 3 Thomas Wells (Sco).

1938: 1 William Butler (Eng), 2 Hendrik Knoesen (SA), 3 Jack Dillon (Aus).

1950: 1 Jan van Rensburg (SA), 2 Albert Perera (Cey), 3 Len Walters (Can).

1954: 1 John Smillie (Sco), 2 Gordon Smith (SRho), 3 Abubakar Idi Garuba (Nig).

1958: 1 Howard Winstone (Wal), 2 Ollie Taylor (Aus), 3 Richard Hanna (NI), Alfred Owen (Sco).

1962: 1 Jeff Dynevor (Aus), 2 Sammy Abbey (Gha), 3 Peter Bennyworth (Eng), John Sentongo (Uga).

1966: 1 Edward Ndukwu (Nig), 2 Darryl Norwood (Aus), 3 Brian Kendall (NZ), Nderu Mwaura (Ken).

1970: 1 Sulley Shittu (Gha), 2 Samuel Mbogwa (Ken), 3 Courtney Atherly (Guy), Stewart Ogilvie (Sco).

1974: 1 Pat Cowdell (Eng), 2 Ali Rojo (Uga), 3 Newton Chisanga (Zam), Isaac Maina (Ken).

1978: 1 Barry McGuigan (NI), 2 Tumat Sugolik (PNG), 3 Douglas Maina (Ken), William Rannelli (Can).

1982: 1 Joe Orewa (Nig), 2 Roy Webb (NI), 3 Ray Gilbody (Eng), Richard Reilly (Aus).

1986: 1 Sean Murphy (Eng), 2 Roy Nash (NI), 3 Glen Brooks (Sco), John Sollitoe (Jer).

1990: 1 Mohammed Sabo (Nig), 2 Geronimo Bie (Can), 3 Justin Chikwanda (Zam), Wesley Christmas (Guy).

1994: 1 Robert Peden (Aus), 2 Spencer Oliver (Eng), 3 Fred Muteweta (Uga), Godson Sowah (Gha).

1998: 1 Michael Yomba (Tan), 2 Herman Ngoudjo (Cam), 3 Andrew Kooner (Can), Adnan Yusoh (Mal).

Featherweight (57kg):

1930: 1 F.R. Meacham (Eng), 2 Lawrence Stevens (SA), 3 Alex Lyons (Sco).

1934: 1 Charles Catterall (SA), 2 J.D. Jones (Wal), 3 William Fulton (Rho).

1938: 1 Ansdale Henricus (Cey), 2 James Watson (Sco), 3 Kenneth Moran (NZ).

1950: 1 Henry Gilliland (Sco), 2 Andy Verceuil (Rho), 3 Peter Brander (Eng).

1954: 1 Len Leisching (SA), 2 Malcolm Collins (Wal), 3 Dave Charnley (Eng).

1958: 1 Wally Taylor (Aus), 2 Malcolm Collins (Wal), 3 Gert Coetzee (SA), John McClory (NI).

1962: 1 John McDermott (Sco), 2 Ali Juma (Ken), 3 Turori George (NZ), Ted Stone (Aus).

1966: 1 Philip Waruinge (Ken), 2 Pat Maguire (NI), 3 Amos Ajoo (Gha), Harold West (Jam).

1970: 1 Philip Waruinge (Ken), 2 Deogratias Musoke (Uga), 3 Alan Richardson (Eng).

Note: only one bronze medal awarded (one semi-finalist did not appear).

1974: 1 Edward Ndukwa (Nig), 2 Shadrack Odhiambo (Uga), 3 Dale Anderson (Can), Samuel Mbugua (Ken).

1978: 1 Azumah Nelson (Gha), 2 John Sichula (Zam), 3 Guy Boutin (Can), Maurice O'Brien (Eng).

1982: 1 Peter Konyegwachie (Nig), 2 Peter Hanlon (Eng), 3 Rodney Harberger (Aus), Winfred Kabunda (Zam).

1986: 1 Billy Downey (Can), 2 Peter English (Eng), 3 Chris Carleton (NI), Johnny Wallace (NZ).

1990: 1 John Irwin (Eng), 2 Haji Ally (Tan), 3 David Gakuha (Ken), James Nicolson (Aus).

1994: 1 Casey Patton (Can), 2 Jason Cook (Wal), 3 Matumla Hassan (Tan), James Swan (Aus).

1998: 1 Alex Arthur (Sco), 2 Marty O'Donnell (Can), 3 Lynch Ipera (PNG), James Swan (Aus).

Lightweight (60kg):

1930: 1 James Rolland (Sco), 2 Cosmos Canzano (Can), 3 Albert Love (Eng).

1934: 1 Leslie Cook (Aus), 2 Frank Taylor (Wal), 3 H.J. May (Eng).

1938: 1 Harry Groves (Eng), 2 Harry Hurst (Can), 3 William Fulton (Rho).

1950: 1 Ronny Latham (Eng), 2 Bill Barber (Aus), 3 Eddie Haddad (Can).

1954: 1 Piet van Staden (SRho), 2 Frank McQuillan (Sco), 3 Brian Cahill (Aus).

1958: 1 Dick McTaggart (Sco), 2 James Jordan (NI), 3 John Cooke (Eng), Thomas Donovan (NZ).

1962: 1 Eddie Blay (Gha), 2 Kesi Odongo (Uga), 3 Thomas Donovan (NZ), Brian Whelan (Eng).

1966: 1 Anthony Andeh (Nig), 2 Ron Thurston (Eng), 3 Stephen Baraza (Ken), Samuel Lockhart (NI).

1970: 1 Abayomi Adeyemi (Nig), 2 John Gillan (Sco), 3 Tatu Ghionga (Mlw), Moses Mbogwa (Ken).

1974: 1 Ayub Kalule (Uga), 2 Kayin Amah (Nig), 3 Robert Colley (NZ), Muniswami Venu (Ind).

1978: 1 Gerard Hamil (NI), 2 Patrick Waweru (Ken), 3 John McAllister (Sco), Teddy Makofi (Zam).

1982: 1 Hussein Khalili (Ken), 2 James McDonnell (Eng), 3 Stephen Larrimore (Bah), Brian Tink (Aus).

1986: 1 Asif Dar (Can), 2 Neil Hadcock (Wal), 3 Joe Jacobs (Eng), Leyton

Mphande (Mlw).

1990: 1 Godfrey Nyakana (Uga), 2 Justin Rowsell (Aus), 3 Davie Anderson (Sco), Bakari Mambeya (Tan).

1994: 1 Mike Strange (Can), 2 Martin Renaghan (NI), 3 Kalolo Fiaui (NZ), Hussein Arshad (Pak).

1998: 1 Raymond Narh (Gha), 2 Ali Ashgar (Pak), 3 Giovanni Frontin (Mau), Andrew McLean (Eng),

Light-Welterweight (63.5kg)

First held 1954

1954: 1 Mickey Bergin (Can), 2 Aubrey Harris (SRho), 3 Des Duguid (Aus).

1958: 1 Henry Loubscher (SA), 2 Robert Kane (Sco), 3 Raymond Galante (Can), Joseph Jacobs (Eng).

1962: 1 Clement Quartey (Gha), 2 Dick McTaggart (Sco), 3 Brian Brazier (Eng), Harvey Reti (Can).

1966: 1 Jim McCourt (NI), 2 Aaron Popoola (Gha), 3 Ray Maguire (Aus), Alex Odhiambo (Uga).

1970: 1 Muhammad Muruli (Uga), 2 Dai Davies (Wal), 3 Paul Kayula (Zam), Odartey Lawson (Gha).

1974: 1 Obisia Nwakpa (Nig), 2 Anthony Martey (Gha), 3 James Douglas (Sco), Philip Mathenge (Ken).

1978: 1 Winfield Braithwaite (Guy), 2 James Douglas (Sco), 3 Michael Mawangi (Ken), John Rafferty (Can).

1982: 1 Christopher Ossai (Nig), 2 Charles Owiso (Ken), 3 David Chibuye (Zam), Clyde McIntosh (Eng).

1986: 1 Howard Grant (Can), 2 Derek Clencie (Aus), 3 Solomon Kondowe (Mlw), Brendan Lowe (NI).

1990: 1 Charlie Kane (Sco), 2 Nicodemus Odore (Ken), 3 Duke Chinyadza (Zim), Stefan Scriggins (Aus).

1994: 1 Peter Richardson (Eng), 2 Mark Winters (NI), 3 Timani Moro (Gha), Trevor Shailer (NZ).

1998: 1 Mike Strange (Can), 2 Gerry Legras (Sey), 3 Casey Johns (Aus), Davie Mwale (Zam).

Welterweight (67kg):

1930: 1 Leonard Hall (SA), 2 Howard Williams (Can), 3 F. Brooman (Eng).

1934: 1 David McCleave (Eng), 2 Richard Barton (SA), 3 William Duncan (NI).

1938: 1 Bill Smith (Aus), 2 Darcy Heeney (NZ), 3 Andrew Tsirindonis (Rho).

1950: 1 Terry Ratcliffe (Eng), 2 Bill Seewitz (NZ), 3 Alex Obeyesekere (Cey).

1954: 1 Nicky Gargano (Eng), 2 Rodney Litzow (Aus), 3 Hendrik van der Linde (SA).

1958: 1 Joseph Greyling (SA), 2 Thomas Kawere (Uga), 3 Brian Nancurvis (Eng), Robert Scott (Sco).

1962: 1 Wallace Coe (NZ), 2 John Pritchett (Eng), 3 Albert Turmel (Jer).

Note: only one bronze medal awarded (one semi-finalist disqualified).

1966: 1 Eddie Blay (Gha), 2 Bobby Arthur (Eng), 3 Andy Peace (Sco), Frank Young (NI).

1970: 1 Emma Ankudey (Gha), 2 John Olulu (Ken), 3 Shivaji Bhonsle (Ind),

Thomas Joyce (Sco).

1974: 1 Muhammad Muruli (Uga), 2 Errol McKenzie (Jam), 3 Steve Cooney (Sco), John Rodgers (NI).

1978: 1 Michael McCallum (Jam), 2 Ken Beattie (NI), 3 Anthony Freal (Wal), Derrick Hoyt (Can).

1982: 1 Chris Pyatt (Eng), 2 Laston Mukobe (Zam), 3 Chenanda Machaiah (Ind), Charles Nwokolo (Nig).

1986: 1 Darren Dyer (Eng), 2 John McAllister (Sco), 3 Damien Denny (NI), Joe Shaw (Can).

1990: 1 David Defiagbon (Nig), 2 Greg Johnson (Can), 3 Grahame Cheney (Aus), Anthony Mwamba (Zam).

1994: 1 Neil Sinclair (NI), 2 Albert Eromosele (Nig), 3 Wald Fleming (Can), Richard Rowles (Aus).

1998: 1 Jeremy Molitor (Can), 2 Absolom Okoth (Ken), 3 Lynden Hosking (Aus), Colin McNeil (Sco).

Light-Middleweight (71kg):

First held 1954

1954: 1 Wilf Greaves (Can), 2 Freddy Wright (Rho), 3 Bruce Wells (Eng).

1958: 1 Grant Webster (SA), 2 Stuart Pearson (Eng), 3 Bill Brown (Wal), James Walters (Can).

1962: 1 Harold Mann (Can), 2 Brian Benson (Rho & N), 3 Kenneth Hopkins (PNG), Francis Nyangweso (Uga).

1966: 1 Mark Rowe (Eng), 2 Tom Imrie (Sco), 3 Nojim Maiyegun (Nig), Robert Okine (Gha).

1970: 1 Tom Imrie (Sco), 2 Julius Luipa (Zam), 3 David Attan (Ken), Patrick Doherty (NI).

1974: 1 Lotti Mwale (Zam), 2 Alex Harrison (Sco), 3 Robert Davies (Eng), Lance Revill (NZ).

1978: 1 Kelly Perlette (Can), 2 Abdurahman Athuman (Ken), 3 Enock Chama (Zam), Ropoti Samu (WS).

1982: 1 Shawn O'Sullivan (Can), 2 Nick Croombes (Eng), 3 Tommy Carr (NI), Roland Omoruyi (Nig).

1986: 1 Dan Sherry (Can), 2 Rick Finch (Aus), 3 Alex McMullen (Sco), Lyn Thomas (Wal).

1990: 1 Richie Woodhall (Eng), 2 Ray Downey (Can), 3 Andy Creery (NZ), Silio Figota (WS).

1994: 1 Jimmy Webb (NI), 2 Bob Gasio (WS), 3 Rival Cadeau (Sey), Joe Townsley (Sco).

1998: 1 Chris Bessey (Eng), 2 Scott Macintosh (Can), 3 James Tony (Gha), Jackie Townsley (Sco).

Note: Joe Townsley and Jackie Townsley were brothers

Middleweight (75kg):

1930: 1 Frederick Mallin (Eng), 2 Dudley Gallagher (Aus), 3 Teddy Phillips (Can).

1934: 1 Alf Shawyer (Eng), 2 Leonard Wadsworth (Can), 3 Jimmy Magill (NI).

1938: 1 Dennis Reardon (Wal), 2 Maurice Dennis (Eng), 3 Rex Carey (Can).

1950: 1 Theunis van Schalkwyk (SA), 2 Jim Beal (NZ), 3 Bill Pinkus (Can).

1954: 1 Jan van der Kolff (SA), 2 Arthur Crawford (Rho), 3 Marcel Piau (Can).

1958: 1 Terry Milligan (NI), 2 Philippus du Plessis (SA), 3 John Caiger (Eng), Robert Piau (Can).

1962: 1 Cephas Colquhoun (Jam), 2 Thomas Arimi (Gha), 3 Moses Evans (Fij). Note: only one bronze medal awarded (one semi-finalist disqualified).

1966: 1 Joe Darkey (Gha), 2 Arthur Trout (Jam), 3 Mathias Ouma (Uga), John Turpin (Eng).

1970: 1 John Conteh (Eng), 2 Titus Simba (Tan), 3 Samuel Kasongo (Zam), Robert Murphy (Aus).

1974: 1 Frankie Lucas (StV), 2 Julius Luipa (Zam), 3 Les Rackley (NZ), Carl Speare (Eng).

1978: 1 Philip McElwaine (Aus), 2 Delroy Parkes (Eng), 3 Richard Betham (WS), Roddy MacDonald (Can).

1982: 1 Jimmy Price (Eng), 2 Douglas Sam (Aus), 3 Kevin McDermott (Can), Jeremiah Okorodudu (Nig).

1986: 1 Rod Douglas (Eng), 2 Jeff Harding (Aus), 3 Gordon Ferrie (Sco), Pat Tinney (NI).

1990: 1 Chris Johnson (Can), 2 Ashiao Joseph Laryea (Gha), 3 Mark Edwards (Eng), Charles Matata (Uga).

1994: 1 Ron Donaldson (Can), 2 Rasmus Ojemaye (Nig), 3 Mike Penniston-John (Tri), Peter Wanyoike (Ken).

1998: 1 John Pearce (Eng), 2 Jitender Kumar (Ind), 3 Brian Magee (NI), Trevor Stewardson (Can).

Light-Heavyweight (81kg):

1930: 1 Joe Goyder (Eng), 2 Al Pitcher (Can), 3 Joey Basson (SA).

1934: 1 George Brennan (Eng), 2 George Holton (Sco), 3 Sydney Leibrandt (SA).

1938: 1 Nicolaas Wolmarans (SA), 2 Cecil Overell (Aus), 3 Joseph Wilby (Eng).

1950: 1 Don Scott (Eng), 2 Chris Rollinson (NZ), 3 Jack Taylor (Aus).

1954: 1 Piet van Vuuren (SA), 2 Tony Madigan (Aus), 3 Bill Misselbrooke (Can).

1958: 1 Tony Madigan (Aus), 2 Robert Higgins (Wal), 3 William Bannan (Sco), Gerhardus de Bruyn (SA).

1962: 1 Tony Madigan (Aus), 2 Jojo Miles (Gha), 3 Hans Christie (NI), Tom Menzies (Sco).

1966: 1 Roger Tighe (Eng), 2 Fatai Ayinla (Nig), 3 Dennis Booth (Aus), Sylvester Hines (Jam).

1970: 1 Fatai Ayinla (Nig), 2 Oliver Wright (Jam), 3 Victor Attivor (Gha), John Rafferty (Sco).

1974: 1 Billy Knight (Eng), 2 William Byrne (NZ), 3 Gordon Ferris (NI), Isaac Ikhuoria (Nig).

1978: 1 Roger Fortin (Can), 2 Ron Smith (Eng), 3 Faitala Su'A (WS), Edward Thande (Ken).

1982: 1 Fine Sani (Fij), 2 Jonathan Kirisa (Uga), 3 Kevin Barry (NZ), Joseph Poto (Zam).

1986: 1 Jim Moran (Eng), 2 Harry Lawson (Sco), 3 Brett Kosolofski (Can), Brian Pullen (Wal).

1990: 1 Joseph Akhasamba (Ken), 2 Dale Brown (Can), 3 Abdu Kaddu (Uga), Nigel Anderson (NZ).

1994: 1 Dale Brown (Can), 2 John Wilson (Sco), 3 Francis Mabiletsa (Bot), Odhiambo Opiyo (Ken).

1998: 1 Courtney Fry (Eng), 2 Troy Amos (Can), 3 Charles Adamu (Gha), Samuel Odindo (Ken).

Heavyweight (over 81kg 1930-1982, 91kg since):

1930: 1 Victor Stuart (Eng), 2 William Skimming (Can).

Note: only two contestants.

1934: 1 Pat Floyd (Eng), 2 Jan van Rensburg (SA), 3 Lord David Douglas-Hamilton (Sco).

1938: 1 Thomas Osborne (Can), 2 Claude Sterley (SA), 3 Les Harley (Aus).

1950: 1 Frank Creagh (NZ), 2 Sid Cousins (Aus).

Note: only two contestants.

1954: 1 Brian Harper (Eng), 2 Gerry Buchanan (Can), 3 George Jenkins (SA).

1958: 1 Daniel Bekker (SA), 2 David Thomas (Eng), 3 Robert Pleace (Wal), Gbadegesin Salawu (Nig).

1962: 1 George Oywello (Uga), 2 Bill Kini (NZ), 3 Holgar Johansen (Fij), Graham Robinson (Aus).

1966: 1 Bill Kini (NZ), 2 Adonis Ray (Gha), 3 Danny McAlinden (NI), Benson Ocan (Uga).

1970: 1 Benson Masanda (Uga), 2 John McKinty (NI), 3 Jack Meda (Can), Leslie Stevens (Eng).

1974: 1 Neville Meade (Eng), 2 Fatai Ayinla (Nig), 3 Benson Masanda (Uga), Vai Samu (WS).

1978: 1 Julius Awome (Eng), 2 Adamah Mensah (Gha), 3 George Stankovich (NZ). Note: only one bronze medal awarded (one semi-finalist did not appear).

1982: 1 Willie de Wit (Can), 2 Harold Hylton (Eng), 3 Willy Isangura (Tan), Mohamed Abdallah (Ken).

1986: 1 Jimmy Peau (NZ), 2 Douggie Young (Sco), 3 Eric Cardouza (Eng), Domenic D'Amico (Can).

1990: 1 George Onyango (Ken), 2 Pat Jordan (Can), 3 Emerio Fainuulua (WS), Kevin Onwuka (Nig).

1994: 1 Omaar Ahmed (Ken), 2 Steve Gallinger (Can), 3 Charles Kizza (Uga), Ezwell Ndlovu (Zim).

1998: 1 Mark Simmons (Eng), 2 Roland Raforme (Sey), 3 Garth Da Silva (NZ), Kevin Evans (Wal).

Super-Heavyweight (over 91kg):

First held 1986

1986: 1 Lennox Lewis (Can), 2 Aneurin Evans (Wal), 3 James Oyebola (Eng). Note: only three contestants.

1990: 1 Michael Kenny (NZ), 2 Liadi Alhassan (Gha), 3 Paul Douglas (Nig), Vernon Linklater (Can).

1994: 1 Duncan Dokiwari (Nig), 2 Miriambo Anyim (Ken), 3 Danny Williams (Eng), Paea Wolfgramm (Ton).

1998: 1 Audley Harrison (Eng), 2 Michael Macaque (Mau), 3 Aloryi Moyoyo (Gha), Justin Whitehead (Aus).

CYCLING

Aussie speedsters triumph in the Test match on wheels

By any reckoning the outcome of Commonwealth Games cycling is too much like that of Test cricket for English comfort. Australia has won 54 gold medals and England 22, and the gap is widening. In 1994 and 1998 Australia won 18 of the 23 available titles - and England merely one.

Considering that only six other countries have produced the two dozen or so other gold-medallists between them, it may be wondered how it is that cycling has survived at all as such an exclusive Games sport since it was introduced in 1934, but then there are a number of good reasons to explain the situation.

Those first cycling events actually took place in Manchester - at the former Fallowfield track - because London had no available facilities, and it would have been a travesty in 2002 if cycling had not come back to the same city, now that it is proud possessor of one of the World's finest and fastest indoor velodromes. In any case, many of the champions at the

Commonwealth Games have also gained the highest honours in the sport at World or Olympic level.

Some amongst them have gone on to professional fame as Tour de France riders, including most notably Australians such as Phil Anderson, Brad McGee and Stuart O'Grady. Others from Australia have also won individual Olympic titles: Edgar "Dunc" Gray and Russell Mockridge on the track, Kathy Watt on the road. Yet more have been World track champions: Gordon Johnson, John Nicholson, Gary Niewand and Darryn Hill in the sprint; Shane Kelly in the time-trial; England's Hugh Porter in the individual pursuit (on four occasions); Gary Sutton in the points race; Tanya Dubnicoff, of Canada, in the women's sprint.

The most famous name of all among racing cyclists from anywhere in the Commonwealth over the past decade does not figure at all in the above lists of merit. Chris Boardman - World and Olympic champion in the individual pursuit and the fastest man ever in that event and World record-holder for one hour - was never a winner at the Commonwealth Games. After taking three bronze medals in the team time-trials and pursuit in 1986 and 1990 he turned his attentions to riding in the Tour de France with the professional teams, Gan and then Crédit Agricole, and gained further renown as a prologue time-triallist.

Back in 1934 at Fallowfield the only events contested were a sprint, a 1000 metres time-trial and a 10 miles track race for men, and it was a South African, Ed Clayton, who achieved a feat which will most likely never be matched by winning three medals during the single day of racing. The programme has now expanded to 12 races, including four for women, though the most spectacular track event of all - the tandem sprint - has fallen by the wayside since it was contested from 1970 to 1978.

A glimpse of what the future may hold for Commonwealth cycle-racing was provided in the men's road race in Kuala Lumpur in 1998 when a totally unheralded local rider, Rosli Effandy, took 2nd place, losing out only to the Australian professional road sprint specialist, Jay Sweet. In the early stages of that race competitors from Kenya - the dominant nation in distance-running - were prominent, and it is reported that the Kenyan authorities are keen to develop the sport.

Now that would make an interesting Tour de France! The thought of a Paul Tergat or a Noah Ngeny on a bicycle should send a tremor down the spine of even the most hardened of Aussie pedal pushers !

Leading countries:

Australia 54 gold medals; England 21; New Zealand 12; Canada 9; South Africa, Trinidad & Tobago 2 each; Isle of Man, Wales 1 each.

Leading gold-medallists:

4 Jocelyn Lovell (Can) 1970-78, Brad McGee (Aus) 1990-94; 3 Kevin Nichols (Aus) 1978-82, Gary Niewand (Aus) 1986-94, Gary Anderson (NZ) 1990, Kathy Watt (Aus) 1994.

Highlights - Games by Games

1934: Cycling made its debut in Manchester, 200 miles away from the other Games venues, with three track events - the sprint, the time-trial and a 10 miles race - held on the same afternoon, and Australia, England and South Africa each won titles. Edgar Gray, who had won the Olympic time-trial for Australia in Los Angeles two years previously and had been the bronze-medallist in 1928, duly took the gold in that event. The most active rider of the day was the South African, Ed Clayton, who did not win gold but took silver or bronze in all three competitions.

1938: Edgar Gray became the first double winner in the Games, taking the sprint final on this occasion from his compatriot, Bob Porter, who won the time-trial. Gray, commonly known as "Dunc", was to become a legend of Australian cycling and the velodrome used for the 2000 Olympic Games was named after him. England sent four riders on the long sea voyage to Australia and William Maxfield, who was the national 25-mile time-trial champion on the road, won the 10 miles track race. A road race was held for the first time and Hendrik Binneman, of South Africa, won in a sprint finish.

1950: Australian riders won four of the five events, with Russell Mockridge taking the sprint/time trial double. The country's only loss was in the newly-introduced individual pursuit in which Mockridge again reached the final but was well beaten by England's Cyril Cartwright, the World Championships silver-medallist. Mockridge improved the 1938 Games record in the time-trial by over two seconds and three other riders were also inside the previous best. In a six-man finish to the road race astute Australian planning saw their sprint specialist, Hec Sutherland, home to victory.

1954: The specially-constructed 250-metre yellow cedarwood track drew maximum crowds of almost 5000 to the four evening sessions and the spectators had plenty of drama for their money. The Australian team withdrew - fortunately, only temporarily - after a series of disputes in the sprint event, and as their riders, Lionel Cox and Dick Ploog, failed to appear for their deciding races the gold and bronze medals were won unopposed. The time-trial, happily, was run off without controversy and resulted in a rare tie between 17-year-old Ploog and the South African, Jimmy Swift. A gallant but outclassed Pakistani trio contested every event from the sprint to the 100km road race and actually won a race - when Muhammad Saleem Farooqi beat his team-mate, Ghulam Baloch, in a sprint repechage.

1958: England won three of the five golds and Australia the other two. Dick Ploog made amends for four years earlier by triumphing in the sprint and England's Norman Sheil became the first man to defend a Games title in the individual pursuit, where he beat Tommy Simpson, who was to become Britain's leading professional road-racer until his sad death in the saddle during the Tour de France. Another of Sheil's team-mates, Ray Booty, achieved the rare feat of winning the road race by means of a lone breakaway, and a Manxman, Stuart Slack, took the bronze.

1962: On home ground Australia won all four track titles and had 1-2 in both the time-trial and the individual pursuit. By contrast they won no medals at all in the road race, in which 21-year-old Sheffield postman Wes Mason delivered England's solitary title. Malayan riders took on the role of courageous underdogs at these Games, losing all four of their sprint races and taking the last three places of 17 riders in the time-trial and of 16 in the individual pursuit, but one of their team managed 15th place of 18 finishers in the road race.

1966: Both the sprint and time-trial titles went to Roger Gibbon, breaking new ground as a Games cycling gold-medallist from Trinidad, but it was no great surprise. He had ridden a 1min 9sec time-trial already and recorded 1:09.6 to break the Games record and win by a huge margin. Australia's six medals did not include a single gold, and instead there were English victories for Hugh Porter and Ian Alsop in the individual pursuit and 10 miles respectively and a runaway success by over six minutes for Peter Buckley, from the Isle of Man, in the road race.

1970: The weather for the road race round 31 laps of Edinburgh's Holyrood Park was predictable: a biting wind and drenching rain driving in from across the North Sea. Only 18 riders finished, and the Canadian and the Scot who came in together in 17th and 18th places probably deserved a medal as much as the two who fought out the finish 12 minutes earlier. Bruce Biddle won for New Zealand and broke the mould in the process because fellow-Kiwis had finished 2nd in five of the six previous Games road races. On the track the honours were widely shared as Australia, Canada, England and New Zealand each won gold and Trinidad got a silver and two bronzes.

1974: With the team pursuit added, there were now six track titles on offer, and Australia and England each won three. John Nicholson, for Australia, and Ian Hallam, of England, successfully defended their sprint and individual pursuit golds respectively, and Hallam was also in the winning pursuit team and won two bronzes for a record medals total at a single Games. The only track medals which these two countries did not take away were silver and bronze in the sprint - both to Trinidadians - and the bronze in the team pursuit. It was the same story in the road race which Australia won (for the first time in 24 years, as it happened) and took the bronze, while England's Phil Griffiths split the Aussies for the silver.

1978: Deterioration in the weather first delayed and then threatened to distort the individual time-trial, but Canada's Jocelyn Lovell, coming out late at night after a long wait, rode a marvellous 1:06.00 which broke the Games record and gave him gold by 0.96sec. Lovell, a triple medallist in 1970 (including gold at 10 miles), then went on to win the tandem event with team-mate Gordon Singleton and to prevail once more in a mass finish to the 10 miles race. No one had previously won three cycling gold medals in the same Games and Lovell, naturally, became one of the heroes of Edmonton. A pair of brothers, Gary and Shane Sutton, figured in Australia's winning pursuit team, and in the road race Phil Anderson - on the eve of a long and successful European road-racing career - made the gold-medal tally a tie. Australia 3 Lovell 3.

1982: Australia won four of the five track titles and England took both gold medals on the road. Kenrick Tucker took the sprint for a second consecutive Games and there were double successes for team pursuiters Kevin Nichols and Michael Turtur, who also won individual golds at 10 miles and in the individual pursuit respectively. In the 10 miles event Australians took all the medals, and that was the first time there had been a clean sweep in Games cycling history. England beat Australia by less than seven seconds in a new event, the 100km road team time-trial, and Malcolm Elliott outsprinted Canada's Steve Bauer for the individual road title. Bauer's was the only medal not won by Australia, England or New Zealand.

1986: Australia went one better than in Brisbane by winning all five track events, and it seemed as if their only sustained challenge was coming

from New Zealand's Gary Anderson, who collected two silvers and two bronzes. England again won both road titles and Australia only came 4th in the team time-trial as a Northern Ireland quartet earned an unprecedented medal. Paul Curran became the fifth English winner of the individual road race in the usual cavalry charge for the finishing-line.

1990: Gary Niewand and Martin Vinnicombe retained track titles for Australia and a team-mate, Robert Burns, won the newly-introduced points race, but the rest of the Games cycling belonged to New Zealand and its star rider, Gary Anderson. Anderson won the individual pursuit and 10 miles and was also in the winning pursuit team (plus a silver in the time-trial). Two other members of the pursuit team, Graeme Miller and Brian Fowler, also took gold and silver in the individual road race. England won only two bronzes - in the track team pursuit and the road team time-trial. Women were awarded a token presence with a sprint and an individual pursuit, and Louise Jones won the first Welsh cycling gold in the former and Madonna Harris gave New Zealand another success in the latter, while her team-mate, Sue Golder, was good enough for sprint bronze at the age of 43.

1994: Australia steamrollered the opposition in every event except the road race. Gary Niewand took his third successive sprint title, while the team pursuit winners between them took home 10 medals: Brad McGee also individual pursuit gold; Brett Aitken also points gold; Tim O'Shannessey also time-trial bronze; and Stuart O'Grady, scarcely ever off the track, also 10 miles gold, points silver and individual pursuit bronze ! The road time-trial team welcomed back Phil Anderson, 16 years after his individual road-race win in the Games, and he played a key role in speeding them to victory by the best part of four minutes over England. The road race went to New Zealand's Mark Rendell, with his team-mate, Brian Fowler, taking a third successive silver and his fifth Games medal in total. In the women's programme, now extended to five events, the dominant figure was Australia's Olympic road-race champion, Kathy Watt, who had been 2nd in the 1990 individual pursuit and now won golds in that event, the road team time-trial and the road race. Canada's World champion, Tanya Dubnicoff, won the women's sprint.

1998: This was yet another Games dominated by Australian riders on the track. They took five of the six available titles, losing only the points race, and Brad McGee won two further golds in the pursuits. The individual time-trial was of the very highest class with Shane Kelly beating his own Games record by more than a second with a time of 1:04.018 and the other medallists both within six-tenths of him. On the road the team time-trial had been replaced by an individual time-trial and the winner by 15sec was Eric Wohlberg, of Canada, after the favourite, Stuart O'Grady, had uncharacteristically fallen off at a bend. The individual road race did produce an Australian winner in French-based professional Jay Sweet, but the big story of the race was the silver medal for the local boy, Rosli Effandy. Overseas visitors to the Games were left wondering how any racing cyclist could ever train seriously and safely on the Kuala Lumpur roads commandeered by kamikaze motor-scooter riders. Canada's Tanya Dubnicoff again beat the Australian, Michelle Ferris, in the women's sprint final, and Australia and Canada shared the road titles.

CYCLING MEDALLISTS

MEN
Sprint (1000 metres):
1934: 1 Ernest Higgins (Eng), 2 Horace Pethybridge (Aus), 3 Ed Clayton (SA).
1938: 1 Edgar Gray (Aus), 2 Bob Porter (Aus), 3 George Giles (NZ).
1950: 1 Russell Mockridge (Aus), 2 Sid Patterson (Aus), 3 George Avery (NZ).
1954: 1 Cyril Peacock (Eng), 2 Not awarded - Lionel Cox (Aus) did not start in final, 3 Tom Shardelow (SA).
1958: 1 Dick Ploog (Aus), 2 Karl Barton (Eng), 3 Lloyd Binch (Eng).
1962: 1 Tom Harrison (Aus), 2 Karl Barton (Eng), 3 Ian Browne (Aus).
1966: 1 Roger Gibbon (Tri), 2 Jim Booker (Eng), 3 Daryl Perkins (Aus).
1970: 1 John Nicholson (Aus), 2 Gordon Johnson (Aus), 3 Leslie King (Tri).
1974: 1 John Nicholson (Aus), 2 Xavier Mirander (Tri), 3 Ian Atherley (Tri).
1978: 1 Kenrick Tucker (Aus), 2 Trevor Gadd (Eng), 3 David Weller (Jam).
1982: 1 Kenrick Tucker (Aus), 2 Michael McRedmond (NZ), 3 Murray Steele (NZ).
1986: 1 Gary Niewand (Aus), 2 Alex Ongaro (Can), 3 Eddie Alexander (Sco).
1990: 1 Gary Niewand (Aus), 2 Curt Harnett (Can), 3 Jon Andrews (NZ).
1994: 1 Gary Niewand (Aus), 2 Curt Harnett (Can), 3 Darryn Hill (Aus).
1998: 1 Darryn Hill (Aus), 2 Sean Eddie (Aus), 3 Barry Forde (Bar).

Time-trial (1000 metres):
1934: 1 Edgar Gray (Aus) 1:16.4, 2 Robert McLeod (Can) 1:18.0, 3 Ed Clayton (SA) 1:18.6.
1938: 1 Bob Porter (Aus) 1:15.2, 2 Tasman Johnson (Aus) 1:15.7, 3 Ernie Mills (Eng) 1:15.9.
1950: 1 Russell Mockridge (Aus) 1:13.4, 2 Sid Patterson (Aus) 1:13.5, 3 Tommy Godwin (Eng) 1:13.6.
1954: 1= Dick Ploog (Aus) & Jimmy Swift (SA) 1:12.5, 3 Keith Harrison (Eng) 1:12.7.
1958: 1 Neville Tong (Eng) 1:12.1, 2 Warren Scarfe (Aus) 1:12.4, 3 Warwick Dalton (NZ) 1:12.6.
1962: 1 Peter Bartels (Aus) 1:12.9, 2 Ian Chapman (Aus) 1:13.2, 3 Roger Whitfield (Eng) 1:13.5.

1966: 1 Roger Gibbon (Tri) 1:09.6, 2 Philip Bristow-Stagg (Aus) 1:10.9, 3 Richard Hine (Aus) 1:11.0.

1970: 1 Harry Kent (NZ) 1:08.69, 2 Leslie King (Tri) 1:10.40, 3 Jocelyn Lovell (Can) 1:10.53.

1974: 1 Dick Paris (Aus) 1:11.85, 2 John Nicholson (Aus) 1:11.92, 3 Ian Hallam (Eng) 1:12.15.

1978: 1 Jocelyn Lovell (Can) 1:06.00, 2 Kenrick Tucker (Aus) 1:06.96, 3 Gordon Singleton (Can) 1:07.56.

1982: 1 Craig Adair (NZ) 1:06.954, 2 Chris Wilson (Aus) 1:07.926, 3 Terry Tinsley (Eng) 1:07.932.

1986: 1 Martin Vinnicombe (Aus) 1:06.230, 2 Gary Anderson (NZ) 1:06.334, 3 Maxwell Rainsford (Aus) 1:07.346.

1990: 1 Martin Vinnicombe (Aus) 1:05.572, 2 Gary Anderson (NZ) 1:06.196, 3 Jon Andrews (NZ) 1:06.516.

1994: 1 Shane Kelly (Aus) 1:05.386, 2 Darryn Hill (Aus) 1:05.632, 3 Tim O'Shannessey (Aus) 1:06.789.

1998: 1 Shane Kelly (Aus) 1:04.018, 2 Jason Queally (Eng) 1:04.427, 3 Josh Kersten (Aus) 1:04.618.

Individual Pursuit (4000 metres):

First held 1950

Note: winning time in rideoff for 3rd place in 1950, 1954, 1974 and 1990 was faster than the 2nd place time in the final. No time taken for 3rd place in 1970 (opponent did not start) and 1998 (caught opponent).

1950: 1 Cyril Cartwright (Eng) 5:16.3, 2 Russell Mockridge (Aus) 5:27.0, 3 Leslie Lock (NZ) 5:26.7.

1954: 1 Norman Sheil (Eng) 5:03.5, 2 Peter Brotherton (Eng) 5:09.1, 3 Robert Fowler (SA) 5:06.9.

1958: 1 Norman Sheil (Eng) 5:10.2, 2 Tommy Simpson (Eng) 5:10.5, 3 Warwick Dalton (NZ) 5:14.7.

1962: 1 Max Langshaw (Aus) 5:08.2, 2 Richard Hine (Aus) 5:13.2, 3 Harry Jackson (Eng) 5:14.2.

1966: 1 Hugh Porter (Eng) 4:56.6, 2 John Bylsma (Aus) 4:59.0, 3 Richard Hine (Aus) 5:03.7.

1970: 1 Ian Hallam (Eng) 5:01.41, 2 Danny Clark (Aus) 5:04.93, 3 Blair Stockwell (NZ).

1974: 1 Ian Hallam (Eng) 5:05.46, 2 Bill Moore (Eng) 5:11.81, 3 Gary Sutton (Aus) 5:09.17.

1978: 1 Michael Richards (NZ) 4:49.74, 2 Gary Campbell (Aus) 4:55.68, 3 Tony Doyle (Eng) 4:55.87.

1982: 1 Michael Turtur (Aus) 4:50.990, 2 Shaun Wallace (Eng) 4:51.347, 3 Alex Stieda (Can) 4:54.254.

1986: 1 Duncan Woods (Aus) 4:43.92, 2 Colin Sturgess (Eng) 4:51.23, 3 Gary Anderson (NZ) 4:54.35.

1990: 1 Gary Anderson (NZ) 4:44.610, 2 Mark Kingsland (Aus) 4:52.750, 3 Darren Winter (Aus) 4:51.610.

1994: 1 Brad McGee (Aus) 4:31.371, 2 Shaun Wallace (Eng) 4:34.662, 3 Stuart O'Grady (Aus) 4:35.203.

1998: 1 Brad McGee (Aus) 4:30.594, 2 Luke Roberts (Aus) 4:33.337, 3 Matt Illingworth (Eng).

Tandem Sprint (1000 metres):

First held 1970, Not held since 1978

1970: 1 Gordon Johnson & Rob Jonker (Aus), 2 Jocelyn Lovell & Barry Harvey (Can), 3 John Hatfield & John Beswick (Wal).

1974: 1 Geoff Cooke & Ernie Crutchlow (Eng), 2 John Rush & Danny O'Neil (Aus), 3 Paul Medhurst & Phil Harland (NZ).

1978: 1 Jocelyn Lovell & Gordon Singleton (Can), 2 Trevor Gadd & David Le Grys (Eng), 3 Ron Boyle & Stephen Goodall (Aus).

Team Pursuit (4000 metres):

First held 1974

1974: 1 England (Mick Bennett, Richard Evans, Ian Hallam, Bill Moore) 4:40.50, 2 Australia (Murray Hall, Kevin Nichols, Garry Reardon, Gary Sutton) 4:49.22, 3 New Zealand (Paul Brydon, Rene Hyde, Russell Nant, Blair Stockwell) - caught their opponents, no time taken.

1978: 1 Australia (Colin Fitzgerald, Kevin Nichols, Gary Sutton, Shane Sutton) 4:29.43, 2 New Zealand (Kevin Blackwell, Anthony Cuff, Neil Lyster, Jack Swart) 4:37.73, 3 England (Tony Doyle, Paul Fennell, Tony James, Glen Mitchell) 4:51.18.

1982: 1 Australia (Michael Grenda, Kevin Nichols, Michael Turtur, Gary West) 4:26.090, 2 New Zealand (Clem Captein, Brian Fowler, Graeme Millar, Murray Steele) 4:29.733, 3 England (Paul Curran, Anthony Mayer, Gary Sadler, Darryl Webster) 4:34.783.

1986: 1 Australia (Glenn Clarke, Brett Dutton, Wayne McCarney, Dean Woods) 4:26.94, 2 New Zealand (Gary Anderson, Andrew Whitford, Stephen Swart, Steven Cox) 4:34.03, 3 England (Chris Boardman, Gary Colman, Rob Muzio, Jon Walshaw) - caught their opponents, no time taken.

1990: 1 New Zealand (Nigel Connelly, Glenn McLeay, Stu Williams, Gary Anderson) 4:22.760, 2 Australia (Brett Aitken, Steve McGlede, Shaun O'Brien, Darren Winter) 4:25.580, 3 England (Chris Boardman, Simon Lillistone, Glen Sword, Bryan Steel) 4:27.160.

1994: 1 Australia (Brett Aitken, Brad McGee, Stuart O'Grady, Tim O'Shannessey) 4:10.485, 2 England (Tony Doyle, Rob Hayles, Chris Newton, Bryan Steel) caught by their opponents, no time taken, 3 New Zealand (Brendon Cameron, Julian Dean, Glen Thomson, Lee Vertongen) 4:22.425.

1998: 1 Australia (Brad McGee, Luke Roberts, Timothy Lyons, Brett Lancaster) 4:13.405, 2 England (Colin Sturgess, Jon Clay, Rob Hayles, Matt Illingworth) 4:14.298, 3 New Zealand (Lee Vertongen, Greg Henderson, Timothy Carswell, Brendon Cameron) 4:17.930.

Track 20 kilometres:

10 miles 1934-1994.

Note: no times recorded after 1st place 1934-1962

1934: 1 Robert McLeod (Can) 24:26.2, 2 Ed Clayton (SA), 3 William Harvell

CYCLING

(Eng).

1938: 1 William Maxfield (Eng) 24:44.0, 2 Ray Hicks (Eng), 3 Syd Rose (SA).

1950: 1 William Heseltine (Aus) 23:23.4, 2 Leslie Lock (NZ), 3 Ken Caves (Aus).

1954: 1 Lindsay Cocks (Aus) 21:59.5, 2 Keith Harrison (Eng), 3 Don Skene (Wal).

1958: 1 Ian Browne (Aus) 21:40.2, 2 Warren Johnston (NZ), 3 Don Skene (Wal).

1962: 1 Doug Adams (Aus) 22:10.8, 2 Warren Johnston (NZ), 3 John Clarey (Eng).

1966: 1 Ian Alsop (Eng) 21:46.0, 2 Hilton Clarke (Aus) 21:46.4, 3 Trevor Bull (Eng) 21:46.8.

1970: 1 Jocelyn Lovell (Can) 20:46.72, 2 Brian Temple (Sco) 20:47.56, 3 Vernon Stauble (Tri) 20:47.72.

1974: 1 Stephen Heffernan (Aus) 20:51.25, 2 Murray Hall (Aus) 20:51.61, 3 Ian Hallam (Eng) 20:51.66.

1978: 1 Jocelyn Lovell (Can) 20:05.81, 2 Shane Sutton (Aus) 20:06.00, 3 Gary Sutton (Aus) 20:06.10.

1982: 1 Kevin Nichols (Aus) 19:56.559, 2 Gary Hammond (Aus) 19:56.639, 3 Michael Turtur (Aus) 19:56.660.

1986: 1 Wayne McCarney (Aus) 19:40.61, 2 Duncan Woods (Aus) 19:40.61, 3 Gary Anderson (NZ) 19:40.61.

1990: 1 Gary Anderson (NZ) 19:44.20, 2 Shaun O'Brien (Aus) 19:44.22, 3 Steve McGlede (Aus) 19:44.26.

1994: 1 Stuart O'Grady (Aus) 18:50.520, 2 Glenn McLeay (NZ) 18:50.520, 3 Brian Walton (Can) 18:50.520.

1998: 1 Michael Rogers (Aus) 25:18.340, 2 Shaun Wallace (Eng) 25:18.340, 3 Timothy Carswell (NZ) 25:18.340.

Track Points Race:

First held 1990, 50 km 1990, 40 km 1994-1998

1990: 1 Robert Burns (Aus) 81pts, 2 Craig Connell (NZ) 72, 3 Alistair Irvine (NI) 39.

1994: 1 Brett Aitken (Aus) 38, 2 Stuart O'Grady (Aus) 37, 3 Dean Woods (Aus) 23.

1998: 1 Glen Thomson (NZ) 35, 2 Rob Hayles (Eng) 29, 3 Greg Henderson (NZ) 24.

Road Team Time-Trial (100 kilometres):

First held 1982

1982: 1 England (Robert Downs, Malcolm Elliott, Stephen Lawrence, Joe Waugh) 2:09:27.00, 2 Australia (Ricky Flood, Michael Lynch, Remo Sansonetti, John Watters) 2:09:33.62, 3 New Zealand (Steven Carton, Stephen Cox, Blair Stockwell, Jack Swart) 2:10:55.96.

1986: 1 England (Paul Curran, Deno Davie, Alan Gornall, Keith Reynolds) 2:13:16, 2 New Zealand (Graeme Miller, Paul Leitch, Greg Fraine, Blair Cox) 2:14:50, 3 Northern Ireland (Joe Barr, Alastair Irvine, Cormac McCann, Martin Quinn) 2:16:13.

1990: 1 New Zealand (Brian Fowler, Graeme Miller, Ian Richards, Gavin Stevens) 2:06:46.55, 2 Canada (Scott Goguen, Chris Koberstein, Perry Scaletta, David

Spears) 2:09:19.59, 3 England (Chris Boardman, Peter Longbottom, Ben Luckwell, Wayne Randle) 2:09:33.17.

1994: 1 Australia (Brett Dennis, Henk Vogels, Phil Anderson, Damian McDonald) 1:53:19.13, 2 England (Matt Illingworth, Paul Jennings, Simon Lillistone, Peter Longbottom) 1:56:40.76, 3 New Zealand (Brian Fowler, Paul Leitch, Timothy Pawson, Mark Rendell) 1:56:52.82.

1998: Not held

Road Race:

First held 1938, 100km 1938-1954, 193km 1958-1966, 164.6km 1970, 183km 1974, 188km 1978, 184km 1982, 168km 1986, 173km 1990, 181.9km 1994, 184km 1998

1938: 1 Hendrik Binneman (SA) 2:53:29.6, 2 John Brown (NZ) 2:53:29.8, 3 Ray Jones (Eng) 2:53:29.9.

1950: 1 Hector Sutherland (Aus) 3:13:06.4, 2 Richard Carter (NZ) 3:13:06.5, 3 Jack Fowler (Aus) 3:13:06.6

1954: 1 Eric Thompson (Eng) 2:44:08.1, 2 John Baird (NZ) no time taken, 3 Bernard Pusey (Eng) no time taken.

1958: 1 Ray Booty (Eng) 5:16:33.7, 2 Frank Brazier (Aus) 5:19:21.7, 3 Stuart Slack (IoM) 5:19:21.7.

1962: 1 Wes Mason (Eng) 5:20:26.2, 2 Anthony Walsh (NZ) 5:20:27.0, 3 Laurie Byers (NZ) 5:20:27.2.

1966: 1 Peter Buckley (IoM) 5:07:52.5, 2 Des Thompson (NZ) 5:12:11.2, 3 Laurie Byers (NZ) 5:12:19.8.

1970: 1 Bruce Biddle (NZ) 4:38:05.8, 2 Ray Bilney (Aus) 4:39:05.9, 3 John Trevorrow (Aus) 4:40:03.0.

1974: 1 Clyde Sefton (Aus) 5:07:16.87, 2 Phil Griffiths (Eng) 5:07:45.95, 3 Remo Sansonetti (Aus) 5:17:26.80.

1978: 1 Phil Anderson (Aus) 4:22:34.41, 2 Pierre Harvey (Can) 4:22:34.55, 3 Garry Bell (NZ) 4:22:35.06.

1982: 1 Malcolm Elliott (Eng) 4:34:40.06, 2 Steve Bauer (Can) 4:34:41.00, 3 Roger Sumich (NZ) 4:34:41.35.

1986: 1 Paul Curran (Eng) 4:08:50, 2 Brian Fowler (NZ) 4:08.50, 3 Jeff Leslie (Aus) 4:08:50.

1990: 1 Graeme Miller (NZ) 4:34:00.19, 2 Brian Fowler (NZ) 4:34:00.39, 3 Scott Goguen (Can) 4:34:05.45.

1994: 1 Mark Rendell (NZ) 4:46:07.91, 2 Brian Fowler (NZ) 4:48:09.76, 3 Willem Engelbrecht (SA) 4:48:10.23.

1998: 1 Jay Sweet (Aus) 4:31:56, 2 Rosli Effandy (Mal) 4:31:56, 3 Eric Wohlberg (Can) 4:31:56.

Road Individual Time-Trial:

First held 1998 (42km)

1998: 1 Eric Wohlberg (Can) 53:15, 2 Stuart O'Grady (Aus) 53:30, 3 David George (SA) 53:56

CYCLING

WOMEN

Sprint (1000 metres):
First held 1990

1990: 1 Louise Jones (Wal), 2 Julie Speight (Aus), 3 Sue Golder (NZ).

1994: 1 Tanya Dubnicoff (Can), 2 Michelle Ferris (Aus), 3 Donna Wynd (NZ).

1998: 1 Tanya Dubnicoff (Can), 2 Michelle Ferris (Aus), 3 Lori Ann Muenzer (Can).

Individual Pursuit (3000 metres):
First held 1990

1990: 1 Madonna Harris (NZ) 3:54.670, 2 Kathy Watt (Aus) 3:54.780, 3 Kelly-Ann Way (Can) 4:00.390.

1994: 1 Kathy Watt (Aus) 3:48.522, 2 Sarah Ulmer (NZ) 3:50.953, 3 Jacqueline Nelson (NZ) 3:55.241.

1998: 1 Sarah Ulmer (NZ) 3:41.667, 2 Alayna Burns (Aus) 3:42.968, 3 Yvonne McGregor (Eng) 3:53.977.

Track Points Race:
First held 1994, 25 kilometres 1990, 24 kilometres 1998

1994: 1 Yvonne McGregor (Eng) 5, 2 Jacqueline Nelson (NZ) 32, 3 Sally Hodge (Wal) 28.

Note: the winner gained a lap on the other competitors.

1998: 1 Alayna Burns (Aus) 34, 2 Sarah Ulmer (NZ) 31, 3 Anne Gariepy (Can) 19.

Road Individual Time-Trial:
First held 1998, 28km 1998

1998: 1 Anna Wilson (Aus) 37:34, 2 Linda Jackson (Can) 38:34, 3 Kathy Watt (Aus) 38:39.

Road Team Time-Trial (50km):
First held 1994

1994: 1 Australia (Jillian Nolan, Cathy Reardon, Rachel Victor, Kathy Watt) 1:04:03.20, 2 Canada (Clare Hughes, Anne Samplonius, Alison Sydor, Lesley Tomlinson) 1:04:18.92, 3 England (Maxine Johnson, Maria Lawrence, Yvonne McGregor, Julia Freeman) 1:06:32.85.

1998: Not held

Road Race:
First held 1994, 96.3km 1994, 92km 1998

1994: 1 Kathy Watt (Aus) 2:48:04.73, 2 Linda Jackson (Can) 2:48:34.75, 3 Alison Sydor (Can) 2:50:17.45.

1998: 1 Lynne Bessette (Can) 2:24:59, 2 Susannah Pryde (NZ) 2:24:59, 3 Anna Wilson (Aus) 2:24:59.

GYMNASTICS

Andrei sweeps the floor
- and almost all besides

Artistic gymnastics first featured in the Commonwealth Games when they were held in Edmonton, Alberta, in 1978 and Canadians duly won the four titles at stake for individuals and teams in the all-round competition. It was another 12 years before the sport reappeared in its fuller form of the all-round events and team competitions for men and women and six separate exercises for men and four for women.

In a sport which has been traditionally dominated by Eastern Europeans, the Commonwealth has produced no more than a handful of genuine World-class competitors. There has yet to be a Nelli Kim, a Nadia Comaneci, an Olga Korbut, or a Boris Shakhlin emerging from the Games, but it could happen. Gymnasts born in Hungary and Russia have won gold medals.

GYMNASTICS

Leading countries:

Canada 27 gold medals; Australia 22; England 10; New Zealand 2; Malaysia, South Africa 1 each.

Leading gold-medallists:

5 Curtis Hibbert (Can) 1990, Andrei Kravtsov (Aus) 1998, 4 Alan Nolet (Can) 1990-94, Lori Strong (Can) 1990); 3 Neil Thomas (Eng) 1990-94, Stella Umeh (Can) 1994, Annika Reeder (Eng) 1994-98.

Highlights - Games by Games

1978: For Canada Philip Delesalle and 4ft 6in (1.37m) tall Elfi Schlegel each won two golds and only one non-Canadian figured among the six individual medallists. Most of the sessions at the 16,000-capacity Edmonton Coliseum were a sell-out, but even the Canadian hosts thought that gymnastics would be a "one time only event".

1990: Despite the long break Canada remained the leading nation. In the men's events the Jamaican-born Curtis Hibbert took four individual gold medals and a fifth gold as a member of the winning team. In the women's competition Lori Strong was the winner of the all-round competition and two of the exercises, and like Hibbert was a member of the winning team.

1994: The men's honours were more widely spread with Neil Thomas, of England, winning the all-round title but only one of the exercises, and each of the remaining five exercises going to a different gymnast. Australia's Brennon Dowrick again won on the pommeled horse, while Thomas took gold in the floor exercises, as in 1990. Thomas had become the first British gymnast to win a medal at the highest level when he placed 2nd in his floor speciality at the 1993 World Championships. Canada's Stella Umeh won the women's all-round title and the vault, but England - including the floor exercises champion, Anika Reeder - took the team title.

1998: The Russian emigré, Andrei Kravtsov, was the totally dominant male gymnast, winning the all-round title and four of the exercises for Australia, though it was England who triumphed in the team event. South African gymnasts intruded at last on the Anglo-Australian monopoly of the sport, with two silver medals and a bronze in the various exercises.

Though Australia and England continued to dominate the women's events, there were five different winners and Zeena McLaughlin, of Australia, took the all-round title without winning any of the individual exercises.

GYMNASTICS MEDALLISTS

MEN

All-round competition only in 1978; individual exercises added since 1990

Individual All-Round:
1978: 1 Philip Delesalle (Can) 56.40pts, 2 Lindsay Nylund (Aus) 54.95, 3 Jean Choquette (Can) 54.25.
1982-1986: Not held
1990: 1 Curtis Hibbert (Can) 57.950, 2 Alan Nolet (Can) 57.800, 3 James May (Eng) 57.400.
1994: 1 Neil Thomas (Eng) 55.950, 2 Brennon Dowrick (Aus) 55.525, 3 Peter Hogan (Aus) 54.950.
1998: 1 Andrei Kravtsov (Aus) 54.675, 2 Andrew Atherton (Eng) 54.025,
3 Brennon Dowrick (Aus) 52.500.

Floor:
1990: 1 Neil Thomas (Eng) 9.750, 2 Alan Nolet (Can) 9.675, 3 Curtis Hibbert (Can) 9.600.
1994: 1 Neil Thomas (Eng) 9.662, 2 Kristan Burley (Can) 9.437, 3 Alan Nolet (Can) 9.150.
1998: 1 Andrei Kravtsov (Aus) 9.325, 2 Christian Brezeanu (SA) 8.950, 3 John Smethurst (Eng) 8.737.

Pommeled Horse:
1990: 1 Brennon Dowrick (Aus) 9,825, 2 Tim Lees (Aus) 9.725, 3 James May (Eng) 9.700.
1994: 1 Brennon Dowrick (Aus) 9.425, 2 Nathan Kingston (Aus) 9.400, 3 Richard Ikeda (Can) 9.225.
1998: 1 Andrei Kravtsov (Aus) 9.325, 2 Richard Ikeda (Can) 9.462, 3 Brennon Dowrick (Aus) 9.137.

Rings:
1990: 1 Curtis Hibbert (Can) 9.775, 2 James May (Eng) 9.750, 3 Ken Meredith (Aus) 9.725.
1994: 1 Lee McDermott (Eng) 9.475, 2 Peter Hogan (Aus) 9.275, 3 Brennon Dowrick (Aus) 9.150.
1998: 1 Pavel Mamine (Aus) 9.337, 2 Andrew Atherton (Eng) 9.325, 3 Athol Myhill (SA) 9.112.

GYMNASTICS

Vault:

1990: 1 James May (Eng) 9.625, 2 Curtis Hibbert (Can) 9.575, 3 Tim Lees (Aus) 9.250.

1994: 1 Bret Hudson (Aus) 9.375, 2 Kristan Burley (Can) 9.312, 3 Neil Thomas (Eng) 9.306.

1998: 1 Simon Hutcheon (SA) 9.537, 2 Christian Brezeanu (SA) 9.281, 3 Bret Hudson (Aus) 9.268.

Parallel Bars:

1990: 1 Curtis Hibbert (Can) 9.800, 2 Ken Meredith (Aus) 9.675, 3 Peter Hogan (Aus) 9.600.

1994: 1 Peter Hogan (Aus) 9.400, 2 Kristan Burley (Can) 9.350, 3 Brennon Dowrick (Aus) 9.250.

1998: 1 Andrei Kravtsov (Aus) 9.637, 2 Richard Ikeda (Can) 9.112, 3 Bret Hudson (Aus) 8.887.

Horizontal Bar:

1990: 1= Curtis Hibbert (Can), Alan Nolet (Can) 9.850, 3 Brennon Dowrick (Aus) 9.800.

1994: 1 Alan Nolet (Can) 9.512, 2 Richard Ikeda (Can) 9.500, 3 Nathan Kingston (Aus) 9.325.

1998: 1 Andrei Kravtsov (Aus) 9.425, 2 Kristan Burley (Can) 9.000, 3 Lee McDermott (Eng) 8.950.

Team:

1978: 1 Canada (Jean Choquette, Philip Delesalle, Nigel Rothwell, Owen Walstrom)165.55, 2 England (Eddie Arnold, Jeff Davis, Ian Neale, Tommy Wilson) 161.95, 3 Australia (Lambert Ariens, Warwick Forbes, Lindsay Nylund, Rudy Starosta) 158.50.

1982-1986: Not held

1990: 1 Canada (Lorne Bobkin, Curtis Hibbert, Claude Latendresse, Alan Nolet) 171.800, 2 England (Terry Bartlett, David Cox, James May, Neil Thomas) 170.450, 3 Australia (Brennon Dowrick, Peter Hogan, Tim Lees, Ken Meredith) 169.500.

1994: 1 Canada (Kristan Burley, Richard Ikeda, Alan Nolet, Travis Romagnoli) 164.700, 2 Australia (Brennon Dowrick, Peter Hogan, Bret Hudson, Nathan Kingston) 164.500, 3 England (Robert Barber, Paul Bowler, Lee McDermott, Neil Thomas) 162.375.

1998: 1 England (Andrew Atherton, Craig Heap, Lee McDermott, John Smethurst) 162.275, 2 Australia (Brennon Dowrick, Bret Hudson, Andrei Kravtsov, Pavel Mamine) 162.150, 3 Canada (Kristan Burley, Richard Ikeda, Alexander Jeltkov, Peter Schmid) 155.825.

WOMEN

Individual All-Round:
1978: 1 Elfi Schlegel (Can) 38.25, 2= Monica Goermann (Can), Sherry Hawco (Can) 37.25.
1982-1986: Not held
1990: 1 Lori Strong (Can) 38.912, 2 Monique Allen (Aus) 38.687, 3 Kylie Shadbolt (Aus) 38.499.
1994: 1 Stella Umeh (Can) 38.400, 2 Rebecca Stoyel (Aus) 38.037, 3 Zita Lusack (Eng) 37.725.
1998: 1 Zeena McLaughlin (Aus) 37.917, 2 Allana Slater (Aus) 37.324, 3 Trudy McIntosh (Aus) 36.636.

Floor:
1990: 1 Lori Strong (Can) 9.887, 2 Larissa Lowing (Can) 9.762, 3 Kylie Shadbolt (Aus) 9.675.
1994: 1 Annika Reeder (Eng) 9.750, 2 Jackie Brady (Eng) 9.662, 3 Lisa Simes (Can) 9.550.
1998: 1 Annika Reeder (Eng) 9.675, 2 Allana Slater (Aus) 9.587, 3 Zeena McLaughlin (Aus) 9.487.

Vault:
1990: 1 Nikki Jenkins (NZ) 9.712, 2 Lori Strong (Can) 9.643, 3 Monique Allen (Aus) 9.506
1994: 1 Stella Umeh (Can) 9.556, 2 Sonia Lawrence (Wal) 9.543, 3 Lisa Simes (Can) 9.506.
1998: 1 Lisa Mason (Eng) 9.231, 2 Trudy McIntosh (Aus) 9.162, 3 Annika Reeder (Eng) 9.124

Asymmetric Bars:
1990: 1 Monique Allen (Aus) 9.875, 2 Lori Strong (Can) 9.850, 3 Michelle Telfer (Aus) 9.737.
1994: 1 Rebecca Stoyel (Aus) 9.525, 2 Stella Umeh (Can) 9.450, 3 Sara Thompson (NZ) 9.337.
1998: 1 Lisa Skinner (Aus) 9.612, 2 Véronique Leclerc (Can) 9.550, 3 Zeena McLaughlin (Aus) 9.512.

Balance Beam:
1990: 1 Lori Strong (Can) 9.850, 2 Larissa Lowing (Can) 9.762, 3 Kylie Shadbolt (Aus) 9.700.
1994: 1 Salli Wills (Aus) 9.075, 2 Zita Lusack (Eng) 8.987, 3 Ruth Moniz (Aus) 8.900.
1998: 1 Trudy McIntosh (Aus) 9.550, 2 Zeena McLaughlin (Aus) 9.375, 3 Lisa Leveille (Can) 9.350.

Team:
1978: 1 Canada (Monica Goermann, Sherry Hawco, Karen Kelsall, Elfi Schlegel)

113.25, 2 England (Susanne Cheeseborough, Lisa Jackman, Karen Robb, Joanne Sime) 107.40, 3 New Zealand (Lynette Brake, Rowena Davis, Kirsty Durward, Deborah Hurst) 106.35.

1982-1986: Not held

1990: 1 Canada (Larissa Lowing, Janet Morin, Lori Strong, Stella Umeh) 116.784, 2 Australia (Monique Allen, Lisa Read, Kylie Shadbolt, Michelle Telfer) 115.272, 3 England (Lisa Elliott, Lisa Grayson, Lorna Mainwaring, Louise Redding) 114.046.

1994: 1 England (Jackie Brady, Zita Lusack, Annika Reeder, Karin Szymko) 114.225, 2 Canada (Stacey Galloway, Jaimie Hill, Lisa Simes, Stella Umeh) 113.650, 3 Australia (Joanna Hughes, Ruth Moniz, Rebecca Stoyel, Salli Wills) 113.625.

1998: 1 Australia (Katarina Freketic, Trudy McIntosh, Zeena McLaughlin, Allana Slater) 111.408, 2 England (Kelly Hackman, Lisa Mason, Annika Reeder, Melissa Wilcox) 110.640, 3 Canada (Emilie Fournier, Véronique Leclerc, Lisa Leveille, Katie Rowland) 108.884.

HOCKEY

The "hockeyroos" run riot at the super stadium

Of the 18 Olympic men's hockey tournaments which had taken place from 1908 to 1996, India had won eight, Great Britain and Pakistan three each, and New Zealand one, leaving just three for the rest of the World. Of the five women's tournaments since 1980 Australia had won two and Zimbabwe one. So it was perhaps not before time that hockey eventually made its Commonwealth Games debut as one of the team sports introduced in Kuala Lumpur in 1998.

It was a logical choice for the Malaysians, who had themselves demonstrated considerable talent for the game and had built at the massive sports complex at Bukit Jalil a 13,000-capacity dedicated hockey stadium which was acclaimed by the participating teams as the finest in the World. Thirteen nations were invited and they represented as fine a Commonwealth cross-section as one could wish for: from the Home Countries - England, Scotland and Wales; from Asia - Bangladesh, India,

HOCKEY

Malaysia and Pakistan; from Africa - Kenya and South Africa; from the Americas - Canada and Trinidad & Tobago; from Oceania - Australia and New Zealand.

The Malaysian men aroused their exuberant supporters to feverish delight by reaching the final before they were finally outclassed by the physically and technically superior "hockeyroos" from Australia. England's women - including Karen Brown, Mandy Nicholson and Jane Sixsmith, who had all played in the Great Britain team which won bronze medals at the 1992 Olympics - fulfilled their hopes of reaching the final but were then routed by the Australian women.

HOCKEY MEDALLISTS

MEN

1998: 1 Australia (Michael Brennan, Adam Commens, Stephen Davies, Damon Diletti, Jason Duff, James Elmer, Paul Gaudoin, Mark Hickman, Jeremy Hiskins, Steven Holt, Brent Livermore. Matthew Smith, Daniel Sproule, Jay Stacy, Lachlan Vivian-Taylor, Michael York),
2 Malaysia (Calvin Fernandez, Chairal Anwar Aziz, Chua Boon Huat, K. Keevan Raj, K.Logan Raj, Lam Mun Fatt, Maninderjit Singh, Mirnawan Nawawi, M.Kaliswaran, Nasihin Nubli, Nor Azlan Bakar, Nor Saiful Zaini, R. Shankar, Roslan Jamaluddin, S. Kuhan, Suhaimi Ibrahim),
3 England (Bobby Crutchley, Guy Fordham, Russell Garcia, Brett Garrard, Julian Halls, Stuart Hrad, Michael Johnson, David Luckes, Simon Mason, Mark Pearn, Justin Piddock, Ben Sharpe, Jimmy Wallis, Billy Waugh, Duncan Woods, Julian Wyatt).

Results:
Final: Australia 4 Malaysia 0.
Third-place playoff: England 1 India 1 (England won 4-2 on penalties).
Semi-finals: Australia 3 England 2 (after extra time), Malaysia 1 India 0.

WOMEN

1998: 1 Australia (Kate Allen, Michelle Andrews, Alyson Annan, Louise Dobson, Juliet Haslam, Rechelle Hawkins, Rachel Imison, Bianca Langham, Claire Mitchell-Taverner, Nicole Mott, Alison Peek, Katrina Powell, Lisa Powell, Justine Sowry, Kate Starre, Kristen Towers).
2 England (Jennie Bimson, Kirsty Bowden, Karen Brown, Melanie Clewlow, Tina Cullen, Jacqueline Empson, Fiona Greenham, Denise Marston-Smith, Kerry Moore, Lucy Newcombe, Mandy Nicholson, Carolyn Reid, Hilary Rose, Jane Sixsmith, Jane Smith, Lucilla Wright),
3 New Zealand (Tina Bell-Kake, Sandy Bennett, Helen Clarke, Jenny Duck, Emily Gillam, Skippy Hamahona, Anna Lawrence, Robyn Matthews, Suzanne

Pearce, Moira Senior, Jenny Shepherd, Karen Smith, Mandy Smith, Kate Trolove, Lisa Walton, Diana Weavers).

Results:

Final: Australia 8 England 1.
Third-place playoff: New Zealand 3 India 0.
Semi-finals: Australia 7 New Zealand 3, England 2 India 0.

JUDO

Elvis books his rivals into Heartbreak Hotel

Considering that British judokas had enjoyed some considerable success at World level over the years it may seem surprising that the sport's only previous appearance at the Games was in New Zealand in 1990. Brian Jacks had won bronze and David Starbrook silver at the 1972 Olympics, while Neil Adams had been a World champion in 1981, and British women had been consistently in the forefront with Diane Bell, Jane Bridge, Karen Briggs, Loretta Doyle, Ann Hughes and Sharon Rendle winning 10 World titles between them during the 1980s.

Women's judo had been introduced as a demonstration sport at the Olympic Games in 1988 and Diane Bell, Sharon Rendle and Australia's Suzanne Williams all won their events. For the 1990 Commonwealth Games eight divisions were contested by men and women, and England won 14 of the 16 titles, losing only the men's half-lightweight and the women's lightweight, with Elvis Gordon taking both the heavyweight and Open (unlimited weight) titles.

Diane Bell, Karen Briggs and Sharon Rendle all won titles for

England, and yet another World title-winner, Loretta Cusack (nee Doyle), was the lone intruder for Scotland in an exceptionally competitive lightweight division ahead of Suzanne Williams and Ann Hughes. Sharon Lee, like her team-mate, Elvis Gordon, took both the heavyweight and open titles. At half-middleweight a bronze was earned by Laurie Pace, who thus became Malta's first Games medal-winner in any sport.

There were further British successes when women's judo was officially recognised at the 1992 Olympics and Sharon Rendle won bronze and Nicola Fairbrother silver. The next year the latter was World champion. More recently, Graeme Randall became only Britain's second male World champion in half-a-century when he won the light-middleweight title in 1999.

Leading countries:

England 14 gold medals; New Zealand, Scotland 1 each.

JUDO MEDALLISTS

Note: both losing semi-finalists awarded bronze medals.

MEN

Extra Lightweight (60kg):
1990: 1 Carl Finney (Eng), 2 Kevin West (Can), 3 James Charles (Wal), Narender Singh (Ind).

Half Lightweight (65kg):
1990: 1 Brent Cooper (NZ), 2 Mark Preston (Sco), 3 Mark Adshead (Eng), Jean-Pierre Cantin (Can).

Lightweight (71kg):
1990: 1 Roy Stone (Eng), 2 Majemite Omagbaluwaje (Nig), 3 William Cusack (Sco), Colin Savage (NI).

Half Middleweight (78kg):
1990: 1 David Southby (Eng), 2 Graeme Spinks (NZ), 3 Roger Coté (Can), Gavin Kelly (Aus).

Middleweight (86kg):
1990: 1 Densign White (Eng), 2 Winston Sweatman (Sco), 3 Chris Bacon (Aus), Rajender Dhanger (Ind).

Half Heavyweight (95kg):
1990: 1 Ray Stevens (Eng), 2 Dean Lampkin (Aus), 3 Graham Campbell (Sco), James Kendrick (Can).

Heavyweight (over 95kg):
1990: 1 Elvis Gordon (Eng), 2 Tom Greenway (Can), 3 Wayne Watson (NZ). Note: only one bronze medal awarded.

Open (unlimited weight):
1990: 1 Elvis Gordon (Eng), 2 Mario Laroche (Can), 3 Graham Campbell (Sco), Majemite Omagbaluwaje (Nig).

WOMEN

Extra Lightweight (48kg):
1990: 1 Karen Briggs (Eng), 2 Helen Duston (Wal), 3 Julie Reardon (Aus), Donna Robertson (Sco).

Half Lightweight (52kg):
1990: 1 Sharon Rendle (Eng), 2 Claire Shiach (Sco), 3 Catherine Grainger (Aus), Lisa Griffiths (Wal).

Lightweight (56kg):
1990: 1 Loretta Cusack (Sco), 2 Suzanne Williams (Aus), 3 Ann Hughes (Eng), Moira Sutton (Wal).

Half Middleweight (61kg):
1990: 1 Diane Bell (Eng), 2 Donna Guy-Halkyard (NZ), 3 Mandy Clayton (Can), Laurie Pace (Mlt).

Middleweight (66kg):
1990: 1 Sharon Mills (Eng), 2 Karen Hayde (Can), 3 Joyce Malley (NI), Narelle Hill (Aus).

Half Heavyweight (72kg):
1990: 1 Jane Morris (Eng), 2 Alison Webb (Can), 3 Philippa Knowles (Wal), Christy Obekpa (Nig).

Heavyweight (over 72kg):
1990: 1 Sharon Lee (Eng), 2 Geraldine Dekker (Aus), 3 Linda Konkol (Can), Ruth Vondy (IoM).

Open (unlimited weight):
1990: 1 Sharon Lee (Eng), 2 Jane Patterson (Can), 3 Geraldine Dekker (Aus), Nicola Morris (NZ).

NETBALL

Where the Commonwealth rules the World

The World Championships for netball were first held in 1963 and then regularly on a four-yearly basis. Of the nine tournaments to 1995, Australia had won six and New Zealand two, and on the only other occasion there had been a three-way tie between those two countries and Trinidad & Tobago. Such total Commonwealth dominance made netball a natural for inclusion in the Games when team sports came into the reckoning in 1998. Australia's pre-eminence is based on the fact that the country has 750,000 affiliated players of the game.

The 12 teams invited to Kuala Lumpur were from Australia, Barbados, Canada, Cook Islands, England, Jamaica, Malawi, Malaysia, New Zealand, South Africa, Sri Lanka and Wales. The final between Australia and New Zealand was close, with only three points in it, and the third-place match was even closer, with two points deciding the result, but the semi-final wins showed how superior the finalists were to the rest. Australia had 30 points to spare and New Zealand 40.

The 1999 World Championships final involved the same two countries - and Australia won by a single point, 42-41, with England beating Jamaica 57-43 for 3rd place. The World rankings for the year 2001 listed the 12 leading nations as follows: 1 Australia, 2 New Zealand, 3 England, 4 Jamaica, 5 South Africa, 6 Fiji, 7 Cook Islands, 8 Trinidad & Tobago, 9 Samoa, 10 Barbados, 11 Malawi, 12 Singapore. The highest placed non-Commonwealth country was the USA, and they were 15th.

NETBALL MEDALLISTS

First held 1998

1998: 1 Australia (Jenny Borlase, Nicole Cusack, Liz Ellis, Kathryn Harby, Janine Ilitch, Simone McKinnis, Sharelle McMahon, Shelley O'Donnell, Rebecca Sanders, Sarah-Louise Sutter, Carissa Tombs, Vicki Wilson),
2 New Zealand (Belinda Blair, Belinda Colling, Julie Dawson, Sonya Hardcastle, Donna Loffhagen, Bernice Mene, Lesley Nicol, Anna Rowberry, Jo Steed, Lorna Suafoa, Noeline Taurua, Linda Vagana),
3 England (Karen Aspinall, Lyn Carpenter, Lorraine Law, Hellen Manufor, Olivia Murphy, Fiona Murtagh, Tracey Neville, Amanda Newton, Lucia Sdao, Naomi Siddall, Lisa Stanley, Joanne Zinzan).

Results:
Final: Australia 42 New Zealand 39
Third-place playoff: England 56 South Africa 54
Semi-finals: Australia 68 South Africa 38, New Zealand 70 England 30.

RUGBY UNION SEVENS

Lomu the magnificent

Rugby football is largely a Commonwealth preserve, with only France offering a persistently serious challenge. The seven-a-side version of the game was originally regarded as no more than an entertaining end-of-season diversion, but a World Cup competition began in 1993 following the growing success over the years of an international invitation tournament organised in Hong Kong.

England and then Fiji were the first World Cup winners, and the latter have made a speciality of the format in succeeding years, but when it came to the inaugural Commonwealth Games rugby sevens in Kuala Lumpur the traditional power and strength of the New Zealand All-Blacks prevailed ... and no single player was more impressive than their massively-built wing-threequarter, Jonah Lomu. With Lomu and his colleagues casually brushing aside the opposition, many of the matches were foregone conclusions, and yet the whole series proved immensely popular with large and excited crowds.

RUGBY UNION SEVENS MEDALLISTS

Seven-a-side tournament:

First held 1998

1998: 1 New Zealand (Christian Cullen, Rico Gear, Jonah Lomu, Caleb Ralph, Roger Randle, Bruce Reihana, Eric Rush, Dallas Seymour, Amasio Valence, Joeli Vidiri),

2 Fiji (Eparama Bose, Alifereti Doviverata, Sirilo Lala, Bruce Rauqe, Saimoni Rokini, Waisale Serevi, Seta Tawake, Jope Tuikabe, Akuila Tuinasau, Marika Vunibaka),

3 Australia (David Campese, Matthew Dowling, Ipolito Fenukitau, Richard Graham, Tryon Mandrusiak, Rick Nalatu, Cameron Pither, Marc Stcherbina, Brendan Williams, Jim Williams).

Results:

Final: New Zealand 21 Fiji 12.

Third-place playoff: Australia 33 Samoa 12.

Semi-finals: New Zealand 19 Samoa 14, Fiji 28 Australia 14.

SHOOTING

The day that Yvonne's aim outscored the men

First held in 1966, when there were five events for men, shooting has grown and grown at the Commonwealth Games so that by 1998 the programme had expanded six-fold to 30 events, with 10 of them for women. This expansion reflects the widespread appeal of the sport.

Altogether, there are 20 countries which have won shooting medals at the Games: England, Northern Ireland, Scotland, Wales, the Isle of Man, Guernsey and Jersey; Australia, New Zealand and Papua New Guinea; Canada, Jamaica and Trinidad & Tobago; Bangladesh, Hong Kong, India, Malaysia and Sri Lanka; and finally Cyprus and South Africa. Of these, all but Papua New Guinea, Jamaica and Trinidad & Tobago have also won gold.

Shooting is one of the very few sports in which women can compete on equal terms with the men in mixed competition. In 1974 Yvonne Gowland, of Australia, won the Small-Bore Rifle Prone event, and in 1982 Hazel Mackintosh won a bronze in the Full-Bore Rifle Pairs event for Northern Ireland. Then in 1986 Sarah Cooper joined forces with her multi-medallist husband, Malcolm, to win the Small-Bore Rifle Pairs Three Positions event for England, and Sharon Bowes partnered Guy Lorion to victory for Canada in the Air Rifle Pairs competition. In the same event in 1990 Soma Dutta was one of the Indian bronze-medal pair.

The increase in events has also created numerous medal opportunities for the leading competitors and there are four men who have each won 10 or more medals. By far the most prolific of them is the Australian pistol marksman, Phil Adams, with 17 in individual and pairs events.

Leading countries:

Australia 38 gold medals; Canada 35; England 26; New Zealand 11; India 8; Scotland 6; Cyprus, Northern Ireland, Wales 3 each; Bangladesh, Guernsey, Hong Kong, Isle of Man, Jersey, Malaysia, South Africa, Sri Lanka 1 each.

Leading gold-medallists:

7 Phil Adams (Aus) 1982-90; 6 Christine Trefry (Aus) 1994-98; 5 Michael Gault (Eng) 1994-98; 4 Malcolm Cooper (Eng) 1982-86, Guy Lorion (Can) 1986-90, Bengt Sandstrom (Aus) 1990-94, Steve Petterson (NZ) 1990-98, Sharon Bowes (Can) 1994-98, Jaspel Rana (Ind) 1994-98; 3 Alister Allan (Sco) 1978-82, Jean-Francois Sénécal (Can) 1982-94, Ian Peel (Eng) 1986-90, Mart Klepp (Can) 1990, Ashok Pandit (Ind) 1990-98, Pat Murray (Aus) 1990-98, Christina Ashcroft (Can) 1994-98, Chris Hector (Eng) 1994-98, Annette Woodward (Aus) 1994-98.

Highlights - Games by Games

1966: Shooting was given an aristocratic welcome to the Commonwealth Games as Lord John Swansea - competing, naturally, for Wales - won the inaugural Full-Bore Rifle event. Of the five titles Canada and England won two each, and there were other medals for Australia, Jamaica, New Zealand and Papua New Guinea.

1974: After an eight-year gap shooting returned, with six events to be contested. Canada won four of them, but it was Mrs Gowland who achieved the historic victory over the men. One of the Canadian winners, Dr Jules Sobrian, became the first of what was to be a long list of multiple medallists, with gold and silver in pistol competition.

1978: Dr Sobrian won another pistol gold, and brothers Desmond and Patrick Vamplew took gold and bronze in the Full-Bore Rifle event as Canada again won four of the six events. The Isle of Man, Trinidad & Tobago and Wales were among those to provide medallists.

1982: Malcolm Cooper won two gold medals, three silver and a bronze for England as the number of events increased to 20. Phil Adams, for Australia, collected two golds, a silver and a bronze. Alister Allan, for Scotland, won two golds and a bronze, having already been World champion in the Small-Bore Rifle Prone event in 1978 with a record score of 599 and then double European Champion in 1981 with a perfect score of 600 in the Three Positions event. Lord Swansea returned after 16 years to add a silver to his earlier gold, and there was a first gold for Asia, won by Solomon Lee, of Hong Kong, in the Rapid-Fire Pistol event.

1986: There was a sense of inevitability about Malcolm Cooper's two further gold-medal successes (one of them in the company of his wife, Sarah). Cooper had won the Olympic title for the Small-Bore Rifle Three Positions event at the 1984 Games (and would do so again in 1988). He had collected four World titles for Free Rifle from 1978 onwards, setting five World records. At the 1985 European Championships he had won all five of his individual events. The Canadian air-rifle marksman, Guy Lorion, also won two golds - and one of them in the Pairs with Sharon Bowes. The Isle of Man took gold in the Skeet Individual through Nigel Kelly.

1990: Australia triumphed in seven of the 22 events, with Phil Adams collecting three golds. Canada won four events (three golds for versatile rifleman Mart Klepp), and England and New Zealand one each, but the most striking feature of shooting at these Games was the emergence of other winning countries: Bangladesh, India, Scotland, Guernsey and Jersey. Adrian Breton won Guernsey's first gold in any Games sport in Rapid Fire Pistol, having been 2nd in 1986, and Colin Mallett took the Full-Bore Rifle gold for Jersey and combined with his father, Clifford, for the Pairs bronze.

1994: India won three titles - the Trap Individual and the Centre-Fire Pistol Individual and Pairs - and Cyprus took the Skeet Pairs. The Running Target Pairs went to the Bedlington brothers from Canada. Women had their own events for the first time and Australia's Christine Trefry won gold in three of the pistol events. Sharon Bowes added two more golds for Canada to the one she had won in open competition eight years earlier, and there were acclaimed victories in the Air Rifle finals for Fani Theofanous, of Cyprus, and for Pushpamali Ramanayake and Malee Wickremasinghe, of Sri Lanka.

1998: India and Cyprus were again event winners and England's Michael Gault was the most successful competitor, accumulating four golds in the Free Pistol and Air Pistol events. The Trap winner, Michael Diamond, of Australia, had also won the 1996 Olympic title. Christine Trefry repeated her triple success and Sharon Bowes was again a double winner, while the hosts, Malaysia, provided the champion in the Air Rifle, in the person of Nurul Huda Baharin, who was a 25-year-old policewoman and won despite having injured her trigger arm in a motor-cycle accident a month previously. Youngest of all the winners was Australia's 17-year-old Susan McCready in the Sport Rifle Three Positions event.

SHOOTING MEDALLISTS

MEN

Small-Bore Rifle - Individual, Prone:
1966: 1 Gilmour Boa (Can) 587, 2 Brian Lacey (NZ) 585, 3 John Murphy (Aus) 584.
1970: Not held
1974: 1 Yvonne Gowland (Aus) 594, 2 Bill Watkins (Wal) 591, 3 Alister Allan (Sco) 591.
1978: 1 Alister Allan (Sco) 1194, 2 Bill Watkins (Wal) 1191, 3 Stewart Watterson (IoM) 1187.
1982: 1 Alan Smith (Aus) 1184, 2 Malcolm Cooper (Eng) 1184, 3 Bill Watkins (Wal) 1177.
1986: 1 Alan Smith (Aus) 599, 2 Alister Allan (Sco) 598, 3 John Knowles (Sco) 597.
1990: 1 Roger Harvey (NZ) 591, 2 Steve Petterson (NZ) 590, 3 Philip Scanlan (Eng) 590.
1994: 1 Steve Petterson (NZ) 694.4, 2 Jim Cornish (Eng) 693.9, 3 Michel Dion (Can) 693.6.
1998: 1 Steve Petterson (NZ) 697.4, 2 David Moore (IoM) 694.6, 3 Gavin van Rhyn (SA) 694.1.

Small-Bore Rifle - Individual, Three Positions:
First held 1982
1982: 1 Alister Allan (Sco) 1146, 2 Malcolm Cooper (Eng) 1145, 3 Guy Lorion (Can) 1144.
1986: 1 Malcolm Cooper (Eng) 1170, 2 Alister Allan (Sco) 1167, 3 Jean-Francois Sénécal (Can) 1150.
1990: 1 Mart Klepp (Can) 1157, 2 Malcolm Cooper (Eng) 1154, 3 Soma Dutta

(Ind) 1143.

1994: 1 Michael Dion (Can) 1234.2, 2 Wayne Sorensen (Can) 1228.7, 3 Alister Allan (Sco) 1224.8.

1998: 1 Tim Lowndes (Aus) 1235.3, 2 Wayne Sorensen (Can) 1234.4, 3 Kenneth Parr (Eng) 1225.6.

Small-Bore Rifle - Pairs, Prone:

First held 1982

1982: 1 Malcolm Cooper & Mike Sullivan (Eng) 1187, 2 Colin Harris & Bill Watkins (Wal) 1183, 3 Patrick Vamplew & Ernest Sopsich (Can) 1180.

1986: 1 Michael Ashcroft & Gale Stewart (Can) 1175, 2 Donald Brook & Alan Smith (Aus) 1171, 3 Terry Wakefield & Colin Harris (Wal) 1165.

1990: 1 Steve Petterson & Roger Harvey (NZ) 1185, 2 Barry Sutherland & Michael Ashcroft (Can) 1184, 3 Bob Jarvis & Philip Scanlan (Eng) 1180.

1994: 1 Steve Petterson & Lindsay Arthur (NZ) 1181, 2 Donangoda Chandrasiri & Lakshman Rajasinghe (SriL) 1177, 3 David Clifton & Dean Turley (Aus) 1176.

1998: 1 Gavin van Rhyn & Michael Thiele (SA) 1189, 2 Philip Scanlan & Neil Day (Eng) 1188, 3 Tim Lowndes & Warren Potent (Aus) 1178.

Small-Bore Rifle - Pairs, Three Positions:

First held 1982

1982: 1 Malcolm Cooper & Barry Dagger (Eng) 2301, 2 Guy Lorion & Jean-Francois Sénécal (Can) 2279, 3 Alister Allan & Bill MacNeill (Sco) 2277.

1986: 1 Malcolm Cooper & Sarah Cooper (Eng) 2278, 2 Jean-Francois Sénécal & Michel Dion (Can) 2276, 3 Alister Allan & Bill MacNeill (Sco) 2241.

1990: 1 Jean-Francois Sénécal & Mart Klepp (Can) 2272, 2 Malcolm Cooper & Robert Smith (Eng) 2268, 3 William Murray & Robert Law (Sco) 2258.

1994: 1 Wayne Sorensen & Michel Dion (Can) 2300, 2 Alister Allan & William Murray (Sco) 2271, 3 Chris Hector & Trevor Langridge (Eng) 2259.

1998: 1 Michel Dion & Wayne Sorensen (Can) 2276, 2 Les Imgrund & Tim Lowndes (Aus) 2266, 3 Chris Hector & Kenneth Parr (Eng) 2255.

Full-Bore Rifle - Individual:

1966: 1 Lord John Swansea (Wal) 394, 2 Robert Stewart (PNG) 381, 3 Tom Sutherland (NZ) 381.

1970: Not held

1974: 1 Maurice Gordon (NZ) 387.26, 2 Colin McEachran (Sco) 386.27, 3 James Spaight (Eng) 383.35.

1978: 1 Desmond Vamplew (Can) 391, 2 James Spaight (Eng) 388, 3 Patrick Vamplew (Can) 387.

1982: 1 Arthur Clarke (Sco) 387, 2 Lord John Swansea (Wal) 385, 3 Charles Trotter (Gue) 384.

1986: 1 Stan Golinski (Aus) 396, 2 Alain Marion (Can) 396, 3 John Bloomfield (Eng) 395.

1990: 1 Colin Mallett (Jer) 394, 2 Andrew Tucker (Eng) 390, 3 James Corbett (Aus) 390.

1994: 1 David Calvert (NI) 398, 2 Geoffrey Smith (NZ) 398, 3 Glyn Barnett

(Eng) 397.

1998: 1 James Paton (Can) 402, 2 Zainal Abidin Zain (Mal) 400, 3 Andrew Luckman (Eng) 400.

Full-Bore Rifle - Pairs:

First held 1982

1982: 1 Keith Affleck & Geoffrey Ayling (Aus) 572, 2 John Bloomfield & Dick Rosling (Eng) 570, 3 David Calvert & Hazel Mackintosh (NI) 563.

1986: 1 Bill Baldwin & Alain Marion (Can) 583, 2 James Corbett & Stan Golinski (Aus) 583, 3 David Calvert & Martin Millar (NI) 582.

1990: 1 Simon Belither & Andrew Tucker (Eng) 580, 2 James Corbett & Barry Wood (Aus) 565, 3 Clifford Mallett & Colin Mallett (Jer) 564.

1994: 1 Bert Bowden & Geoffrey Grenfell (Aus) 593, 2 Glyn Barnett & Anthony Ringer (Eng) 588, 3 David Calvert & Martin Millar (NI) 584.

1998: 1 David Calvert & Martin Millar (NI) 299, 2 James Paton & Alain Marion (Can) 298, 3 David Davies & Christopher Hockley (Wal) 298.

Air Rifle - Individual:

First held 1982

1982: 1 Jean-Francois Sénécal (Can) 574, 2 Matthew Guille (Gue) 572, 3 Malcolm Cooper (Eng) 570.

1986: 1 Guy Lorion (Can) 588, 2 Sharon Bowes (Can) 583, 3 Malcolm Cooper (Eng) 582.

1990: 1 Guy Lorion (Can) 583, 2 Chris Hector (Eng) 578, 3 Mart Klepp (Can) 577.

1994: 1 Chris Hector (Eng) 685.9, 2 Jean-Francois Sénécal (Can) 683, 3 Nigel Wallace (Eng) 680.

1998: 1 Chris Hector (Eng) 690, 2 Mohamed Zakaria (Mal) 687.2, 3 Steve Beneta (Aus) 686.2.

Air Rifle - Pairs:

First held 1982

1982: 1 Alister Allan & Bill MacNeill (Sco) 1137, 2 Malcolm Cooper & Barry Dagger (Eng) 1126, 3 Norbert Jahn & Anton Wurfel (Aus) 1123.

1986: 1 Guy Lorion & Sharon Bowes (Can) 1167, 2 Wolfgang Jobst & Anton Wurfel (Aus) 1151, 3 Malcolm Cooper & Robert Smith (Eng) 1146.

1990: 1 Guy Lorion & Mart Klepp (Can) 1163. 2 Chris Hector & Robert Smith (Eng) 1155, 3 Soma Dutta & Bhagirath Samai (Ind) 1148.

1994: 1 Jean-Francois Sénécal & Wayne Sorensen (Can) 1166, 2 Chris Hector & Nigel Wallace (Eng) 1161, 3 David Rattray & Robin Law (Sco) 1145.

1998: 1 Chris Hector & Nigel Wallace (Eng) 1173, 2 Mutalip Razak & Mohamed Zakaria (Mal) 1167, 3 David Rattray & Robin Law (Sco) 1163.

Running Target - Individual:

First held 1990

1990: 1 Colin Robertson (Aus) 539, 2 John Maddison (Eng) 539, 3 Tony Clarke (NZ) 535.

1994: 1 Bryan Wilson (Aus) 657.9, 2 Mark Bedlington (Can) 656.0, 3 Paul Carmine (NZ) 650.7.
1998: Not held

Running Target - Pairs:
First held 1990
1990: 1 Paul Carmine & Tony Clarke (NZ) 1091, 2 David Lee & Mark Bedlington (Can) 1070, 3 David Chapman & John Maddison (Eng) 1064.
1994: 1 Mark Bedlington & Matthew Bedlington (Can) 1088, 2 Bryan Wilson & Peter Zutenis (Aus) 1088, 3 Paul Carmine & Tony Clarke (NZ) 1079.
1998: Not held

Trap - Individual:
First held 1974
1974: 1 John Primrose (Can) 196, 2 Brian Bailey (Eng) 193, 3 Philip Lewis (Wal) 191.
1978: 1 John Primrose (Can) 186, 2 George Leary (Can) 185, 3 Terry Rumbel (Aus) 183.
1982: 1 Peter Boden (Eng) 191, 2 Terry Rumbel (Aus) 190, 3 Peter Croft (Eng) 190.
1986: 1 Ian Peel (Eng) 195, 2 Peter Boden (Eng) 192, 3 Roland Phillips (Wal) 192.
1990: 1 John Maxwell (Aus) 184, 2 Kevin Gill (Eng) 183, 3 Ian Peel (Eng) 179.
1994: 1 Mansher Singh (Ind) 141, 2 George Leary (Can) 140, 3 Andreas Anglou (Cyp) 137.
1998: 1 Michael Diamond (Aus) 144, 2 Ian Peel (Eng) 144, 3 Desmond Coe (NZ) 141.

Trap - Pairs:
First held 1982
1982: 1 Jim Ellis & Terry Rumbel (Aus) 190, 2 Peter Croft & Peter Boden (Eng) 186, 3 James Young & Martin Girvan (Sco) 183.
1986: 1 Peter Boden & Ian Peel (Eng) 185, 2 Tom Hewitt & Eamon Furphy (NI) 183, 3 Terry Rumbel & Domingo Diaz (Aus) 183.
1990: 1 Kevin Gill & Ian Peel (Eng) 181, 2 Colin Evans & James Birkett-Evans (Wal) 178, 3 Russell Mark & John Maxwell (Aus) 178.
1994: 1 Thomas Hewitt & Samuel Allen (NI) 188, 2 Ron Bonotto & George Leary (Can) 187, 3 Bob Borsley & John Grice (Eng) 186.
1998: 1 Mansher Singh & Manavjit Singh (Ind) 192, 2 Michael Diamond & Ben Kelley (Aus) 190, 3 Bob Borsley & Ian Peel (Eng) 189.

Skeet - Individual:
First held 1974
1974: 1 Harry Willsie (Can) 194, 2 Joe Neville (Eng) 191, 3 Robin Bailey (Aus) 189.
1978: 1 John Woolley (NZ) 193, 2 Paul Bentley (Eng) 191, 3 Joe Neville (Eng) 190.
1982: 1 John Woolley (NZ) 197, 2 Ian Hale (Aus) 196, 3 Wally Sykes (Eng) 195.

SHOOTING

1986: 1 Nigel Kelly (IoM) 196, 2 Joe Neville (Eng) 195, 3 Brian Gabriel (Can) 195.

1990: 1 Ken Harman (Eng) 187, 2 Georgios Sakellis (Cyp) 187, 3 Andy Austin (Eng) 184.

1994: 1 Ian Hale (Aus) 144, 2 Christos Kourtellas (Cyp) 143, 3 Andy Austin (Eng) 143.

1998: 1 Desmond Davies (Wal) 145, 2 Joe Trinci (Can) 144, 3 David Cunningham (Aus) 143.

Skeet - Pairs:

First held 1982

1982: 1 Brian Gabriel & Fred Altmann (Can) 191, 2 Jim Sheffield & Wally Sykes (Eng) 190, 3 Alex Crikis & Ian Hale (Aus) 190.

1986: 1 Joe Neville & Ken Harman (Eng) 195, 2 Brian Gabriel & Don Kwasyncia (Can) 193, 3 John Woolley & Jeff Farrell (NZ) 189.

1990: 1 Ian Marsden & James Dunlop (Sco) 189, 2 Andy Austin & Ken Harman (Eng) 185, 3 Tim Dodds & John Woolley (NZ) 183.

1994: 1 Antonis Andreou & Christos Kourtellas (Cyp) 189, 2 Brian Thomson & Geoffrey Jukes (NZ) 186, 3 Michael Thomson & Ian Marsden (Sco) 186.

1998: 1 Costas Stratis & Antonis Nicolaides (Cyp) 188, 2 Andy Austin & Drew Harvey (Eng) 187, 3 Douglas McCutcheon & Joe Trinci (Can) 186.

Free Pistol - Individual:

1966: 1 Charles Sexton (Eng) 544, 2 Jules Sobrian (Can) 538, 3 Garfield McMahon (Can) 536.

1970: Not held

1974: 1 Jules Sobrian (Can) 549, 2 Norman Harrison (Aus) 549, 3 Laslo Antal (Eng) 543.

1978: 1 Yvon Trempe (Can) 543, 2 Edward Jans (Can) 540, 3 Bertram Manhim (Tri) 536.

1982: 1 Tom Guinn (Can) 553, 2 Geoffrey Robinson (Eng) 543, 3 Phil Adams (Aus) 540.

1986: 1 Greg Yelavich (NZ) 551, 2 Phil Adams (Aus) 549, 3 Kar Fai Ho (HK) 549.

1990: 1 Phil Adams (Aus) 554, 2 Bengt Sandstrom (Aus) 549, 3 Gilbert U (HK) 549.

1994: 1 Michael Gault (Eng) 654.1, 2 Phil Adams (Aus) 647.0, 3 Bengt Sandstrom (Aus) 642.5.

1998: 1 Michael Gault (Eng) 646.3, 2 Francois van Tonder (SA) 642.5, 3 Bruce Quick (Aus) 640.3.

Free Pistol - Pairs:

First held 1982

1982: 1 Phil Adams & John Tremelling (Aus) 1077, 2 Barrie Wickens & Rex Hamilton (NZ) 1075, 3 Geoffrey Robinson & Frank Wyatt (Eng) 1074.

1986: 1 Tom Guinn & Claude Beaulieu (Can) 1099, 2 Paul Leatherdale & Richard Wang (Eng) 1090, 3 Phil Adams & Bengt Sandstrom (Aus) 1085.

1990: 1 Phil Adams & Bengt Sandstrom (Aus) 1106, 2 Brian Read & Greg Yelavich (NZ) 1084, 3 Ateequr Rahman & Abdus Sattar (Ban) 1078.

1994: 1 Phil Adams & Bengt Sandstrom (Aus) 1104, 2 Julian Lawton & Greg Yelavich (NZ) 1094, 3 Michael Gault & Paul Leatherdale (Eng) 1082.

1998: 1 Nick Baxter & Michael Gault (Eng) 1093, 2 David Moore & Bruce Quick (Aus) 1084, 3 John Rochon & Jean-Pierre Huot (Can) 1080.

Centre Fire Pistol - Individual:

1966: 1 James Lee (Can) 576, 2 Tony Clark (Eng) 575, 3 Julio Machado (Jam) 571.
1970-1978: Not held
1982: 1 John Cooke (Eng) 580, 2 James Cairns (Sco) 579, 3 Noel Ryan (Aus) 577.
1986: 1 Bob Northover (Eng) 583, 2 Phil Adams (Aus) 582, 3 Rod Hack (Aus) 580.
1990: 1 Ashok Pandit (Ind) 583, 2 Surinder Marwah (Ind) 577, 3 Bruce Quick (Aus) 576.
1994: 1 Jaspal Rana (Ind) 581, 2 Michael Gault (Eng) 581, 3 Greg Yelavich (NZ) 575.
1998: 1 Jaspal Rana (Ind) 581, 2 Allan McDonald (SA) 581, 3 John Rochon (Can) 576.

Centre Fire Pistol - Pairs:

First held 1982
1982: 1 Noel Ryan & Alexander Taransky (Aus) 1151, 2 Mohinder Lal & Ashok Pandit (Ind) 1138, 3 John Cooke & John Gough (Eng) 1131.
1986: 1 Phil Adams & Rod Hack (Aus) 1165, 2 Bob Northover & Michael Cutler (Eng) 1157, 3 Rex Hamilton & Barry O'Neale (NZ) 1153.
1990: 1 Phil Adams & Bruce Quick (Aus) 1155, 2 Barry O'Neale & Greg Yelavich (NZ) 1144, 3 Ashok Pandit & Surinder Marwah (Ind) 1142.
1994: 1 Jaspal Rana & Ashok Pandit (Ind) 1168, 2 Kelvin Vickers & Phil Adams (Aus) 1149, 3 Stanley Wills & John Rochon (Can) 1148.
1998: 1 Jaspal Rana & Ashok Pandit (Ind) 1154, 2 John Rochon & Metodi Igorov (Can) 1150, 3 Mike Giustiniano & Bruce Quick (Aus) 1149.

Rapid Fire Pistol - Individual:

1966: 1 Tony Clark (Eng) 585, 2 Michael Papps (Aus) 578, 3 Jules Sobrian (Can) 572.
1970: Not held
1974: 1 William Hare (Can) 586, 2 Jules Sobrian (Can) 583, 3 Bruce McMillan (NZ) 581.
1978: 1 Jules Sobrian (Can) 587, 2 John Cooke (Eng) 581, 3 Jeff Farrell (NZ) 581.
1982: 1 Solomon Lee (HK) 583, 2 Jim Timmerman (Can) 583, 3 John Cooke (Eng) 582.
1986: 1 Pat Murray (Aus) 591, 2 Adrian Breton (Gue) 588, 3 Mark Howkins (Can) 585.
1990: 1 Adrian Breton (Gue) 583, 2 Pat Murray (Aus) 582, 3 Michael Jay (Wal) 579.
1994: 1 Michael Jay (Wal) 670.2, 2 Robert Dowling (Aus) 668.4, 3 Pat Murray

(Aus) 668.1.

1998: 1 Metodi Igorov (Can) 674.8, 2 Allan McDonald (SA) 669.7, 3 Bhanwar Dhaka (Ind) 668.9.

Rapid Fire Pistol - Pairs:

First held 1982

1982: 1 Peter Heuke & Alexander Taransky (Aus) 1160, 2 James Cairns & Hugh Hunter (Sco) 1152, 3 Sharad Cahuran & Ramakrishnan Vij (Ind) 1151.

1986: 1 Brian Girling & Terry Turner (Eng) 1169, 2 Pat Murray & Jack Mast (Aus) 1152, 3 Mark Howkins & André Chevrefils (Can) 1150.

1990: 1 Bruce Favell & Pat Murray (Aus) 1153, 2 Stanley Willis & Mark Howkins (Can) 1138, 3 Brian Girling & John Rolfe (Eng) 1133.

1994: 1 Pat Murray & Robert Dowling (Aus) 1148, 2 Richard Craven & Michael Jay (Wal) 1142, 3 Adrian Breton & Graham Le Maitre (Gue) 1129.

1998: 1 Mike Giustiniano & Pat Murray (Aus) 1138, 2 Jason Wakeling & Alan Earle (NZ) 1133, 3 Allan McDonald & André van Emmenis (SA) 1123.

Air Pistol - Individual:

First held 1982

1982: 1 George Darling (Eng) 576, 2 Phil Adams (Aus) 573, 3 Tom Guinn (Can) 571.

1986: 1 Greg Yelavich (NZ) 575, 2 Tom Guinn (Can) 574, 3 Gilbert U (HK) 574.

1990: 1 Bengt Sandstrom (Aus) 580, 2 Phil Adams (Aus) 574, 3 David Lowe (Eng) 574.

1994: 1 Jean-Pierre Huot (Can) 672.4, 2 Jaspal Rana (Ind) 670.7, 3 Greg Yelavich (NZ) 668.5.

1998: 1 Michael Gault (Eng) 679.9, 2 Jaspal Rana (Ind) 677.4, 3 Greg Yelavich (NZ) 677.4.

Air Pistol - Pairs:

First held 1982

1982: 1 Phil Adams & Gregory Colbert (Aus) 1128, 2 Geoffrey Robinson & George Darling (Eng) 1126, 3 Jim Timmerman & Tom Guinn (Can) 1125.

1986: 1 Paul Leatherdale & Ian Reid (Eng) 1143, 2 Phil Adams & Bruce Favell (Aus) 1143, 3 Greg Yelavich & Barrie Wickens (NZ) 1140.

1990: 1 Ateequr Rahman & Abdus Sattar (Ban) 1138, 2 Phil Adams & Bengt Sandstrom (Aus) 1138, 3 Julian Lawton & Greg Yelavich (NZ) 1137.

1994: 1 Mike Giustiniano & Bengt Sandstrom (Aus) 1137, 2 Jean-Pierre Huot & John Rochon (Can) 1135, 3 Jaspal Rana & Vivek Singh (Ind) 1133.

1998: 1 Nick Baxter & Michael Gault (Eng) 1145, 2 Jaspal Rana & Satendra Kumar (Ind) 1143, 3 John Rochon & Jean-Pierre Huot (Can) 1138.

WOMEN

Sport Rifle - Individual, Prone:

1994: 1 Shirley McIntosh (Sco) 586, 2 Sylvia Purdie (Aus) 58.5, 3 Patricia Littlechild (Sco) 585.

1998: 1 Roopa Unikrishnan (Ind) 590, 2 Carrie Quigley (Aus) 590, 3 Sally Johnston (NZ) 587.

Sport Rifle - Individual, Three Positions:
1994: 1 Sharon Bowes (Can) 666.4, 2 Roopa Unikrishnan (Ind) 662.5, 3 Christina Ashcroft (Can) 661.6.
1998: 1 Susan McCready (Aus) 667.3, 2 Sharon Bowes (Can) 666.4, 3 Roslina Bakar (Mal) 666.3.

Sport Rifle - Pairs, Prone:
1994: 1 Kim Frazer & Sylvia Purdie (Aus) 1160, 2 Shirley McIntosh & Patricia Littlechild (Sco) 1158, 3 Christina Ashcroft & Linda Szulga (Can) 1158.
1998: 1 Kim Frazer & Carrie Quigley (Aus) 1174, 2 Christina Ashcroft & Maureen Spinney (Can) 1172, 3 Shirley McIntosh & Susan Bell (Sco) 1170.

Sport Rifle - Pairs, Three Positions:
1994: 1 Sharon Bowes & Christina Ashcroft (Can) 1143, 2 Karen Morton & Lindsay Volpin (Eng) 1132, 3 Roopa Unikrishnan & Kuheli Gangulee (Ind) 1110.
1998: 1 Sharon Bowes & Christina Ashcroft (Can) 1133, 2 Val Martin & Donna Potgieter (SA) 1115, 3 Shirley McIntosh & Janis Thomson (Sco) 1112.

Air Rifle - Individual:
1994: 1 Fani Theofanous (Cyp) 488.7, 2 Malee Wickremasinghe (SriL) 488.5, 3 Sharon Bowes (Can) 488.4.
1998: 1 Nurul Huda Baharin (Mal) 494.8. 2 Sharon Bowes (Can) 493.3, 3 Louise Minett (Eng) 491.7.

Air Rifle - Pairs:
1994: 1 Pushpamali Ramanayake & Malee Wickremasinghe (SriL) 771, 2 Karen Morton & Louise Minett (Eng) 771, 3 Christina Ashcroft & Sharon Bowes (Can) 766.
1998: 1 Christina Ashcroft & Sharon Bowes (Can) 778, 2 Belinda Muehlberg & Noemi Rostas (Aus) 774, 3 Louise Minett & Rebecca Spicer (Eng) 772.

Air Pistol - Individual:
1994: 1 Helen Smith (Can) 474.2, 2 Annette Woodward (Aus) 466.1, 3 Sharon Cozzarin (Can) 465.8.
1998: 1 Annemarie Forder (Aus) 480.6, 2 Christine Trefry (Aus) 476.9, 3 Tania Corrigan (NZ) 476.3.

Air Pistol - Pairs:
1994: 1 Annette Woodward & Christine Trefry (Aus) 747, 2 Jocelyn Lees & Gerd Barkman (NZ) 745, 3 Margaret Thomas & Carol Page (Eng) 744.
1998: 1 Annemarie Forder & Christine Trefry (Aus) 748, 2 Tania Corrigan & Jocelyn Lees (NZ) 747, 3 Kamisah Abdul Jalal & Suriani Othman (Mal) 743.

Sport Pistol - Individual:

1994: 1 Christine Trefry (Aus) 679.4, 2 Margaret Thomas (Eng) 675.0, 3 Annette Woodward (Aus) 674.0.

1998: 1 Christine Trefry (Aus) 672.8, 2 Bibiana Ng Peichin (Mal) 672.1, 3 Kimberley Eagles (Can) 671.0.

Sport Pistol - Pairs:

1994: 1 Christine Trefry & Annette Woodward (Aus) 1134, 2 Sharon Cozzarin & Helen Smith (Can) 1132, 3 Margaret Thomas & Carol Page (Eng) 1129.

1998: 1 Christine Trefry & Annette Woodward (Aus) 1140, 2 Tania Corrigan & Jocelyn Lees (NZ) 1138, 3 Pei Chin Ng & Norsita Mahmud (Mal) 1116.

SQUASH

A Scots single, but doubles are the orders of the day

Squash had been a worthy candidate for inclusion in the Commonwealth Games for some 30 years before it was accepted by the Kuala Lumpur organisers in 1998. The first World Championships for amateurs had been held in 1967 and Australia and Pakistan won all 10 titles until the World Open Championships took precedence from 1985 onwards.

These two countries continued to dominate both the men's and women's games, together with Great Britain and New Zealand. The outstanding men during this era were Pakistan's Jansher Khan and Jahangir Khan, with eight and six World titles respectively, and Australia's Geoff Hunt, with seven. The leading women were Heather McKay, also of Australia, who remained unbeaten from 1962 to 1980 and won 16 British Open titles, and Susan Devoy, of New Zealand, who was five times World champion between 1985 and 1992.

The year before the 1998 Commonwealth Games the World Open

titles had been won by the Australians, Rodney Eyles and Sarah Fitz-Gerald, and England had taken the men's World Team Championship. Eyles had beaten Peter Nicol, of Scotland, in straight sets in the men's tournament, which had been held in Kuala Lumpur, while Fitz-Gerald had retained her title in winning the women's final in Sydney from her compatriot, Michelle Martin, who had herself been World champion in 1993-94-95. England's team of Del Harris, Simon Parke and Chris Walker overwhelmed Canada 3-0 in the men's team final without losing a set.

1998 Games highlights

The squash facility built by the Malaysian organisers was described by the Australian team manager, Phil Trenorden, as "far superior to any other I have seen". He also concluded that the standard of play "was as high as the World Championships or the British Open, but the real bonus was that media coverage greatly exceeded the level we receive in those events".

In the Men's Singles eight of the top 10 players in the World rankings took part and the gold medal went to the 25-year-old Scotsman, Peter Nicol, who had taken over as No.1 from Jansher Khan earlier in the year and had become the first player from the Home Countries since Jonah Barrington a quarter-of-a-century before to win the British Open title. Nicol beat the talented but tempestuous World No.3, Jonathon Power, of Canada, in the final, while the World title-holder, Rodney Eyles, failed to advance beyond the last eight. Australia's other World champion, Sarah Fitz-Gerald, fared better in the Women's Singles before losing in the final to her team-mate, Michelle Martin.

Doubles play was an innovative venture because it was not until the announcement had been made that squash would figure in the 1998 Games that the World ruling body gave recognition to a form of the game which until then had not been widely played. Even in Australia, where the sport was so strong, there were only two doubles courts in existence. So perhaps understandably, in view of their limited prepara-tion, Australian pairings lost both the Men's Doubles and Women's Doubles finals to English opposition. Unabashed, England player Paul Johnson (who had also won a Singles bronze) described the success in which he shared as "probably the best moment in my life".

In the Mixed Doubles the new Australian partnership of Craig Rowland and Michelle Martin improved throughout the tournament to win the gold medals, but silver for Simon Parke, of England, alongside Suzanne Horner was a personal triumph over daunting adversity. Parke had suffered from testicular cancer in 1995 but had recovered health and

173

form so remarkably that he had regained World No.4 ranking by 1997 and had shared in England's World team title that year.

SQUASH MEDALLISTS

First held 1998

Men's singles:
1998: 1 Peter Nicol (Sco), 2 Jonathon Power (Can), 3 Alex Gough (Wal), Paul Johnson (Eng).

Men's doubles:
1998: 1 Paul Johnson & Mark Chaloner (Eng), 2 Rodney Eyles & Byron Davis (Aus), 3 Peter Nicol & Stuart Cowie (Sco), Chris Walker & Mark Cairns (Eng).

Women's singles:
1998: 1 Michelle Martin (Aus), 2 Sarah Fitz-Gerald (Aus), 3 Cassie Jackman (Eng), Sue Wright (Eng).

Women's doubles:
1998: 1 Sue Wright & Cassie Jackman (Eng), 2 Robyn Cooper & Rachael Grinham (Aus), 3 Sarah Fitz-Gerald & Carol Owens (Aus), Claire Nitch & Natalie Grainger (SA).

Mixed doubles:
1998: 1 Craig Rowland & Michelle Martin (Aus), 2 Simon Parke & Suzanne Horner (Eng), 3 Glen Wilson & Sarah Cook (NZ), Rodney Durbach & Natalie Grainger (SA).

TABLE TENNIS

Barna and Bergmann:
the "ping pong" innovators

Table Tennis was probably invented in England in the 1880s. Certainly by 1902 a "Ping Pong Association" had been formed and by 1927 the English Table Tennis Association had taken over the sport's domestic administration. There then came a spell just after the Second World War when British players were among the best in the World.

The initiators of this era of dominance were two wartime refugees from Nazi Europe - Viktor (later Victor) Barna and Richard Bergmann. Barna had already won 15 World titles for Hungary, including the Men's Singles on five occasions from 1930 to 1935, and Bergmann had also been the winner of that event for Austria in 1937 before the two of them joined forces to win the Men's Doubles in 1939.

After the war Bergmann won the singles again in 1948 and 1950 for England and Britain's first home-grown talent, Johnny Leach, did the same in 1949 and 1951. Margaret Franks and Vera Thomas had won the

Women's Doubles in 1948, but it was the identical Rowe twins - Diane and Rosalind - who became national celebrities with their successes in that event in 1951 and 1954.

Subsequently, only a handful of British players - or, for that matter, players from anywhere in the Commonwealth - have reached the highest level. Jamaican-born Desmond Douglas won a record total of 26 English closed titles and Denis Neale won 18, while Jill Hammersley was the leading woman player, winning the European Championships singles in 1976. Supremacy in the game had by then passed largely into the hands of players from China and Japan, and even the four women players who represented Australia in the Sydney 2000 Olympics were all Chinese born - Jian Fang Lay, Miao Miao and the unrelated Shirley Zhou and Stella Zhou.

Table Tennis comes to the Commonwealth Games for the first time in Manchester in an unusual situation in that Commonwealth Championships are a firmly established fixture, and Desmond Douglas was one of the most notable winners of a singles title in that tournament back in 1985. When the 14th edition of these Championships was held in Singapore in February 2000 there were 14 nations taking part: Australia, Canada, Cyprus, England, India, Malaysia, Mauritius, New Zealand, Northern Ireland, Scotland, Singapore, South Africa, Sri Lanka and Wales.

TRIATHLON

Swim, bike, run:
a new challenge for the Games

Combining swimming, cycling and running, the sport of triathlon has already had a highly successful try-out at the Commonwealth Games. It was staged as a demonstration event in Auckland in 1990, attracting wildly enthusiastic crowds of tens of thousands along the harbour-area route, and it is perhaps surprising that it has taken another dozen years for it to be accepted as a full-scale event.

In that Auckland competition, involving a 1500-metre swim, a 40-kilometre cycle ride, and a 10-kilometre run, the women's event was won by the then current World champion, Erin Baker, and the men's by her fellow New Zealander, Ric Wells. The sport has continued to be dominated ever since at the highest level by athletes from Commonwealth countries.

The Britons, Simon Lessing and Spencer Smith, between them won every annual World Championships from 1992 to 1996, and when the

title was contested in Edmonton, Alberta, in 2001 the winner was Peter Robertson, of Australia, with another Australian, Chris Hall, 2nd and a New Zealander, Craig Watson, 3rd. Seven of the leading nine places were taken by Commonwealth countries, with Andrew Johns (GB) 5th, Simon Whitfield (Canada) 6th, Bevan Docherty (NZ) 7th and Miles Stewart (Australia) 9th. Whitfield had won the inaugural Olympic triathlon title the previous year and Stewart had been World champion back in 1991.

The women's World title in Canada was taken by Siri Lindley, of the USA, with Michellie Jones, of Australia, in 2nd place. Jones had been World champion in 1992 and 1993 and had also finished 2nd to Brigette McMahon, of Switzerland, in the 2000 Olympics. Five other Commonwealth competitors took top 12 places in Edmonton: Australian-born Rina Hill (NZ) 4th, Jill Savage (Canada) 6th, Loretta Harrop (Australia) 8th, Evelyn Williamson (NZ) 9th and Carol Montgomery (Canada) 12th.

WEIGHTLIFTING

Rebuilding an image after the records were scrapped

Many of weightlifting's champions over the years have produced wondrous feats of strength, but the sport has had an odd and chequered career. It can be traced back to the Ancient Olympic Games and was featured in the first Modern Olympics in Athens in 1896. Retrospective recognition by the international authorities means that World Championships can be traced back to 1898.

Yet weightlifting did not gain a foothold in the Empire Games until 1950, and that may be attributed to its lack of international success and perhaps to its Victorian vaudeville image. A Briton, Launceston Elliott, had won the one-handed competition at the 1896 Olympics after coaching from the professional strongman, Eugen Sandow, as a teenager, but it was not until the London Games of 1948 that any Empire competitor was again a medallist. The British lifters, Julian Creus and Jim Halliday, took silver and bronze respectively in the Bantamweight and Lightweight divisions, while Rodney Wilkes had also won a silver at Featherweight for Trinidad. Halliday's achievement was particularly notable because he had spent four years in a Japanese prisoner-of-war camp.

Wilkes went on to win another medal at the 1952 Olympics, when there were four Empire medallists in the various weights, but standards relative to the rest of the World steadily slipped away over the years, and when Louis Martin took Middle-heavyweight silver at the 1964 Games no other Commonwealth lifter finished higher than 8th. There have been occasional successes since - such as the win for Australia's Super-heavyweight, Dean Lukin, in Los Angeles in 1984 - but Martin remains the pre-eminent competitor. He won the World title at Middle-heavyweight on four occasions between 1959 and 1965, and with his dramatic on-stage presence and his penchant for quoting lines of poetry to explain his motivation he raised weightlifting to a new level of public awareness.

Yet by 1993 the International Weightlifting Federation felt impelled to rewrite the record-books and annul all previous performances in an attempt to distance the sport from past accusations of widespread drug-taking. Whether or not the authorities have been successful in their clean-up efforts is a matter of debate, and the remarks of one Commonwealth Games competitor are a chilling testament to the sport's reputation.

Despite having just won three gold medals at the 1990 Games David Morgan, a 25-year-old Welshman, remained disillusioned. Announcing his immediate retirement from the sport at the press conference afterwards he told reporters dolefully: "When I go home people will say, 'You won three gold medals. Do you take steroids?' " Four years later, lighter in weight and his spirits revived, he won two more Commonwealth Games gold medals.

Leading countries:

Australia 43 gold medals; England 38; India 20; Canada 17; Wales 15; New Zealand, Nigeria 7 each; Nauru 6; Singapore 4; Malaysia 3; Scotland, Trinidad & Tobago 2 each; Barbados, South Africa 1 each.

Leading gold-medallists:

6 David Morgan (Wal) 1986-94, Marcus Stephen (Nau) 1990-98, Kirk Kounev (Aus) 1994-98; 4 Precious McKenzie (Eng) 1966-78, Chandersekharan Raghavan (Ind) 1990-94.

WEIGHTLIFTING

Highlights - Games by Games

1950: The confidence of the New Zealand organisers was rewarded by an entry of 28 lifters from eight nations. Jim Halliday, the Lightweight bronze-medallist from the Olympics of two years previously, won his division and set three Empire records in the process, but his England team-mate, Julian Creus, was beaten at Featherweight by Koh Eng Tong, one of the members of an astonishingly capable team of four from Malaya. Making their first international appearance the Malayans also took the bantamweight title and two other medals to win the unofficial team contest by one point from Canada.

1954: Rodney Wilkes had won Olympic silver and bronze but missed out on the 1950 Empire Games because Trinidad did not send a team. In Vancouver he made up for lost time with Featherweight gold, and two other titles were won by 1952 Olympic medallists: Vern Barberis (Australia) at Lightweight and Gerry Gratton (Canada) at Light-heavyweight. Canada also took the Middle-heavyweight title with Keevil Daly, who had been born in British Guiana, and the Heavyweight title when Doug Hepburn - weighing in at 21st 5½lb (136kg) - beat his team-mate, Dave Baillie, who was a mere stripling 9½lb (4kg) lighter !

1958: Australia, England, Scotland and South Africa won titles, but so, too, did Barbados and Singapore, and there were other medals for British Guiana, Canada, Malaya and Trinidad. Rodney Wilkes had been the most successful Empire lifter at the 1956 Olympics, placing 4th at Featherweight, but was beaten into 3rd place in Cardiff behind Singapore's Tan Ser Cher, and Singapore also won at Lightweight. The Bantamweight title went to South Africa's Reg Gaffley, but a better lifter had been left at home - and that was to become a tale with many a sequel over the years.

1962: England won three of the seven gold medals, with the most decisive success coming for Louis Martin at Middle-heavyweight, but then he had started as the strongest of favourites, having already won two World titles and an Olympic bronze. Tan Howe Liang, who had been the Olympic silver-medallist for Singapore in 1960, won the Lightweight title, and Singapore again had a second gold, while the Scotsman, Phil Caira, who earned his living as a newsagent, made his own headlines by becoming the first man to retain an Empire Games weight-lifting title.

1966: The pressure was on Louis Martin, by now four times a World champion, who was back in his birthplace of Kingston, Jamaica, but competing for England. Despite suffering the shock of having one of his chosen weights overloaded by mistake by 22lb (10kg), Martin duly won, and England's other success had an even greater sense of poignancy about it. The title in this instance went to 4ft 11in (1.50m) tall Bantamweight Precious McKenzie, who was the same man who had been omitted from South Africa's team eight years before because of the country's apartheid policy but was now living in England. Another successful emigrant was Chan Kum Weng, a Featherweight silver-medallist for Malaysia in 1958 and now a winner for his adopted country, Wales.

1970: Louis Martin won the Middle-heavyweight gold for the third time and Precious McKenzie retained the Bantamweight title. Ray Rigby, for Australia, became the first winner of the Super-heavyweight division (over 110kg in bodyweight) which had been introduced to accommodate ever bigger throwers - and was to return for the 1974 Games as a shot-putter, finishing 6th. India and Pakistan also provided medal-winners.

1974: It was like an old boys' reunion in Christchurch. Precious McKenzie won at Flyweight, having twice been Bantamweight champion. George Vasiliades, of Australia, won at Featherweight, having been McKenzie's predecessor as Flyweight champion. George Newton, of England, won again at Lightweight, having also been Featherweight champion in 1962. Another Australian, Nicolo Ciancio, won at Middle-heavyweight, having been Light-heavyweight champion four years earlier. Tony Ebert, of Canada, won at Middleweight, having been 2nd in 1970.

1978: Precious McKenzie became the first man to win four titles in Commonwealth Games weightlifting, and it was as if by Royal Command because the Queen of England had specially requested to be there throughout to watch him do it. Australia and Canada predominated in the heavier weights with five wins between them, and at Heavyweight a Canadian, Russ Prior, was champion for the second time in succession.

1982: England took four titles, Australia three and Wales two, but perhaps the most significant victory was for a Nigerian, Oliver Orok, at Sub-heavyweight. His predecessor as champion at that weight was John Burns, of Wales, who was this time successful at Heavyweight. Dean Lukin, of Australia, had 30kg to spare over his nearest rival at Super-heavyweight, and in 3rd place was the aptly-named Bassey Ironbar, for Nigeria, while two of his team-mates also won bronze. India had silver medals in each of the three lightest weights.

WEIGHTLIFTING

1986: No Nigerians at these Games, so Australia won four golds and Canada, England and Wales two each. Dean Lukin, having been Olympic champion in the interim, won again at Super-heavyweight, and by an even greater margin on this occasion of 45kg. Despite the absence of the boy-cotting countries, winning totals were higher than 1982 in eight of the 10 events.

1990: Separate medals were awarded for the snatch, the jerk and totals, but if the intention was to spread the awards more widely it did not work. Three English lifters, three Indian lifters and two Welsh lifters each won all three gold medals available in their events and only at Featherweight and Middleweight was there any shareout. India, in fact, won 11 gold medals, seven silver and five bronze, which was no doubt encouraging for the further development of the sport there, and neither was there any questioning of the calibre of their team. Their Flyweight champion, Chandersekharan Raghavan, won overall by fully 20kg, but there was a much closer contest at Featherweight, where Marcus Stephen, from the Pacific island of Nauru, finished only 2.5kg behind Parvesh Chander Sharma, of India. Nauru is 8.2 square miles in size (21 sq km) with an estimated population of 9,000 at the time. India is 1,269,346 square miles (3,287,590 sq km) with a population of 844 million.

1994: Different weight levels were introduced and the familiar descrip-tions of events were dropped. Marcus Stephen, benefiting from coaching in Australia, won two more gold medals in the 59kg division, and the Australians with whom he trained picked up 14 wins between them, of which nine went to a quartet of recent arrivals from the Bulgarian and Rumanian national teams. This caused some muttering in other camps that medals were being "bought", but no one apparently thought of objecting to the fact that another Aussie triple winner, Harvey Goodman, had been born in Bolton! For Wales David Morgan won two gold medals in the 76kg class to bring his total of Games golds at three different weights since 1982 to seven.

1998: The one-man team from Nauru took all three gold medals available to him this time. Otherwise, Australia had six golds, Canada five, and England, India and New Zealand three each. In the 69kg event a Malaysian, Muhamad Hidayat Hamidon, won the jerk lift to rekindle memories of those first successes by his fellow-countrymen almost half-a-century before.

WEIGHTLIFTING MEDALLISTS

NOTE: From 1950 to 1970 competitions consisted of three separate lifts - Press, Snatch and Jerk - but since 1974 the Press has been omitted. From 1950 to 1986 medals were awarded for the totals achieved in all or both lifts, as applicable. Since 1990 separate medals have been awarded for each lift and for the totals, as indicated in the results which follow (S Snatch, J Jerk, T Total). Bodyweight categories have been altered twice and have been as follows:

1950-1986: up to 52kg, 56, 60, 67.5, 75, 82.5, 90, 100, 110, over 110.

1994: up to 54kg, 59, 64, 70, 76, 83, 91, 99, 108, over 108.

1998: up to 56kg, 62, 69, 77, 85, 94, 105, over 105.

52kg (Flyweight):
First held 1970

1970: 1 George Vasiliades (Aus) 290kg, 2 Abdul Ghafoor (Pak) 287.5, 3 John McNiven (Sco) 265.

1974: 1 Precious McKenzie (Eng) 215, 2 Anil Mondal (Ind) 200, 3 John McNiven (Sco) 192.5.

1978: 1 Ekambaram Karunakaran (Ind) 205, 2 Charlie Revolta (Sco) 197.5, 3 Roger Crabtree (Aus) 190.

1982: 1 Nick Voukelatos (Aus) 207.5, 2 Grunadan Kambiah (Ind) 200, 3 Lawrence Tom (Nig) 192.5.

1986: 1 Greg Hayman (Aus) 212.5, 2 Charlie Revolta (Sco) 185, 3 Alan Ogilvie (Sco) 177.5.

1990:

S: 1 Chandersekharan Raghavan (Ind) 105, 2 Velu Govindarj (Ind) 95, 3 Greg Hayman (Aus) 90.

J: 1 Chandersekharan Raghavan (Ind) 127.5, 2 Greg Hayman (Aus) 117.5, 3 Velu Govindraj (Ind) 117.5.

T:1 Chandersekharan Raghavan (Ind) 232.5, 2 Velu Govindraj (Ind) 212.5, 3 Greg Hayman (Aus) 207.5.

54kg:
1994:

S: 1 Murgesan Veerasamy (Ind) 105, 2 Badathala Adisekhar (Ind) 105, 3 Francois Lagace (Can) 105.

J: 1 Badathala Adisekhar Ind) 132.5, 2 Matin Guntali (Mal) 130, 3 Murgesan Veerasamy (Ind) 127.5.

T: 1 Badathala Adiskehar (Ind) 237.5, 2 Murgesan Veerasamy (Ind) 232.5, Francois Lagace (Can) 227.5.

WEIGHTLIFTING

56kg (Bantamweight):

1950: 1 Tho Fook Hung (Mal) 297, 2 Rosaire Smith (Can) 279, 3 Keith Caple (Aus) 272.

1954: 1 Maurice Megennis (Eng) 281, 2 Frank Cope (Eng) 276.5, 3 Keith Caple (Aus) 274.

1958: 1 Reg Gaffley (SA) 299, 2 Ronald Brownbill (Eng) 285.5, 3 Marcel Gosselin (Can) 274.

1962: 1 Chua Fung Kim (Sin) 322, 2 Allen Salter (Can) 310.5, 3 Martin Dias (BG) 306.

1966: 1 Precious McKenzie (Eng) 319.5, 2 Martin Dias (Guy) 307, 3 Chon Hon Chan (Can) 304.5.

1970: 1 Precious McKenzie (Eng) 335, 2 Tony Phillips (Bar) 317.5, 3 Chye Hong Tung (Sin) 302.5.

1974: 1 Michael Adams (Aus) 222.5, 2 Yves Carignan (Can) 212.5, 3 Shanmug Velliswamy (Ind) 212.5.

1978: 1 Precious McKenzie (Eng) 220, 2 Tamil Selvan (Ind) 220, 3 Jeffrey Bryce (Wal) 215.

1982: 1 Geoff Laws (Eng) 235, 2 Bijar Kumar Satpathy (Ind) 227.5, 3 Lorenzo Orsini (Aus) 222.5.

1986: 1 Nick Voukelatos (Aus) 245, 2 Clayton Chelley (NZ) 217.5, 3 Teo Yong Joo (Sin) 215.

1990:

S: 1 Rangaswamy Punnuswamy (Ind) 110, 2 Alan Ogilvie (Sco) 107.5, 3 Denis Aumais (Can) 102.5.

J: 1 Rangaswamy Punnuswamy (Ind) 137.5, 2 Gopal Maruthachelam (Ind) 125, 3 Alan Ogilvie (Sco) 122.5.

T:1 Rangaswamy Punnuswamy (Ind) 247.5, 2 Alan Ogilvie (Sco) 230, 3 Gopal Maruthachelam (Ind) 227.5.

56kg:

1998:

S: 1 Mehmet Yagci (Aus) 107.5, 2 Arumagam Pandian (Ind) 107.5, 3 Matin Guntali (Mal) 105.

J: 1 Dharmaraj Wilson (Ind) 140, 2 Arumagam Pandian (Ind) 137.5, 3 Matin Guntali (Mal) 135.

T: 1 Arumagam Pandian (Ind) 245, 2 Dharmaraj Wilson (Ind) 242.5, 3 Matin Guntali (Mal) 240.

59kg:

1994:

S: 1 Marcus Stephen (Nau) 115, 2 Chandersekharan Raghavan (Ind) 110, 3= Ben Devonshire (Eng), Denis Aumais (Can) 107.5.

J: 1 Chandersekharan Raghavan (Ind) 147.5, 2 Marcus Stephen (Nau) 145, 3 Ben Devonshire (Eng) 132.5.

T: 1 Marcus Stephen (Nau) 262.5, 2 Chandersekharan Raghavan (Ind) 255, 3 Denis Aumais (Can) 237.5.

60kg (Featherweight):

1950: 1 Koh Eng Tong (Mal) 310.5, 2 Julian Creus (Eng) 304, 3 Barrie Engelbrecht (SA) 290.

1954: 1 Rodney Wilkes (Tri) 313, 2 Jules Sylvain (Can) 297, 3 Ron Jenkins (Wal) 279.

1958: 1 Tan Ser Cher (Sin) 310.5, 2 Chan Kum Weng (Mal) 306, 3 Rodney Wilkes (Tri) 304.

1962: 1 George Newton (Eng) 326.5, 2 Ieuan Owen (Wal) 292.5, 3 Cheong Kam Hong (Mal) 281.

1966: 1 Chan Kum Weng (Wal) 337, 2 Mahon Ghosh (Ind) 334.5, 3 Allen Salter (Can) 324.5.

Note: Chan Kum Weng competed for Malaya in 1958.

1970: 1 George Perrin (Eng) 342.5, 2 Phung Kim Chua (Sin) 340, 3 Alexander Navis (Ind) 335.

1974: 1 George Vasiliades (Aus) 237.5, 2 Gerald Hay (Aus) 235, 3 Brian Duffy (NZ) 232.5.

1978: 1 Michel Mercier (Can) 237.5, 2 Ivan Katz (Aus) 235, 3 Darrell Schultz (Can) 230.

1982: 1 Dean Willey (Eng) 267.5, 2 Tamil Selvan (Ind) 245, 3 Koon Siang Chua (Sin) 242.5.

1986: 1 Ray Williams (Wal) 252.5, 2 David Lowenstein (Aus) 250, 3 Jeffrey Bryce (Wal) 235.

1990:

S: 1 Marcus Stephen (Nau) 112.5, 2 Parvesh Chander Sharma (Ind) 112.5, 3 Kumarasan Sudalaimani (Ind) 110.

J: 1 Parvesh Chander Sharma (Ind) 145, 2 Marcus Stephen (Nau) 142.5, 3 Kumarasan Sudalaimani (Ind) 142.5.

T:1 Parvesh Chander Sharma (Ind) 257.5, 2 Marcus Stephen (Nau) 255, 3 Kumarasan Sudalaimani (Ind) 252.5.

62kg:

1998:

S: 1 Marcus Stephen (Nau) 125, 2 Yurik Sarkisian (Aus) 125, 3 G. Gnanasekar (Ind) 117.5.

J: 1 Marcus Stephen (Nau) 167.5, 2 Yurik Sarkisian (Aus) 157.5, 3 Marugesan Arun (Ind) 155.

T: 1 Marcus Stephen (Nau) 292.5, 2 Yurik Sarkisian (Aus) 282.5, 3 Marugesan Arun (Ind) 272.5.

64kg:

1994:

S: 1 Najite Ogbogu (Nig) 125, 2 Sevdalin Marinov (Aus) 125, 3 Oliver Toby (Nig) 120.

J: 1 Oliver Toby (Nig) 152.5, 2 Sevdalin Marinov (Aus) 152.5, 3 Najite Ogbogu (Nig) 150.

T: 1 Sevdalin Marinov (Aus) 277.5, 2 Najite Ogbogu (Nig) 275, 3 Oliver Toby (Nig) 272.5.

WEIGHTLIFTING

67.5kg (Lightweight):

1950: 1 Jim Halliday (Eng) 344.5, 2 Thong Saw Pak (Mal) 333, 3 Vern Barberis (Aus) 333.

1954: 1 Vern Barberis (Aus) 347, 2 George Nicholls (Bar) 344.5, 3 Jan Pieterse (SA) 333.

1958: 1 Tan Howe Liang (Sin) 358, 2 Harry Webber (SA) 340, 3 Ben Helfgott (Eng) 340.

1962: 1 Carlton Goring (Eng) 351.5, 2 Alan Oshyer (Aus) 340, 3 Jimmy Moir (Sco) 340.

1966: 1 Hugo Gittens (Tri) 367, 2 George Newton (Eng) 354.5, 3 Ieuan Owen (Wal) 349.5.

1970: 1 George Newton (Eng) 372.5, 2 Ieuan Owen (Wal) 355, 3 Bruce Cameron (NZ) 335.

1974: 1 George Newton (Eng) 260, 2 Ieuan Owen (Wal) 255, 3 Bruce Cameron (NZ) 252.5.

1978: 1 Bill Stellios (Aus) 272.5, 2 Adrian Kebbe (Aus) 267.5, 3 Philip Sue (NZ) 262.5.

1982: 1 David Morgan (Wal) 295, 2 Bill Stellios (Aus) 285, 3 Patrick Bassey (Nig) 277.5.

1986: 1 Dean Willey (Eng) 315, 2 Ron Laycock (Aus) 307.5, 3 Langis Côté (Can) 290.

1990:

S: 1 Paramjit Sharma (Ind) 130, 2 Lawrence Iquaibom (Nig) 130, 3 Mark Blair (Aus) 127.5.

J: 1 Paramjit Sharma (Ind) 165, 2 Lawrence Iquaibom (Nig) 160, 3 Mark Roach (Wal) 155.

T: 1 Paramjit Sharma (Ind) 295, 2 Lawrence Iquaibom (Nig) 290, 3 Mark Roach (Wal) 280.

69kg:

1998:

S: 1 Sebastien Groulx (Can) 130, 2 Stewart Cruikshank (Eng) 130, 3 Tony Morgan (Wal) 130.

J: 1 Muhamad Hidayat Hamidon (Mal) 167.5, 2 Sebastien Groulx (Can) 167.5, 3 G. Vadivelu (Ind) 162.5.

T: 1 Sebastien Groulx (Can) 297.5, 2 Muhamad Hidayat Hamidon (Mal) 295, 3 Sandip Kumar (Ind) 285.

70kg:

1994:

S: 1 Lawal Riliwan (Nig) 132.5, 2 Stewart Cruikshank (Eng) 132.5, 3 Moji Oluwa (Nig) 130.

J: 1 Moji Oluwa (Nig) 165, 2 Satish Rai (Ind) 165, 3 Stewart Cruikshank (Eng) 160.

T: 1 Moji Oluwa (Nig) 295, 2 Satish Rai (Ind) 292.5, 3 Stewart Cruikshank (Eng) 292.5.

75kg (Middleweight):

1950: 1 Gerry Gratton (Can) 360.5, 2 Bruce George (NZ) 335.5, 3 Fred Griffin (Aus) 326.5.

1954: 1 Jim Halliday (Eng) 362.5, 2 Lionel De Freitas (Tri) 342, 3 Julius Park (BG) 338.

1958: 1 Blair Blenman (Bar) 360.5, 2 Winston McArthur (BG) 360.5, 3 Adrien Gilbert (Can) 356.

1962: 1 Tan Howe Liang (Sin) 390, 2 Pierre St Jean (Can) 376, 3 Horace Johnson (Wal) 372.

1966: 1 Pierre St Jean (Can) 404.5, 2 Horace Johnson (Wal) 382, 3 Russell Perry (Aus) 372.

1970: 1 Russell Perry (Aus) 412.5, 2 Tony Ebert (NZ) 402.5, 3 Pierre St Jean (Can) 400.

1974: 1 Tony Ebert (NZ) 275, 2 Stanley Bailey (Tri) 275, 3 Robert Wrench (Wal) 270.

1978: 1 Sam Castiglione (Aus) 300, 2 Newton Burrowes (Eng) 290, 3 Steve Pinsent (Eng) 290.

1982: 1 Steve Pinsent (Eng) 312.5, 2 Tony Pignone (Aus) 305, 3 Jacques Demers (Can) 302.5.

1986: 1 Bill Stellios (Aus) 302.5, 2 Louis Payer (Can) 300, 3 Neil Taylor (Wal) 270.

1990:

S: 1 Ricky Chaplin (Wal) 137.5, 2 Karnadhar Mondal (Ind) 135, 3 Karl Jones (Wal) 135.

J: 1 Ron Laycock (Aus) 177.5, 2 Karnadhar Mondal (Ind) 170, 3 Damian Brown (Aus) 167.5.

T:1 Ron Laycock (Aus) 310, 2 Karnadhar Mondal (Ind) 3205, 3 Benoit Gagné (Can) 292.5.

76kg:

1994:

S: 1 David Morgan (Wal) 147.5, 2 Serge Tremblay (Can) 145, 3 Damian Brown (Aus) 142.5.

J: 1 Damian Brown (Aus) 182.5, 2 David Morgan (Wal) 180, 3 Serge Tremblay (Can) 172.5.

T: 1 David Morgan (Wal) 327.5, 2 Damian Brown (Aus) 325, 3 Serge Tremblay (Can) 317.5.

77kg:

1998:

S: 1 Satheesha Rai (Ind) 147.5, 2 David Morgan (Wal) 145, 3 Damian Brown (Aus) 140.

J: 1 Damian Brown (Aus) 187.5, 2 Satheesha Rai (Ind) 175, 3 Alain Bilodeau (Can) 167.5.

T: 1 Damian Brown (Aus) 327.5, 2 Satheesha Rai (Ind) 322.5, 3 Alain Bilodeau (Can) 305.

WEIGHTLIFTING

82.5kg (Light-Heavyweight):

1950: 1 Jim Varaleau (Can) 369.5, 2 Issy Bloomberg (SA) 369.5, 3 Tan Kim Bee (Mal) 347.

1954: 1 Gerry Gratton (Can) 403.5, 2 Louis Greeff (SA) 367, 3 Bruce George (NZ) 353.5.

1958: 1 Phil Caira (Sco) 396.5, 2 Sylvanus Blackman (Bar) 385.5, 3 Jack Kestell (SA) 385.5.

1962: 1 Phil Caira (Sco) 408, 2 George Manners (Eng) 403.5, 3 Peter Arthur (Wal) 392.

1966: 1 George Vakakis (Aus) 419.5, 2 Sylvanus Blackman (Eng) 414.5, 3 Mike Pearman (Eng) 409.5.

Note: Blackman competed for Barbados in 1958.

1970: 1 Nicolo Ciancio (Aus) 447.5, 2 John Bolton (NZ) 445, 3 Peter Arthur (Wal) 427.5.

1974: 1 Tony Ford (Eng) 302.5, 2 Paul Wallwork (WS) 300, 3 Mike Pearman (Eng) 292.5.

1978: 1 Rob Kabbas (Aus) 322.5, 2 Charles Quagliata (Aus) 287.5, 3 Gary Shadbolt (Eng) 277.5.

1982: 1 Newton Burrowes (Eng) 325, 2 Guy Greavette (Can) 320, 3 Cosmas Idioh (Nig) 317.5.

1986: 1 David Morgan (Wal) 350, 2 Rob Kabbas (Aus) 325, 3 Peter May (Eng) 317.5.

1990:

S: 1 David Morgan (Wal) 155, 2 Muyiwa Odusanya (Nig) 152.5, 3 Sylvain Leblanc (Can) 145.

J: 1 David Morgan (Wal) 192.5, 2 Soronomathu Rampaswamy 182.5, 3 Muyiwa Odusanya (Nig) 180.

T: 1 David Morgan (Wal) 347.5, 2 Muyiwa Odusanya (Nig) 332.5, 3 Andy Callard (Eng) 317.5.

83kg:

1994:

S: 1 Kiril Kounev (Aus) 152.5, 2 Stephen Ward (Eng) 147.5, 3 Jim Dan Corbett (Can) 147.5.

J: 1 Kiril Kounev (Aus) 200, 2 Stephen Ward (Eng) 187.5, 3 Jim Dan Corbett (Can) 182.5.

T: 1 Kiril Kounev (Aus) 352.5, 2 Stephen Ward (Eng) 335, 3 Jim Dan Corbett (Can) 300.

85kg:

1998:

S: 1 Stephen Ward (Eng) 157.5, 2 Leon Griffin (Eng) 155, 3 Matam David (Cam) 147.5.

J: 1 Leon Griffin (Eng) 192.5, 2 Stephen Ward (Eng) 187.5, 3 Matam David (Cam) 180.

T: 1 Leon Griffin (Eng) 347.5, 2 Stephen Ward (Eng) 345, 3 Matam David (Cam) 327.5.

90kg (Middle-Heavyweight):

First held 1954

1954: 1 Keevil Daly (Can) 399, 2 Lennox Kilgour (Tri) 392, 3 Joseph Barnett (Eng) 376.5.

1958: 1 Manny Santos (Aus) 403.5, 2 Tan Kim Bee (Mal) 392, 3 Leonard Treganowan (Aus) 378.5.

1962: 1 Louis Martin (Eng) 469.5, 2 Cosford White (Can) 408, 3 Jackie Samuel (Tri) 399.

1966: 1 Louis Martin (Eng) 462, 2 George Manners (Eng) 429.5, 3 Dudley Lawson (Jam) 422.

1970: 1 Louis Martin (Eng) 457.5, 2 Robert Santavy (Can) 425, 3 George Manners (Eng) 410.

1974: 1 Nicolo Ciancio (Aus) 330, 2 Brian Marsden (NZ) 315, 3 Steve Wyatt (Aus) 310.

1978: 1 Gary Langford (Eng) 335, 2 Terry Hadlow (Can) 330, 3 Brian Marsden (NZ) 312.5.

1982: 1 Rob Kabbas (Aus) 337.5, 2 Peter Pinsent (Eng) 335, 3 Mick Sabljak (Aus) 325.

1986: 1 Keith Boxell (Eng) 350, 2 David Mercer (Eng) 342.5, 3 Guy Greavette (Can) 340.

1990:

S: 1 Duncan Dawkins (Eng) 162.5, 2 Keith Boxell (Eng) 152.5, 3 Harvey Goodman (Aus) 150.

J: 1 Duncan Dawkins (Eng) 195, 2 Keith Boxell (Eng) 192.5, 3 Harvey Goodman (Aus) 190.

T: 1 Duncan Dawkins (Eng) 367.5, 2 Keith Boxell (Eng) 345, 3 Harvey Goodman (Aus) 340.

91kg:

1994:

S: 1 Harvey Goodman (Aus) 162.5, 2 Peter May (Eng) 155, 3 Collins Okoth (Ken) 120.

J: 1 Harvey Goodman (Aus) 200, 2 Peter May (Eng) 190, 3 Collins Okoth (Ken) 120.

T: 1 Harvey Goodman (Aus) 362.5, 2 Peter May (Eng) 345, 3 Collins Okoth (Ken) 240.

94kg:

1998:

S: 1 Kiril Kounev (Aus) 165, 2 Anthony Arthur (Eng) 152.5, 3 Simon Heffernan (Aus) 150.

J: 1 Kiril Kounev (Aus) 205, 2 Andy Callard (Eng) 190, 3 Simon Heffernan (Aus) 185.

T: 1 Kiril Kounev (Aus) 370, 2 Andy Callard (Eng) 340, 3 Simon Heffernan (Aus) 335.

WEIGHTLIFTING

99kg:
1994:

S: 1 Christopher Onyezie (Nig) 155, 2 Andrew Saxton (Aus) 155, 3 Phillip Christou (Aus) 152.5.

J: 1 Andy Callard (Eng) 197.5, 2 Andrew Saxton (Aus) 192.5, 3 Christopher Onyezie (Nig) 190.

T: 1 Andy Callard (Eng) 347.5, 2 Andrew Saxton (Aus) 347.5, 3 Christopher Onyezie (Nig) 345.

100kg (Sub-Heavyweight):
First held 1978

1978: 1 John Burns (Wal) 340, 2 Steve Wyatt (Aus) 325, 3 Robert Santavy (Can) 315.

1982: 1 Oliver Orok (Nig) 350, 2 Gary Langford (Eng) 350, 3 Kevin Roy (Can) 340.

1986: 1 Denis Garon (Can) 360, 2 Duncan Dawkins (Eng) 332.5, 3 Andrew Saxton (Eng) 327.5.

1990:

S: 1 Andrew Saxton (Eng) 165, 2 Peter May (Eng) 145, 3 Guy Greavette (Can) 140.

J: 1 Andrew Saxton (Eng) 197.5, 2 Peter May (Eng) 175, 3 Guy Greavette (Can) 175.

T:1 Andrew Saxton (Eng) 362.5, 2 Peter May (Eng) 320, 3 Guy Greavette (Can) 315. Note: Saxton competed for Australia in 1994.

105kg:
1998:

S: 1 Akos Sandor (Can) 167.5, 2 Tommy Yule (Eng) 160, 3 Nigel Avery (NZ) 155.

J: 1 Akos Sandor (Can) 192.5, 2 Tommy Yule (Eng) 190, 3 Karl Grant (Eng) 187.5.

T: 1 Akos Sandor (Can) 360, 2 Tommy Yule (Eng) 350, 3 Nigel Avery (NZ) 340.

Over 105kg:
1998:

S: 1 Darren Liddel (NZ) 165, 2 Giles Greenwood (Eng) 162.5, 3 Chris Rae (Aus) 160.

J: 1 Darren Liddel (NZ) 203, 2 Jean Bilong (Can) 192.5, 3 Chris Rae (Aus) 192.5.

T: 1 Darren Liddel (NZ) 368, 2 Chris Rae (Aus) 352.5, 3 Giles Greenwood (Eng) 352.5.

108kg:
1994:

S: 1 Steven Kettner (Aus) 165, 2 Stefan Botev (Aus) 160, 3 Victor Edem (Nig) 155.

J: 1 Stefan Botev (Aus) 200, 2 Steven Kettner (Aus) 195, 3 Victor Edem (Nig) 190.

T: 1 Stefan Botev (Aus) 360, 2 Steven Kettner (Aus) 360, 3 Victor Edem (Nig)

345.

Over 108kg:
1994:
S: 1 Nicu Vlad (Aus) 185, 2 Innocent Chika (Nig) 160, 3 Gareth Hives (Wal) 130.
J: 1 Nicu Vlad (Aus) 220, 2 Innocent Chika (Nig) 200, 3 Gareth Hives (Wal) 160.
T: 1 Nicu Vlad (Aus) 405, 2 Innocent Chika (Nig) 360, 3 Gareth Hives (Wal) 290.

110kg (Heavyweight):
1950: 1 Harold Cleghorn (NZ) 408, 2 Ray Magee (Aus) 376.
Note: only two competitors.
1954: 1 Doug Hepburn (Can) 471.5, 2 Dave Baillie (Can) 453.5, 3 Harold Cleghorn (NZ) 421.5.
1958: 1 Ken McDonald (Eng) 455.5, 2 Dave Baillie (Can) 446.5, 3 Arthur Shannos (Aus) 394.5.
1962: 1 Arthur Shannos (Aus) 465, 2 Don Oliver (NZ) 465, 3 Brandon Bailey (Tri) 440.
1966: 1 Don Oliver (NZ) 497, 2 Arthur Shannos (Aus) 464.5, 3 Brandon Bailey (Tri) 462.
1970: 1 Russ Prior (Can) 490, 2 Dave Hancock (Eng) 470, 3 Price Morris (Can) 470.
1974: 1 Russ Prior (Can) 352.5, 2 John Bolton (NZ) 340, 3 John Barrett (NZ) 320.
1978: 1 Russ Prior (Can) 347.5, 2 Wayne Smith (Can) 337.5, 3 Andy Drzwiecki (Eng) 335.
1982: 1 John Burns (Wal) 347.5, 2 Joe Kabalan (Aus) 325, 3 Mario Leblanc (Can) 315.
1986: 1 Kevin Roy (Can) 375. 2 Gino Frantangelo (Aus) 372.5, 3 Andrew Davies (Wal) 370.
1990:
S: 1 Mark Thomas (Eng) 160, 2 Jason Roberts (Aus) 152.5, 3 Steve Wilson (Wal) 152.5.
J: 1 Mark Thomas (Eng) 197.5, 2 Jason Roberts (Aus) 192.5, 3 Aled Arnold (Wal) 187.5.
T:1 Mark Thomas (Eng) 357.5, 2 Jason Roberts (Aus) 345, 3 Aled Arnold (Wal) 335.

Over 110kg (Super-Heavyweight):
First held 1970
1970: 1 Ray Rigby (Aus) 500, 2 Terry Perdue (Wal) 500, 3 Grant Anderson (Sco) 432.5.
1974: 1 Graham May (NZ) 342.5, 2 Andy Kerr (Eng) 337.5, 3 Terry Perdue (Wal) 330.
1978: 1 Jean-Marc Cardinal (Can) 365, 2 Bob Edmond (Aus) 322.5, 3 John Hynd (Sco) 305.
1982: 1 Dean Lukin (Aus) 377.5, 2 Bob Edmond (Aus) 347.5, 3 Bassey Ironbar (Nig) 320.
1986: 1 Dean Lukin (Aus) 392.5, 2 David Bolduc (Can) 347.5, 3 Charles

Garzarella (Aus) 342.5.

1990:

S: 1 Andrew Davies (Wal) 180, 2 Aduche Ojadi (Nig) 177.5, 3 Steven Kettner (Aus) 172.5.

J: 1 Andrew Davies (Wal) 222.5, 2 Aduche Ojadi (Nig) 222.5, 3 Steven Kettner (Aus) 205.

T: 1 Andrew Davies (Wal) 402.5, 2 Aduche Ojadi (Nig) 400, 3 Steven Kettner (Aus) 377.5.

WRESTLING

Was the prodigy on the mat really as young as 12?

With a documented history stretching back to the Ancient Olympics of 704BC, wrestling was a natural choice for the traditionalist-minded organisers as one of the sports at the first Empire Games of 1930. From the outset the freestyle form - rather than the Greco-Roman style, where use of the legs to eliminate an opponent is not allowed - was the chosen discipline, and wrestling has survived in the Games ever since with only two recent exceptions.

It is perhaps surprising that it has done so because its foothold - in the figurative sense - was for many years no more than a precarious one. In Hamilton, Ontario, in 1930 there were only sufficient competitors to award all three medals in one of the seven weights, and in five straight finals English visitors lost to Canadian hosts. At Featherweight the Canadian, Cliff Chilcott, became one of the first and least taxed of Empire champions, as no one else was entered in his event.

WRESTLING

As Canada won all seven titles, the sport's inclusion might in hindsight have been dismissed as self-indulgence and it could then have been quietly dropped from future programmes, but the standard of competition was high, despite the limited numbers, and it was not until 1990 and again in 1998 that wrestling was excluded. With multiple successes for the mighty Asian powers of India and Pakistan over the years, and with an established North of England legacy in the sport to support it, wrestling has returned to the schedule for the Manchester Games

Leading countries:

Canada 49 gold medals; India 20; Pakistan 18; Australia 13; South Africa 12; England 4; New Zealand 3; Nigeria, Scotland 1 each.

Leading gold-medallists:

3 Dick Garrard (Aus) 1934-50, Muhammad Akhtar (Pak) 1958-66, Muhammad Bashir (Pak) 1958-66, Muhammad Faiz (Pak) 1962-70.

Highlights - Games by Games

1930: Canada and England fought out what was, in effect, an international match between the two countries, and the hosts won the series of bouts 5-0 and took the two other titles, with only a lone South African otherwise earning a medal. Canada's supremacy was not unexpected because they had won three freestyle medals at the 1928 Olympics and their Bantamweight bronze medallist in Amsterdam, James Trifunov, won at that weight in Hamilton.

1934: The spoils were much more evenly shared. Canada was again the leading nation, with three winners, but Australia had two and Scotland and South Africa one each. Joseph Schleimer, Canada's Welterweight champion, was to be the bronze-medallist at the 1936 Olympics, but the competitor who attracted probably the greatest attention was the Scottish Heavyweight bronze-medallist, Archie Dudgeon, who weighed 21st 7lb (139kg) and was apparently nicknamed "The Loch Ness Monster" !

1938: With 26 entries at seven weights there were only five competitors who did not come away with medals. Three men won gold for the second time: Dick Garrard (Australia) at Lightweight, Terry Evans (Canada) at Middleweight, and Jack Knight (also Australia) at Heavyweight. Another of the six Australian winners, Eddie Scarf, had been an Olympic bronze-medallist in Los Angeles six years earlier.

1950: Dick Garrard returned at the age of 41 to win his third Empire title in 16 years, but it was no surprise as he had been Olympic silver-medallist at Welterweight in 1948. According to the reporter for "The New Zealand Sportsman", Garrard "towered head and shoulders over the remainder as a wrestler of World class". The veteran Australian was also fondly described as being "a trifle battered looking", but neither was this much of a surprise. He had already contested 471 bouts and lost only nine. New Zealand's first choice in Garrard's weight class was dropped at the last minute by his team management for "insubordination", but Garrard beat him as well in an unofficial Sunday morning encounter.

1954: The South African wrestlers in Vancouver deserve consideration as the most successful team in Games history. There were six of them -at every weight except Bantamweight and Heavyweight - and all six won gold medals. The 1952 Olympic bronze medallist at heavyweight, Ken Richmond, defeated his only opponent to win England's solitary title. Richmond later gained permanent celebrity status as the man who appeared on screen before every J. Arthur Rank film, beating the massive gong which was the company's trademark introduction. Dick Garrard made his fourth Games appearance at 45 but lost twice to take bronze and bring his career (now totalling 525 bouts) to a close. He obviously thrived on a competitive life because at the age of 91 he was to make a guest appearance at the 2000 Olympics in Sydney.

1958: South Africa's supremacy was strongly challenged by Pakistan and the two countries shared all but one of the eight golds between them and won 14 of the 24 medals. Abe Geldenhuys and Jacob Theron took their second successive titles. Australia won only two bronze medals and a silver and England only two bronzes.

1962: Pakistan exceeded even the 1954 South African team in their medal haul. Pakistanis appeared in all eight finals and lost only at Light-heavyweight to England's Tony Buck. Muhammad Akhtar and Muhammad Bashir, who had both been 1960 Olympic bronze-medallists, won their second Games titles.

1966: Pakistan sent much the same team of wrestlers as they had four years previously, and Muhammad Akhtar won his third title at three different weights; Muhammad Bashir won his third successive title at the same weight; and Muhammad Faiz won his second successive title. Yet Pakistan's total of four wins was only one more than that of neighbour-

ing India, and the lone break in the Asian monopoly was achieved by Canada's Robert Chamberot at Light-heavyweight - an event which neither Pakistan nor India had ever won in Games history.

1970: The introduction of Light-flyweight at one end of the scale and Super-heavyweight at the other increased the wrestling programme to 10 events, and it was at Light-flyweight that the greatest sensation was caused. It was not so much the agility and subtle skills of India's winner, Ved Prakash, which caught the attention of the press and public as the fact that he was officially said to be 14 years old - and there were confident claims from some Indian sources that he was only 12 ! There was even question of whether he would be allowed to compete at all because of his youthfulness. India won five gold medals and Pakistan four, but the best either country had achieved at any weight at the 1968 Olympics was 6th place.

1974: Again two countries shared nine gold medals, but there was no entry from politically-divided Pakistan and it was Canada who predominated with five titles to India's four. The remaining gold, at Middleweight, went to David Aspin, who was New Zealand's first Games champion in wrestling for 24 years.

1978: Canadians won six of the 10 titles, India three and Australia one. Sudesh Kumar, twice Flyweight champion for India, lost this time to Ray Takahashi, of Canada, and six of the finals were Canada v India contests. The Lightweight decider was the only one in which neither country was represented and Zsigmund Kelevitz won Australia's first wrestling gold for 24 years as England's Joe Gilligan lost his second successive final.

1982: The gold-medal tally was narrowly in Canada's favour over India - five to four. The one other winner was Brian Aspen, from a renowned wrestling family, winning what was only England's third title in the sport at the Games. The Canadians, Richard Deschatelets and Wayne Wishart, and the Indian, Rajinder Singh, were all winners for a second time.

1986: No India, no Pakistan. So Canada had a field day but didn't quite take all ten wickets. Doug Cox, their Light-heavyweight, must have felt himself to be the odd man out on the long flight home because he was the only Canadian who failed to win gold, losing in the final to England's Noel Loban. At Middleweight Chris Rinke beat Australia's Wally Koenig in the final, as he had done in 1982, and in the process Koenig set an unenviable record. It was the fourth consecutive Games at which he had been a silver-medallist.

1994: The Canadian hosts, as anticipated, brought wrestling back after it had missed out in 1990 and were rewarded with nine gold medals, but even if the constant repetition of the strains of "O Canada" at the medal ceremonies might have become a trifle wearing, there was a satisfying spread of other medals elsewhere. The one remaining gold went, significantly, to a Nigerian, Jacob Isaac, at Light-flyweight. Nigerians also won two silvers and a bronze, while India won two silvers and three bronzes, and Pakistan returned to the fold with two bronzes. There was also a first-ever wrestling medal for Cyprus.

WRESTLING MEDALLISTS

Light-Flyweight (48kg):
First held 1970
1970: 1 Ved Prakash (Ind), 2 Ken Shand (Can), 3 Masih Sadiq (Pak), Don Urquhart (Sco).
1974: 1 Mitchell Kawasaki (Can), 2 Wally Koenig (Aus), 3 Radhey Shyam (Ind).
1978: 1 Ashok Kumar (Ind), 2 George Gunouski (Can), 3 Mark Dunbar (Eng).
1982: 1 Ram Chander Sarang (Ind), 2 Steve Reinsfield (NZ), 3 Maldwyn Cooper (Can).
1986: 1 Ron Moncur (Can), 2 Duncan Burns (Eng), 3 David Connelly (Sco).
1990: Not held.
1994: 1 Jacob Isaac (Nig), 2 Paul Ragusa (Can), 3 Ramesh Kumar (Ind).
1998: Not held.

Flyweight (52kg):
First held 1950
1950: 1 Bert Harris (Aus), 2 Eric Matthews (NZ). Note: only two competitors
1954: 1 Louis Baise (SA), 2 Fred Flannery (Aus), 3 Muhammad Din (Pak).
1958: 1 Ian Epton (SA), 2 Shujah-ud-Din (Pak), 3 Fred Flannery (Aus).
1962: 1 Muhammad Niaz (Pak), 2 Peter Michienzi (Can), 3 Warren Nisbet (NZ).
1966: 1 Muhammad Nazir (Pak), 2 Shamrao Sable (Ind), 3 Peter Michienzi (Can).
1970: 1 Sudesh Kumar (Ind), 2 Muhammad Nazir (Pak), 3 David Stitt (Can).
1974: 1 Sudesh Kumar (Ind), 2 Gordon Bertie (Can), 3 John Navie (Aus).
1978: 1 Ray Takahashi (Can), 2 Sudesh Kumar (Ind), 3 Ken Hoyt (Aus).
1982: 1 Mahabir Singh (Ind), 2 Ray Takahashi (Can), 3 Ken Hoyt (Aus).
1986: 1 Charles Woodcroft (Can), 2 James McAlary (Aus), 3 Nigel Donahue (Eng).
1990: Not held.
1994: 1 Selwyn Tam (Can), 2 Andrew Hutchinson (Eng), 3 Kirpa Shankar (Ind).
1998: Not held.

WRESTLING

Bantamweight (57kg):

1930: 1 James Trifunov (Can), 2 Joseph Reid (Eng). Note: only two competitors.

1934: 1 Edward Melrose (Sco), 2 Ted McKinley (Can), 3 Joseph Reid (Eng).

1938: 1 Ted Purcell (Aus), 2 Vernon Blake (Can), 3 Raymond Cazaux (Eng).

1950: 1 Douglas Mudgeway (NZ), 2 Jim Chapman (Aus).
Note: only two competitors.

1954: 1 Geoff Jameson (Aus), 2 Muhammad Amin (Pak), 3 Ian Epton (NR).
Note: Epton competed for South Africa at Flyweight in 1958.

1958: 1 Muhammad Akhtar (Pak), 2 Geoff Jameson (Aus), 3 Daniel van der Walt (SA).

1962: 1 Siraj-ud-Din (Pak), 2 Walter Pilling (Eng), 3 James Turnbull (Sco).

1966: 1 Bishamber Singh (Ind), 2 Kevin McGrath (Aus), 3 Muhammad Saeed (Pak).

1970: 1 Muhammad Sardar (Pak), 2 Herbert Singerman (Can), 3 Terence Robinson (Eng).

1974: 1 Prem Nath (Ind), 2 Amrik Singh (Eng), 3 Kevin Burke (Aus).

1978: 1 Satbir Singh (Ind), 2 Michael Barry (Can), 3 Amrik Singh (Eng).

1982: 1 Brian Aspen (Eng), 2 Ashok Kumar (Ind), 3 Chris Maddock (NZ).

1986: 1 Mitch Ostberg (Can), 2 Steve Reinsfield (NZ), 3 Brian Aspen (Eng).

1990: Not held.

1994: 1 Robert Dawson (Can), 2 Ashok Kumar (Ind), 3 Cory O'Brien (Aus).

1998: Not held.

Featherweight (62kg):

1930: 1 Cliff Chilcott (Can). Note: only one competitor.

1934: 1 Robert McNab (Can), 2 Joe Nelson (Eng), 3 Murdoch White (Sco).

1938: 1 Roy Purchase (Aus), 2 Larry Clarke (Can), 3 Joseph Genet (NZ).

1950: 1 John Armitt (NZ), 2 Roland Milord (Can), 3 Arnold Parsons (Eng).

1954: 1 Abe Geldenhuys (SA), 2 Herb Hall (Eng), 3 John Armitt (NZ).

1958: 1 Abe Geldenhuys (SA), 2 Siraj-ud-Din (Pak), 3 Albert Aspen (Eng).

1962: 1 Ala-ud-Din (Pak), 2 Matti Jutila (Can), 3 Albert Aspen (Eng).

1966: 1 Muhammad Akhtar (Pak), 2 Randhawa Singh (Ind), 3 Albert Aspen (Eng).

1970: 1 Muhammad Saeed (Pak), 2 Patrick Bolger (Can), 3 Randhawa Singh (Ind).

1974: 1 Egon Beiler (Can), 2 Shivaji Chingle (Ind), 3 Ray Brown (Aus).

1978: 1 Egon Beiler (Can), 2 Jagminder Singh (Ind), 3 Brian Aspen (Eng).

1982: 1 Bob Robinson (Can), 2 Chris Brown (Aus), 3 Austin Atasie (Nig).

1986: 1 Paul Hughes (Can), 2 Dan Cumming (Aus), 3 Stephen Bell (NZ).

1990: Not held.

1994: 1 Marty Calder (Can), 2 John Melling (Eng), 3 Aroutioun Barseguian (Cyp).

1998: Not held.

Lightweight (68kg):

1930: 1 Howard Thomas (Can), 2 Harold Angus (Eng).
Note: only two competitors.

1934: 1 Dick Garrard (Aus), 2 G.E. North (Eng), 3 Howard Thomas (Can).

1938: 1 Dick Garrard (Aus), 2 Vernon Thomas (NZ), 3 Alfred Harding (SA).

1950: 1 Dick Garrard (Aus), 2 Morgan Plumb (Can), 3 George Hobson (NZ).

1954: 1 Godfrey Pienaar (SA), 2 Ruby Leibovitch (Can), 3 Dick Garrard (Aus).
1958: 1 Muhammad Ashraf (Pak), 2 Alastair Duncan (Sco), 3 Anthony Ries (SA).
1962: 1 Muhammad Akhtar (Pak), 2 Sid Marsh (Aus), 3 Kurt Boese (Can).
1966: 1 Mukhtiar Singh (Ind), 2 Ray Lougheed (Can), 3 Anthony Greig (NZ).
1970: 1 Udey Chand (Ind), 2 Muhammad Yaqub (Pak), 3 Ole Sorensen (Can).
1974: 1 Jagrup Singh (Ind), 2 Joe Gilligan (Eng), 3 Stephen Martin (Can).
1978: 1 Zsigmund Kelevitz (Aus), 2 Joe Gilligan (Eng), 3 Jagdish Kumar (Ind).
1982: 1 Jagminder Singh (Ind), 2 Zsigmund Kelevitz (Aus), 3 Lloyd Renken (Can).
1986: 1 Dave McKay (Can), 2 Zsigmund Kelevitz (Aus), 3 Stephen Cooper (Eng).
1990: Not held.
1994: 1 Chris Wilson (Can), 2 Ibo Oziti (Nig), 3 Muhammad Umar (Pak).
1998: Not held.

Welterweight (74kg):

1930: 1 Reg Priestley (Can), 2 Harry Johnson (Eng).
Note: only two competitors.
1934: 1 Joseph Schleimer (Can), 2 William Fox (Eng), 3 Rashid Anwar (Ind).
1938: 1 Tom Trevaskis (Aus), 2 Felix Standen (SA), 3 Jeremiah Podjursky (NZ).
1950: 1 Henry Hudson (Can), 2 Jack Little (Aus), 3 Martin Jooste (SA).
1954: 1 Nick Loubscher (SA), 2 Abdul Rashid (Pak), 3 Ray Myland (Eng).
1958: 1 Muhammad Bashir (Pak), 2 Lachmi Kant Pandey (Ind), 3 Coenraad de Villers (SA).
1962: 1 Muhammad Bashir (Pak), 2 Philip Oberlander (Can), 3 Len Allen (Eng).
1966: 1 Muhammad Bashir (Pak), 2 Richard Bryant (Can), 3 Hukum Singh (Ind).
1970: 1 Mukhtiar Singh (Ind), 2 Alfred Wurr (Can), 3 Gordon Mackay (NZ).
1974: 1 Raghunath Pawar (Ind), 2 Tony Shacklady (Eng), 3 Gordon Mackay (NZ).
1978: 1 Rajinder Singh (Ind), 2 Victor Zilberman (Can), 3 Keith Howard (Eng).
1982: 1 Rajinder Singh (Ind), 2 Ken Reinsfield (NZ), 3 Brian Renken (Can).
1986: 1 Gary Holmes (Can), 2 George Marsh (Aus), 3 Fitzlloyd Walker (Eng).
1990: Not held.
1994: 1 David Hohl (Can), 2 Reinold Ozoline (Aus), 3 Calum McNeil (Sco).
1998: Not held.

Middleweight (82kg):

1930: 1 Mike Chepwick (Can), 2 Stanley Bissell (Eng), 3 Max Thiel (SA).
1934: 1 Terry Evans (Can), 2 Stanley Bissell (Eng), 3 Robert Harcus (Sco).
1938: 1 Terry Evans (Can), 2 Peter Sheasby (SA), 3 Leslie Jeffers (Eng).
1950: 1 Maurice Vachon (Can), 2 Bruce Arthur (Aus), 3 Carel Reitz (SA).
1954: 1 Hermanus van Zyl (SA), 2 Jim Christie (Can), 3 Harry Kendall (Eng).
1958: 1 Hermanus van Zyl (SA), 2 George Farquhar (Sco), 3 Ray Myland (Eng).
1962: 1 Muhammad Faiz (Pak), 2 Michael Benarik (Aus), 3 Frederick Thomas (NZ).
1966: 1 Muhammad Faiz (Pak), 2 Sebastien Donison (Can), 3 Michael Benarik (Aus).
1970: 1 Harish Rajindra (Ind), 2 Nick Schori (Can), 3 David Aspin (NZ) & Ron Grinstead (Eng).
1974: 1 David Aspin (NZ), 2 Satpal Singh (Ind), 3 Taras Hryb (Can).
1978: 1 Richard Deschatelets (Can), 2 Wally Koenig (Aus), 3 Tony Shacklady

(Eng).

1982: 1 Chris Rinke (Can), 2 Wally Koenig (Aus), 3 Jai Parkash Kangar (Ind).

1986: 1 Chris Rinke (Can), 2 Wally Koenig (Aus), 3 Anthony Bell (Eng).

1990: Not held.

1994: 1 Justin Abdou (Can), 2 Randhir Singh (Ind), 3 Muhammad Bhola (Pak).

1998: Not held.

Light-Heavyweight (90kg):

1930: 1 Bill McIntyre (Can), 2 Edgar Bacon (Eng).

Note: only two competitors.

1934: 1 Mick Cubbin (SA), 2 Bernard Rowe (Eng), 3 Alex Watt (Can).

1938: 1 Eddie Scarf (Aus), 2 Sidney Greenspan (SA), 3 Thomas Ward (Sco).

1950: 1 Patrick Morton (SA), 2 Arthur Sneddon (NZ), 3 Tom Trevaskis (Aus).

1954: 1 Jacob Theron (SA), 2 Bob Steckle (Can), 3 Dan van Staden (NR).

1958: 1 Jacob Theron (SA), 2 Muhammad Ali (Pak), 3 Bob Steckle (Can).

1962: 1 Tony Buck (Eng), 2 Muhammad Saeed (Pak), 3 Jim Armstrong (Aus).

1966: 1 Robert Chamberot (Can), 2 Wallace Booth (Sco), 3 Bishwanath Singh (Ind).

1970: 1 Muhammad Faiz (Pak), 2 Sajjan Singh (Ind), 3 Claude Pilon (Can).

1974: 1 Terry Paice (Can), 2 Netra Pal Singh (Ind), 3 Maurice Allan (Sco).

1978: 1 Stephen Danier (Can), 2 Mick Pikos (Aus), 3 Kartar Singh (Ind).

1982: 1 Clark Davis (Can), 2 Kartar Singh (Ind), 3 Nigel Sargeant (NZ).

1986: 1 Noel Loban (Eng), 2 Doug Cox (Can), 3 Graeme English (Sco).

1990: Not held.

1994: 1 Scott Bianco (Can), 2 Kodei Victor (Nig), 3 Graeme English (Sco).

1998: Not held.

Heavyweight (100kg):

1930: 1 Earl McCready (Can), 2 Alex Sanguine (Eng).

Note: only two competitors.

1934: 1 Jack Knight (Aus), 2 Pat Meehan (Can), 3 Archie Dudgeon (Sco).

1938: 1 Jack Knight (Aus), 2 James Dryden (NZ), 3 John Whelan (Can).

1950: 1 Jim Armstrong (Aus), 2 Pat O'Connor (NZ), 3 Ken Richmond (Eng).

1954: 1 Ken Richmond (Eng), 2 Keith Maltman (Can).

Note: only two competitors.

1958: 1 Lila Ram (Ind), 2 Jacobus Hanekom (SA), 3 Ray Mitchell (Aus).

1962: 1 Muhammad Niaz (Pak), 2 Ray Mitchell (Aus), 3 Denis McNamara (Eng).

1966: 1 Bhim Singh (Ind), 2 Ikram Ilahi (Pak), 3 Denis McNamara (Eng).

1970: 1 Edward Millard (Can), 2 Bishwanath Singh (Ind), 3 Muhammad Riaz (Pak).

1974: 1 Claude Pilon (Can), 2 Dadu Chaugule (Ind), 3 Ian Duncan (Sco).

1978: 1 Wyatt Wishart (Can), 2 Satpal Singh (Ind), 3 Murray Avery (NZ).

1982: 1 Richard Deschatelets (Can), 2 Satpal Singh (Ind), 3 Murray Avery (NZ).

1986: 1 Clark Davis (Can), 2 Robert Algie (NZ), 3 David Kilpin (Eng).

1990: Not held.

1994: 1 Greg Edgelow (Can), 2 Noel Loban (Eng), 3 Subhash Verma (Ind).

1998: Not held.

Super-Heavyweight (Over 100kg):

First held 1970

1970: 1 Ikram Ilahi (Pak), 2 Maruti Mane (Ind), 3 Denis McNamara (Eng).

1974: 1 Bill Benko (Can), 2 Bishwanath Singh (Ind), 3 Gary Knight (NZ).

1978: 1 Robert Gibbons (Can), 2 Albert Patrick (Sco), 3 Ishwar Singh (Ind).

1982: 1 Wyatt Wishart (Can), 2 Rajinder Singh (Ind), 3 Albert Patrick (Sco).

1986: 1 Wayne Brightwell (Can), 2 Albert Patrick (Sco), 3 Keith Peache (Eng).

1990: Not held.

1994: 1 Andrew Borodow (Can), 2 Bidei Jackon (Nig), 3 Amerjit Singh (Eng).

1998: Not held.

SPORTS PREVIOUSLY PART OF THE COMMONWEALTH GAMES

ARCHERY

Neroli makes history with her wheelchair win

The governing body for archery in Great Britain can claim a long history, scarcely matched in any other sport. The Grand National Archery Society was set up in 1861 and had itself grown out of a self-appointed committee which had organised the first nationwide meeting 17 years before. In terms of equality of the sexes archery's credentials are impeccable because ladies' competition had already begun in 1845.

Archery events were held at the Olympic Games as early as 1900, and at the 1908 Games in London British women took all three medals, with Sybil "Queenie" Newall winning at the age of 53 from Charlotte "Lottie" Dod, who had also been Wimbledon tennis champion at the age of 15 and English ladies' golf champion. The sport then fell out of Olympic favour until 1972, by which time the USA and subsequently South Korea had become the World's leading exponents. The one and only appearance of archery at the Commonwealth Games was in 1982.

Transitory as archery's existence was as a Commonwealth Games sport, it provided one result which remains of momentous significance. The women's event was won by 38-year-old Neroli Fairhall, of New Zealand, who was wheelchair-bound, having been disabled by a motorcycle accident 13 years earlier. Not only that but both Fairhall and the 17-year-old silver-medallist from Northern Ireland, Janet Yates, finished with the same score of 2373 and the gold medal was decided, aptly enough, by the greater number of inner golds hit on the target.

The men's title went by a rather more comfortable margin to England's Mark Blenkarne, who had placed 4th at the 1980 Olympics, and Roger LeMay, of Canada, took the silver to add to the bronze won by his wife, Lucille. Altogether, there were 11 nations represented, and with wins at World Championship and Olympic level for Australian archers in the years since it may be that archery may yet be revived at the Commonwealth Games.

ARCHERY MEDALLISTS

MEN

1982: 1 Mark Blenkarne (Eng) 2446, 2 Roger LeMay (Can) 2426, 3 Michael Coen (Aus) 2411.

WOMEN
1982: 1 Neroli Fairhall (NZ) 2373, 2 Janet Yates (NI) 2373, 3 Lucille LeMay (Can) 2349.

CRICKET

Woolmer's men win, but it's a short Games innings

The inclusion of cricket, hockey, netball and rugby union in the 1998 Commonwealth Games caused some raised eyebrows, but there was no real reason why they should not have been brought in. Admittedly, team sports as such had not formed part of the programme before then, but there had been plenty of examples of team events incorporated into other sports.

Badminton, bowls, cycling, fencing, gymnastics, shooting, squash and rowing had all featured team competitions of two-a-side or more, and if the relay events in athletics and swimming are also taken into consideration there are very few exclusively individual sports left - archery, boxing, judo, weightlifting, wrestling - which have been held at the Games at some time or another.

Cricket was perhaps the oddest choice for Kuala Lumpur as there was no great feeling for the game in the country, but at least half-a-dozen of the 16 countries entered were potential winners of the 11-day tournament, and fresh memories of Sri Lanka taking the 1995 World Cup as 66-1 outsiders added zest to the proceedings. One notable absentee was England, whose administrators decided it was a difficult time of the year to find a truly representative team.

It has to be said that the attendances - in sharp contrast to hockey and the rugby seven-a-aide tournament - were disappointingly sparse, but the level of play was highly competitive. The South African team was coached by former England bowler Bob Woolmer and caused something of an upset by beating Australia in the final. Perhaps surprisingly, considering the Test match tradition at Old Trafford, cricket does not figure on the Manchester 2002 programme but will presumably return when the Games go to Australia in 2006.

CRICKET MEDALLISTS

First held in 1998

1998: 1 South Africa (Paul Adams, Dale Benkenstein, Nicky Boje, Mark Boucher, Derek Crookes, Alan Dawson, Steve Elworthy, Herschelle Gibbs, Andrew Hudson, Jacques Kallis, Makhaya Ntini, Shaun Pollock, Mike Rindel, Henry Williams),
2 Australia (Michael Bevan, Andy Bichel, Damien Fleming, Adam Gilchrist, Brendon Julian, Michael Kasprowicz, Darren Lehmann, Damien Martyn, Tom Moody, Ricky Ponting, Gavin Robertson, Mark Waugh, Steve Waugh, Brad Young),
3 New Zealand (Geoff Allott, Nathan Astle, Mark Bailey, Matthew Bell, Chris Drum, Stephen Fleming, Chris Harris, Matthew Horne, Craig McMillan, Dion Nash, Shayne O'Connor, Adam Parore, Daniel Vettori, Paul Wiseman).

Results:

Final: South Africa (184-6) beat Australia (183) by four wickets.
Third-place playoff: New Zealand (212-7) beat Sri Lanka (161) by 51 runs.
Semi-finals: Australia (62-1) beat New Zealand (58) by nine wickets, South Africa (131-9) beat Sri Lanka (130) by one wicket.

FENCING

The Paul family make their point
- and make it often

The most ancient and elegant art of swordsmanship had first been recorded in Egypt in 1360 BC and the modern version was a fixture at the Commonwealth Games for 20 years from 1950 to 1970 but has not appeared since, and there seems little likelihood that it will return. For right or wrong, it would now be regarded as an "establishment" sport with not much of a look-in for the vast majority of countries.

The bare facts of those two decades of Commonwealth competition certainly on the face of it justify this view. Englishmen have won 14 of the 18 individual titles at foil, sabre and epee and 16 of the 18 team titles. Australia won three gold medals in total, Scotland two and Canada one. Other than the English, the only male fencers to win as individuals were Sandy Leckie, of Scotland, and Ivan Lund, of Australia.

Women's events were held only for the foil weapon - for individuals from 1950 and for teams in 1966 and 1970 - and the story is virtually the same. England won all of the eight titles except the individual in 1962 when Melody Coleman, of New Zealand, briefly broke the sequence. The best known of the champions was Gillian Sheen, whose gold in 1958 came two years after a famously unexpected Olympic victory, and other Englishwomen, Mary Glen-Haig and Janet Wardell-Yerburgh, each won two individual foil titles. Having beaten an 18-year-old Australian, Marion Exelby, in the 1970 final with the prospect of no more Games competition to come in her favoured sport, 30-year-old Ms Wardell-Yerburgh declared that she would take up badminton instead.

The standard was comparably high in the men's events because Bill Hoskyns won the World epee title in 1958 and Allan Jay the World foil title the next year. England's leading fencers collected a treasure trove of medals between them, though it was actually the Australian, Ivan Lund, who won more than anyone else, with 13. A remarkable family record was set by René Paul and his brother, Raymond, to be followed by René's sons, Barry and Graham, who between them won 18 medals, including 13 gold, while Raymond's wife, June (nee Foulds), was an athletics gold-medallist in her own right - in the 4 x 110 yards relay in 1958.

Leading countries:

England 37 gold medals; Australia 3; Scotland 2; Canada, New Zealand 1 each.

Leading gold-medallists:

Bill Hoskyns (Eng) 9 (4 individual, 5 team) 1958-70, Allan Jay (Aus/Eng) 8 (1 individual, 7 team) 1950-66, Ralph Cooperman (Eng) 7 (2 individual, 5 team) 1962-66, René Paul (Eng) 7 (2 individual, 5 team) 1950-58, Janet Wardell-Yerburgh (Eng) 4 (2 individual, 2 team) 1966-70.

Highlights - Games by Games

1950: English fencers won all four individual titles and two of the three team events. The only set of gold medals which eluded them was in the team epee, where they were beaten by an Australian trio which included Allan Jay, who was go on to many more successes - for England. Fencing "proved such a success", according to the official report in "The New Zealand Sportsman" magazine, "that hopes have been expressed that this fast and spectacular sport will become a permanent part of future Empire Games carnivals".

1954: René Paul and Mary Glen-Haig repeated their individual foil wins for England and the former also won gold (with Allan Jay as one of his team-mates) in both team foil and team epee, but an Australian, Ivan Lund, took the individual epee and Canada won the team sabre. Paul was commended for his "whiplike precision and solid technique" in the official games report, "and won rounds of applause not only for his fencing but for his sportsmanship".

1958: Seven golds out of seven for England. Raymond Paul succeeded his brother in the foil and Bill Hoskyns won the other two individual events and was in two winning teams. Gillian Sheen, who had won the Olympic title two years before, took the women's foil. The Jamaican hosts bravely entered everything and had a finalist in the individual sabre.

1962: England's defences were penetrated at last in the intense Western Australian heat as three of the individual titles went elsewhere - to Sandy Leckie for Scotland, Ivan Lund for Australia, and Melody ("Dot") Coleman for New Zealand. In the women's foil England even failed to win a medal of any kind.

1966: Normal service was resumed. Eight events (including the newly-introduced women's team foil) ... eight English wins. Bill Hoskyns won three gold medals and the next generation of the Paul family entered the reckoning with a share in the men's team foil success.

1970: Fencing's final thrust. England won everything except the individual sabre which went to local hero Sandy Leckie. Janet Wardell-Yerburgh completed a perfect record - two individual wins and two team wins in two Games.

FENCING MEDALLISTS

MEN

Individual Foil:
1950: 1 René Paul (Eng), 2 John Fethers (Aus), 3 George Pouliot (Can).
1954: 1 René Paul (Eng), 2 John Fethers (Aus), 3 Allan Jay (Eng).
1958: 1 Raymond Paul (Eng), 2 Ivan Lund (Aus), 3 René Paul (Eng).
1962: 1 Sandy Leckie (Sco), 2 Allan Jay (Eng), 3 Ralph Cooperman (Eng).
1966: 1 Allan Jay (Eng), 2 Bill Hoskyns (Eng), 3 Graham Paul (Eng).
1970: 1 Mike Breckin (Eng), 2 Barry Paul (Eng), 3 Graham Paul (Eng).

Individual Epee:

1950: 1 Charles-Louis de Beaumont (Eng), 2 Robert Anderson (Eng), 3 Ivan Lund (Aus).

1954: 1 Ivan Lund (Aus), 2 René Paul (Eng), 3 Carl Schwende (Can).

1958: 1 Bill Hoskyns (Eng), 2 Mike Howard (Eng), 3 Allan Jay (Eng).

1962: 1 Ivan Lund (Aus), 2 John Pelling (Eng), 3 Peter Jacobs (Eng).

1966: 1 Bill Hoskyns (Eng), 2 John Pelling (Eng), 3 Robert Reynolds (Wal).

1970: 1 Bill Hoskyns (Eng), 2 Lester Wong (Can), 3 Peter Jacobs (Eng).

Individual Sabre:

1950: 1 Arthur Pilbrow (Eng), 2 Robert Anderson (Eng), 3 George Pouliot (Can).

1954: 1 Mike Amberg (Eng), 2 Ralph Cooperman (Eng), 3 John Fethers (Aus).

1958: 1 Bill Hoskyns (Eng), 2 Ralph Cooperman (Eng), 3 Mike Amberg (Eng).

1962: 1 Ralph Cooperman (Eng), 2 Benedek Simo (Can), 3 John Andru (Can).

1966: 1 Ralph Cooperman (Eng), 2 Sandy Leckie (Sco), 3 Gabor Arato (Aus).

1970: 1 Sandy Leckie (Sco), 2 Rodney Craig (Eng), 3 Richard Cohen (Eng).

Team Foil:

Note: teams were not restricted to three fencers.

1950: 1 England (Robert Anderson, René Paul, Arthur Pilbrow), 2 New Zealand (Gordon Dearing, Austen Gittos, Murray Gittos, Malcolm Miller), 3 Canada (Edward Brooke, Robert Desjarlais, George Pouliot).

1954: 1 England (Ralph Cooperman, Allan Jay, René Paul), 2 Australia (John Fethers, Ivan Lund, Roddrick Steel), 3 Canada (Roland Asselin, Edward Brooke, John Howard, Carl Schwende).

1958: 1 England (Harry Cooke, Allan Jay, Raymond Paul, René Paul), 2 Australia (Ivan Lund, Brian McCowage, Michael Sichel), 3 Wales (John Evans, John McCombe, Roger Maunder).

1962: 1 England (Ralph Cooperman, Mike Howard, Allan Jay, René Paul), 2 Australia (Brian McCowage, Ivan Lund, David McKenzie), 3 Canada (John Andru, Carl Schwende, Benedek Simo).

1966: 1 England (Bill Hoskyns, Allan Jay, Graham Paul), 2 Australia (Russell Hobby, John Humphreys, Barry Wasley), 3 Scotland (Joe Rorke, George Sandor, Bobby Wilson).

1970: 1 England (Mike Breckin, Barry Paul, Graham Paul), 2 Australia (Gregory Benko, Bill Ronald, Ernst Simon), 3 Canada (Magdy Conyd, Konrad Widmaier, Gerry Wiedel).

Team Epee:

1950: 1 Australia (Allan Jay, Ivan Lund, Charles Stanmore), 2 England (Robert Anderson, Charles-Louis de Beaumont, René Paul), 3 Canada (Edward Brooke, Robert Desjarlais, George Pouliot).

1954: 1 England (Charles-Louis de Beaumont, Allan Jay, René Paul), 2 Canada (Roland Asselin, Edward Brooke, Carl Schwende), 3 Australia (John Fethers, Ivan Lund, Laurence Smith).

Note: Jay competed for Australia in 1950.

1958: 1 England (Bill Hoskyns, Mike Howard, Allan Jay), 2 Canada (John Andru, Roland Asselin, Carl Schwende), 3 Australia (David Doyle, Ivan Lund, John Simpson).

1962: 1 England (Mike Howard, Peter Jacobs, John Pelling), 2 Australia (Michael Diamond, John Humphreys, Ivan Lund), 3 Canada (Peter Bakonyi, Robert Foxcroft, Carl Schwende).

1966: 1 England (Bill Hoskyns, Peter Jacobs, John Pelling), 2 Canada (John Andru, Peter Bakonyi, Konrad Widmaier), 3 Australia (Peter Hardiman, John Humphreys, Barry Wasley).

1970: 1 England (Bill Hoskyns, Peter Jacobs, William Johnson), 2 Scotland (Ian Hunter, Derek Russell, George Sandor), 3 Canada (Peter Bakonyi, Konrad Widmaier, Lester Wong).

Team Sabre:

1950: 1 England (Robert Anderson, Charles-Louis de Beaumont, Arthur Pilbrow), 2 Canada (Edward Brooke, Robert Desjarlais, George Pouliot), 3 Australia (Norman Booth, Leslie Chillug, Edwin Dean, John Gibson).

1954: 1 Canada (Roland Asselin, Leslie Krasa, Carl Schwende), 2 England (Mike Amberg, William Beatley, Ralph Cooperman), 3 Australia (John Fethers, Ivan Lund, Laurence Smith, Roddrick Steel).

1958: 1 England (Mike Amberg, Ralph Cooperman, Bill Hoskyns, Eugene Verebes), 2 Australia (Ivan Lund, Brian McCowage, Alexander Martonffy, Michael Sichel), 3 Wales (Malcolm Kerslake, Ted Lucas, Roger Maunder, John Preston).

1962: 1 England (Mike Amberg, George Birks, Ralph Cooperman), 2 Canada (John Andru, Robert Foxcroft, Carl Schwende, Benedek Simo), 3 New Zealand (Bob Binning, Mike Henderson, Brian Pickworth).

1966: 1 England (Ralph Cooperman, Richard Oldcorn, William Rayden), 2 Australia (Gabor Arato, Brian McCowage, Laszlo Tornallyay), 3 Canada (John Andru, Robert Foxcroft, Leslie Samek).

1970: 1 England (David Acfield, Richard Cohen, Rodney Craig), 2 Scotland (Sandy Leckie, Gordon Wiles, Tony Mitchell), 3 Australia (Gabor Arato, Gregory Benko, Laszlo Tornallyay).

WOMEN

Individual Foil:

1950: 1 Mary Glen-Haig (Eng), 2 Pat Woodroffe (NZ), 3 Catherine Pym (Aus).

1954: 1 Mary Glen-Haig (Eng), 2 Gillian Sheen (Eng), 3 Aileen Harding (Wal).

1958: 1 Gillian Sheen (Eng), 2 Barbara McCreath (Aus), 3 Mary Glen-Haig (Eng).

1962: 1 Melody Coleman (NZ), 2 Johanna Winter (Aus), 3 Janet Hopner (Aus).

1966: 1 Janet Wardell-Yerburgh (Eng), 2 Shirley Parker (Eng), 3 Gaye McDermitt (NZ).

1970: 1 Janet Wardell-Yerburgh (Eng), 2 Marion Exelby (Aus), 3 Susan Youngs (Sco).

Team Foil:
First held 1966
1966: 1 England (Shirley Parker, Joyce Pearce, Janet Wardell-Yerburgh), 2 Australia (Jeanette Beauchamp, Melody Coleman, Val Winter), 3 New Zealand (Pam French, Joyce Fenton, Gaye McDermitt).
1970: 1 England (Susan Greene, Clare Henley, Janet Wardell-Yerburgh), 2 Scotland (Judith Bain, Paula Robinson, Barbara Williams, Susan Youngs), 3 Canada (Kyoko Aoyama, Fleurette Cameau, Pacita Wiedel).

RHYTHMIC GYMNASTICS

Aided by the Eastern Bloc, Malaysia finally gets gold

A rare sport, in that it is restricted to women, rhythmic gymnastics was first held at World Championships level in 1963. Unlike artistic gymnastics competitors use various forms of hand-held apparatus and the principle is that the body and apparatus must be kept moving in harmony. Acrobatic elements are not allowed. The sport was dominated from the outset by Eastern European nations, but when it appeared at the widely-boycotted Olympic Games of 1984 the all-round gold medal was won by a Canadian, Lori Fung. Rhythmic gymnastics was introduced to the Commonwealth Games in 1990.

Highlights - Games by Games

1990: The star at the Auckland Games was Canada's 15-year-old Hungarian-born Mary Fuzesi, winner of three of the five individual medals on offer, who had placed 9th at the previous year's World Championships. Miss Fuzesi had taken up the sport at the age of seven and was already a national team member by the time she was 11. Had there been a team competition, Canada would surely have won that as well.

1994: It was a Japanese-born Australian, Kasumi Takahashi, aged only 14, who was outstanding on this occasion with victories in all five individual events, but otherwise Canada won seven medals and Australia only one, and it was the greater all-round strength of the Canadians which brought them the team title. Two of the three Canadian team-members were coached by Lori Jackson (nee Fung), the 1984 Olympic champion.

1998: As in so many sports the Malaysian authorities had invested a great deal of money in preparing their competitors for the Kuala Lumpur Games. For artistic and rhythmic gymnastics they had employed nine coaches from Russia and Bulgaria for up to four years beforehand, and the investment finally paid off. As in 1994 one gymnast was far and away the best individual as Erika-Leigh Stirton, of Canada, won five golds, and mostly by decisive margins. She had been the only Commonwealth competitor ranked in the top 25 in the previous year's World Championships, but again as in 1994 the best gymnast did not figure in the winning team, and despite all of Leigh-Stirton's efforts it was Malaysia which narrowly took the title amid the wild excitement of the fervent and relentlessly patriotic spectators.

Leading gold-medallists:

5 Kasumi Takahashi (Aus) 1994, Erika-Leigh Stirton (Can) 1998; 3 Mary Fuzesi (Can) 1990.

RHYTHMIC GYMNASTICS MEDALLISTS

Note: the individual disciplines contested were as follows: 1990 - Hoop, Ball, Ribbon, Rope; 1994 - Hoop, Ball, Ribbon, Clubs; 1998 - Hoop, Ribbon, Rope, Clubs. The Team event was first contested in 1994.

Individual All-Round:
1990: 1 Mary Fuzesi (Can) 37.650pts, 2 Madonna Gimotea (Can) 37.250, 3 Angela Walker (NZ) 36.900.
1994: 1 Kasumi Takahashi (Aus) 36.850, 2 Camille Martens (Can) 36.600, 3= Debbie Southwick (Eng) & Joanne Walker (Sco) 36.350.
1998: 1 Erika-Leigh Stirton (Can) 38.207, 2 Leigh Marning (Aus) 37.865, 3 Shaneez Johnston (Aus) 37.673.

Hoop:
1990: 1 Mary Fuzesi (Can) 9.400, 2 Madonna Gimotea (Can) 9.200, 3= Raewyn Jack (NZ), Anita Sands (Eng), Viva Seifert (Eng) 9.100.
1994: 1 Kasumi Takahashi (Aus) 9.300, 2 Lindsay Richards (Can) 9.050, 3 Aicha McKenzie (Eng) 8.900.
1998: 1 Erika-Leigh Stirton (Can) 9.624, 2 Thye Chee Kiat (Mal) 9.524, 3 Leigh Marning (Aus) 9.500.

Ball:
1990: 1 Madonna Gimotea (Can) 9.450, 2 Mary Fuzesi (Can) 9.400, 3 Angela Walker (NZ) 9.250.
1994: 1 Kasumi Takahashi (Aus) 9.200, 2 Camille Martens (Can) 9.000, 3= Aicha

McKenzie (Eng), Gretchen McLennan (Can) 8.800.
1998: Not held

Ribbon:

1990: 1 Mary Fuzesi (Can) 9.400, 2 Madonna Gimotea (Can) 9.300, 3= Raewyn Jack (NZ), Viva Seifert (Eng), Angela Walker (NZ) 9.200.
1994: 1 Kasumi Takahashi (Aus) 9.200, 2 Camille Martens (Can) 9.050,
3 Gretchen McLennan (Can) 9.000.
1998: 1 Erika-Leigh Stirton (Can) 9.650, 2 Shaneez Johnston (Aus) 9.491,
3 Carolyn Au-Yong (Mal) 9.391.

Rope:

1990: 1 Angela Walker (NZ) 9.300, 2 Madonna Gimotea (Can) 9.275, 3 Mary Fuzesi (Can) 9.250.
1994: Not held
1998: 1 Erika-Leigh Stirton (Can) 9.508, 2 Leigh Marning (Aus) 9.500, 3 Thye Chee Kiat (Mal) 9.466.

Clubs:

1990: Not held
1994: 1 Kasumi Takahashi (Aus) 9.400, 2 Camille Martens (Can) 9.150, 3 Leigh Marning (Aus) 9.000.
1998: 1 Erika-Leigh Stirton (Can) 9.583, 2 Shaneez Johnston (Aus) 9.458,
3 Emilie Livingston (Can) 9.341.

Team:

1990: Not held
1994: 1 Canada (Gretchen McLennan, Camille Martens, Lindsay Richards) 106.900, 2 Australia (Leigh Marning, Kate Mitchell, Kasumi Takahashi) 105.300, 3 England (Aicha McKenzie, Debbie Southwick, Linda Southwick) 103.300.
1998: 1 Malayasia (Carolyn Au-Yong, El Regina Tajudin, Sarina Sindara Rajah, Thye Chee Kiat) 93.023,2 Canada (Katie Iafolla, Emilie Livingston, Erika-Leigh Stirton) 92.962, 3 Australia (Kristy Darrah, Danielle Leray, Shaneez Johnston, Leigh Marning) 92.937

ROWING

Redgrave's triple fails to save the sinking ship

Rowing's limited appeal to the underdeveloped nations has spelled its demise as a Commonwealth Games sport. It disappeared from the schedule when the Games went to Jamaica in 1966, and apart from a brief revival in Edinburgh 20 years later it has no long figured in the programme.

Such a fate would have seemed inconceivable to the organisers of the inaugural 1930 Games. Despite the problems of financing the long journey to Canada for many of the visiting teams, five rowing events were arranged, including the highly labour-intensive Eights event for which both England and New Zealand sent crews.

At those 1930 Games there were no less than two Olympic champions in the Single Sculls - Jack Beresford for England and Bobby Pearce for Canada. Beresford had won at the 1924 Olympics; Pearce succeeded him in 1928 and was to win again in 1932. Pearce beat Beresford for the Empire title, but the Englishman went on to accumulate five Olympic medals (including three golds) at five different Games up to 1936. Half-a-century later his illustrious successor, Steve Redgrave, became the first rower to win three gold medals at a single Commonwealth Games, and he was also to win five Olympic golds over a 16-year period.

Redgrave's partner at Coxed Pairs and Coxless Pairs in 1986 was Andrew Holmes, who also shared in the 1988 Olympic gold in the latter event. Other rowers to have won Olympic gold in addition to medals in the Empire or Commonwealth Games over the years are Arthur "Jumbo" Edwards and Richard Burnell (England), Mervyn Wood and Peter Antonie (Australia), and Donald Arnold, Walter d'Hondt, Lorne Loomer and Archie McKinnon (all of Canada). Beresford, Burnell and Edwards had strong family connections with the sport, as Beresford's father had been an Olympic silver-medallist in 1912 and Burnell's father a gold-medallist in 1908, while Edwards's sons, David and John, won silver and bronze for Wales in the 1958 and 1962 Commonwealth Games.

Leading countries:

Australia 16 gold medals; England 14; New Zealand 9, Canada 7. No other country has won a gold medal.

Leading gold-medallists:

4 Mervyn Wood (Aus) 1950-54; 3 Steve Redgrave (Eng) 1986.

Highlights - Games by Games

1930: England won two events and Australia, Canada and New Zealand one each, which made everyone's journey worthwhile. In the Double Sculls only Canada was represented, so the organisers simply invited a couple of American crews to provide some opposition. There was also, surprisingly, an entry from British Guiana (now Guyana) in the Eights.

1938: Oddly, considering the great tradition established by the Boat Race and the Henley Regatta, there had been no rowing at the 1934 Games in London, but England sent a team of 11 to Australia four years later and they practised their skills en route in a static shell set up on the deck of their ocean liner. The preparation was supervised by the team coach, Julius Beresford (father of Jack), and served the Eights crew excellently because they won a thrilling race by ¾-of-a-length from Australia. Faring less well were the Offer brothers from Kingston Rowing Club, who were beaten by nine lengths in the Double Sculls, and Peter Jackson, who lost the Single Sculls by five lengths - though he had been a member of the winning Eight.

1950: Australia and New Zealand were the only countries entered in all five events. Otherwise, the numbers were made up by England in the Single Sculls, Double Sculls and Eights and a solitary sculler from South Africa. In other words, only a single competitor would not get a medal of some kind. The standard, though, was beyond reproach with Australia beating a youthful New Zealand crew (average age 21) by only one foot in the Eights, and the Olympic champion, Mervyn Wood, winning the Single Sculls and sharing in the Double Sculls success.

1954: Finals day attracted a crowd of 12,000, including the Duke of Edinburgh. Mervyn Wood and his partner, Murray Riley, won the Double Sculls again, and Wood got a fourth gold medal in the Coxed Fours. New Zealanders won the Single Sculls and Coxless Pairs, but the surprise of the day was the victory in the Eights of the inexperienced University of British Columbia team over Thames Rowing Club. For the second successive Games no England rower won gold.

1958: England ended the drought with wins in three of the five events. The coxless pair from New Zealand, Bob Parker and Reg Douglas, repeated their 1954 success. Canada again won the Eights, with a contribution from all four members of the Olympic gold-medal crew at Coxless Fours in 1956. Wales, on home waters, won bronze in the Coxless Fours, with the two sons of "Jumbo" Edwards, a 1930 gold-medallist for England, in the crew.

1962: In what was to be the last Commonwealth Games regatta for 24 years England won three of the events, New Zealand two, and Australia only one - though this was in the prestigious Eights by a mere two-tenths of a second. Both the Coxed Fours, won by New Zealand, and the Coxless Fours, won by England, also provided desperately close races. In the latter the Welsh crew of the Edwards brothers, David and John, and the Luke twins, Jeremy and Tim, led until 150 metres from the end of the 2,000-metre course and were caught by England almost on the finishing-line.

1986: Rowing's swansong was ironically a much grander affair than anything previously in Commonwealth Games history. With lightweight and women's races included for the first (and last) time there were 14 events in all. England won four of the men's finals, and Steve Redgrave had a hand in three of them - Single Sculls, Coxless Pairs and Coxed Fours. Australia, Canada and New Zealand each won two of the women's titles, but the 42 medals were shared out among only five countries.

ROWING MEDALLISTS

MEN

Note: crews are listed, so far as is known, in rowing order.

Single Sculls:
1930: 1 Bobby Pearce (Aus) 8:03.6, 2 Jack Beresford (Eng), 3 Fred Bradley (Eng).
1934: Not held
1938: 1 Herb Turner (Aus) 8:24.0, 2 Peter Jackson (Eng) at five lengths, 3 Robert Smith (NZ) at four lengths.
1950: 1 Mervyn Wood (Aus) 7:46.8, 2 Tony Rowe (Eng) 7:54.0, 3 Ian Stephen (SA) 8:03.0.
1954: 1 Don Rowlands (NZ) 8:28.2, 2 Sidney Rand (Eng) 8:43.4, 3 Bobby Williams (Can) 8:51.3.
1958: 1 Stuart Mackenzie (Aus) 7:20.1, 2 Jack Hill (NZ) 7:23.9, 3 Russell Carver (Eng) 7:26.8.
1962: 1 Jack Hill (NZ) 7:39.7, 2 Bill Barry (Eng) 7:44.9, 3 Ian Tutty (NZ) 7:48.9.
1966-1982: Not held
1986: 1 Steve Redgrave (Eng) 7:28.29, 2 Richard Powell (Aus) 7:32.64, 3 Eric Verdonk (NZ) 7:39.11.

Lightweight Single Sculls:
First held 1986
1986: 1 Peter Antonie (Aus) 7:16.43, 2 Peter Tattersall (Can) 7:26.65, 3 Carl Smith (Eng) 7:27.34.

Double Sculls:
1930: 1 Elswood Boles & Bob Richards (Can) 7:48.0.
Note: US crews finished 2nd and 3rd competing as guests!
1934: Not held
1938: 1 William Bradley & Cecil Pearce (Aus) 7:29.4, 2 Robert Offer & Jack Offer

(Eng), 3 Peter Jackson (Eng) & Robert Smith (NZ).

Note: This was listed as an "invitation event" and no medals were awarded.

1950: 1 Mervyn Wood & Murray Riley (Aus) 7:22.0, 2 Joe Schneider & Des Simonsen (NZ) 7:32.0, 3 Ken Tinegate & Jack Brown (Eng) 7:39.0.

1954: 1 Mervyn Wood & Murray Riley (Aus) 7:54.5, 2 Bob Parker & Reg Douglas (NZ) 8:05.2, 3 Donald Guest & Lawrence Stephan (Can) 8:28.5.

1958: 1 Mike Spracklen & Geoffrey Baker (Eng) 6:56.4, 2 Mervyn Wood & Stuart Mackenzie (Aus) 7:01.4, 3 Norman Suckling & Jack Hill (NZ) at three-quarters of a length.

1962: 1 George Justicz & Nicholas Birkmyre (Eng) 6:52.4, 2 Peter Watkinson & Murray Watkinson (NZ) 6:54.2, 3 Barclay Wade & Graeme Squires (Aus) 7:01.4.

1966-1982: Not held

1986: 1 Bruce Ford & Pat Walter (Can) 6:19.43, 2 Paul Reedy & Brenton Terrell (Aus) 6:21.17, 3 Carl Smith & Alan Whitwell (Eng) 6:33.53.

Coxless Pairs:

First held 1950

1950: 1 Wal Lambert & Jack Webster (Aus) 7:58.0, 2 David Gould & Humphrey Gould (NZ) 8:10.0.

Note: only two crews competed.

1954: 1 Bob Parker & Reg Douglas (NZ) 8:23.9, 2 Tom Christie & Nicholas Clack (Eng) 8:24.1, 3 Dave Anderson & Geoff Williamson (Aus) 8:29.7.

1958: 1 Bob Parker & Reg Douglas (NZ) 7:11.1, 2 Jonathan Hall & Stewart Douglas-Mann (Eng) 7:13.7, 3 Stephen Roll & Kevin Webb (Aus) 7:32.5.

1962: 1 Stewart Farquharson & Jim Lee-Nicholson (Eng) 7:03.7, 2 Graham Lawrence & Murray Lawrence (NZ) 7:08.5, 3 Rodger Ninham & William Hatfield (Aus) 7:10.3.

1966-1982: Not held

1986: 1 Andrew Holmes & Steve Redgrave (Eng) 6:40.48, 2 Barrie Mabbott & Ian Wright (NZ) 6:42.63, 3 Ewan Stuart & David Riches (Sco) 6:43.06.

Coxless Fours:

1930: 1 England (F.M.L. Fitzwilliams, A.J. Halby, Arthur Edwards, Humphrey Boardman) 7:40.6, 2 Canada (J. Gayner, J. Fleming, O.G. Bellew, H.J. Pelham) at two lengths, 3 New Zealand (Barry Johnson, Vic Olsson, Alex Ross, Charley Saunders) -.

1934-1954: Not held

1958: 1 England (Roger Pope, Keith Shakell, David Young, Creighton Redman) 6:34.4, 2 Canada (Glen Smith, Malcolm Turnbull, Richard McClure, John Madden) 6:38.9, 3 Wales (David Edwards, John Fage, David Prichard, John Edwards) 6:47.9.

1962: 1 England (Chris Davidge, Michael Clay, John Beveridge, John Tilbury) 6:31.1, 2 Wales (David Edwards, Jeremy Luke, Richard Luke, John Edwards) 6:32.5, 3 Canada (Eldon Worobieff, Thomas Gray, Thomas Stokes, Ray McIntosh) 6:34.9.

1966-1982: Not held

1986: 1 Canada (Grant Mann, Kevin Neufeld, Paul Steele, Pat Turner) 6:00.56, 2 New Zealand (Andrew Stevenson, Shane O'Brien, Neil Gibson, Don Symon)

6:00.85, 3 England (Graham Faultless, Richard Ireland, Martyn Field, Humphrey Hatton) 6:05.99.

Lightweight Coxless Fours:

First held 1986

1986: 1 England (Christopher Bates, Peter Haining, Neil Staite, Stuart Forbes) 6:25.86, 2 Australia (Simon Cook, Brian Digby, Merrick Howes, Joseph Joyce) 6:27.71, 3 Canada (Dave Henry, Brian Peaker, Bob Thomas, Ryan Tierney) 6:35.66.

Coxed Fours:

1930: 1 New Zealand (Mick Brough, John MacDonald, Ben Waters, Bert Sandos, Arthur Eastwood) 8:02.0 2 Canada (B.L. Gales, R.S. Evans, J.A.Butler, H.R. McCuaig, A. Miles) at two lengths, 3 British Guiana (J.I. Matthews, F.O. Gomes, B. P. Bagley, E.M. Gonsalves, J. Jardine) -.

1934: Not held

1938: 1 Australia (Gordon Freeth, Don Fraser, Stewart Elder, Jack Fisher, Harry Kerr) 7:16.8, 2 New Zealand (Oliver Clayton, Albert Hope, Ken Boswell, John Rigby, George Burns) at 1¼ lengths, 3 Canada (James Temple, Max Winkler, Donald Davis, John MacDonald, Kenneth Jaggard) at ¾ length.

1950: 1 New Zealand (Ted Johnson, John O'Brien, Bill James, Bill Carroll, Charles Johnston) 7:17.2, 2 Australia (Leslie Montgomery, Erwin Elder, Cecil Winkworth, Kenneth Gee, Kevin Fox) 7:24.0.

Note: only two crews competed.

1954: 1 Australia (Lionel Robberds, Dave Anderson, Peter Evatt, Geoff Williamson, Mervyn Wood) 7:58.3, 2 New Zealand (Bruce Culpan, Kerry Ashby, Murray Ashby, William Tinnock, Stanley Gallagher) 8:04.4, 3 England (Geoffrey Page, Roderick Macmillan, Alastair Davidson, Maurice Legg, David Glynne-Jones) 8:04.5.

1958: 1 England (Colin Porter, John Vigurs, Simon Crosse, John Beresford, Richard Gabriel) 6:46.5, 2 Canada (Donald Arnold, Walter d'Hondt, David Helliwell, Lawrence Stapleton, Sohen Biln) 6:53.2, 3 Australia (Graeme Allen, Ralfe Currall, Kevin Evans, Lionel Robberds, Roland Waddington) no time taken.

1962: 1 New Zealand (Winston Stephens, Keith Heselwood, Hugh Smedley, George Paterson, Douglas Pulman) 6:48.2, 2 Australia (David Ramage, Derek Norwood, David Caithness, David John, Phillip Sarah) 6:48.8, 3 England (John Russell, Richard Knight, John Vigurs, Colin Porter, Michael Howard-Johnston) 7:04.9.

1966-1982: Not held

1986: 1 England (Martin Cross, Adam Cliff, Andrew Holmes, Steve Redgrave, Adrian Ellison) 6:08.13, 2 New Zealand (Nigel Atherfold, Chris White, Greg Johnston, Bruce Holden, Andrew Bird) 6:09.89, 3 Australia (Mark Doyle, James Galloway, Michael McKay, James Tomkins, Dale Caterson) 6:10.52.

Eights:

1930: 1 England (J.A. Brown, Terry O'Brien, F.M.L. Fitzwilliams, A.J. Halby, Arthur Edwards, Humphrey Boardman, J.H. Crawford, D.E.L. Howitt, R.G.

Close-Brooks) 6:37.0, 2 New Zealand (Mick Brough, John Gilby, John MacDonald, Vic Olsson, Bert Sandos, Charley Saunders, Fred Thompson, Ben Waters, Arthur Eastwood) at ¾ length, 3 Canada (Leslie McDonald, Earl Eastwood, Albert Taylor, Dan Doal, William Thoburn, Joseph Zabinsky, Harry Fry, Joseph Bowkes, William Moore) at four lengths..

1934: Not held

1938: 1 England (John Burrough, Basil Beazley, Rhodes Hambridge, John Turnbull, Peter Jackson, Jan Sturrock, Desmond Kingsford, J.T. Turner, Thomas Reeve) 6:29.0, 2 Australia (William Thomas, Frank Le Soeuf, Gordon Yewers, Richard Paramor, Edward Bromley, William Dixon, Ainslie Gould, Alfred Gregory, Doug Bowden) at ¾ length, 3 New Zealand (Leslie Pithie, Oswald Denison, John Charters, Howard Benge, Gus Jackson, Bob Stiles, Fred Thompson, Nat Gould, William Stodart) at two lengths.

1950: 1 Australia (Alan Brown, Edward Pain, Eric Longley, Ross Selman, Bruce Goswell, Peter Holmes, Phillip Cayzer, Robert Tinning, James Barnes) 6:27.0, 2 New Zealand (Tom Engel, Kerry Ashby, William Tinnock, Murray Ashby, Graham Jarratt, Don Rowlands, Bruce Culpan, Ted Smith, Don Adam) 6:27.5, 3 England (Patrick Bradley, Michael Lapage, Peter Kirkpatrick, Richard Burnell, Hedley Rushmere, Bill Windham, Peter de Giles, Anthony Butcher, Jack Dearlove) 6:40.0.

1954: 1 Canada (Glen Smith, Thomas Harris, Thomas Toynbee, Douglas McDonald, Lawrence West, Herman Zloklikovits, Kenneth Drummond, Robert Wilson, Ray Sierpina) 6:59.0, 2 England (Geoffrey Page, John Pope, Michael Savage, Alan Watson, Alastair Davidson, Roderick Macmillan, Maurice Legg, Joe Eldeen, David Glynne-Jones) 7:10.5.

Note: only two crews competed.

1958: 1 Canada (Donald Arnold, Wayne Pretty, Glen Mervyn, Walter d'Hondt, William McKerlick, Archie MacKinnon, Lorne Loomer, Robert Wilson, Sohen Biln) 5:51.1, 2 Australia (Graeme Allen, Neville Clinton, Ralfe Currall, Bruce Evans, Kevin Evans, Kenneth Railton, Victor Schweikert, Roland Waddington, Lionel Robberds) 5:56.1, 3 England (Dick Workman, Peter Thomson, John Stephenson, Tony Wober, Tony Hancox, Felix Badcock, Dennis Mount, Don Elliott, Ray Penney) 6:10.2.

1962: 1 Australia (Ian Douglas, Charles Lehman, Dushan Stankovic, Terence Davies, Paul Guest, Graeme McCall, Martin Tomanovits, Walter Howell, David Palfreyman) 5:53.4, 2 New Zealand (Colin Cordes, Darien Boswell, Alistair Dryden, Christian Larsen, Alan Grey, Louis Lobel, Alan Webster, Leslie Arthur, Robert Page) 5:53.6, 3 England (Chris Davidge, Michael Clay, John Russell, Richard Knight, Colin Porter, John Vigurs, John Beveridge, John Tilbury, Michael Howard-Johnston) 6:09.4.

1966-1982: Not held

1986: 1 Australia (Malcolm Batten, Andrew Cooper, Mark Doyle, Stephen Evans, James Galloway, Michael McKay, Ion Popa, James Tomkins, Dale Caterson) 5:44.42, 2 England (Jonathan Spencer-Jones, Patrick Broughton, John Garrett, John Maxey, Terence Dillon, Mark Buckingham, Stephen Peel, Richard Stanhope, Vaughan Thomas) 5:46.35, 3 New Zealand (Mike Burrell, Neil Gibson, Andrew Hay, Barrie Mabbott, Shane O'Brien, Andrew Stevenson, Don Symon, Carl Vincent, Ian Wright) 5:47.97

WOMEN

Single Sculls:
1986: 1 Stephanie Foster (NZ) 7:43.22, 2 Lisa Wright (Can) 7:48.90, 3 Gillian Bond (Eng) 7:52.82.

Lightweight Single Sculls:
1986: 1 Adair Ferguson (Aus) 7:45.49, 2 Philippa Baker (NZ) 7:45.82, 3 Heather Hattin (Can) 7:52.14.

Double Sculls:
1986: 1 Stephanie Foster & Robin Clarke (NZ) 7:21.52, 2 Heather Clarke & Lisa Robertson (Can) 7:48.90, 3 Diane Prince & Claire Parker (Eng) 7:54.71.

Coxless Pairs:
1986: 1 Kathryn Barr & Andrea Schreiner (Can) 7:34.51, 2 Pauline Bird & Fiona Johnson (Eng) 7:42.23, 3 Catherine Hall & Alison Smith (Aus) 7:53.09.

Lightweight Coxless Fours:
1986: 1 England (Alexa Forbes, Gillian Hodges, Linda Clark, Judith Burne) 6:54.70, 2 Australia (Deborah Clingeleffer, Amanda Cross, Virginia Lee, Karin Riedel) 6:59.68, 3 Canada (Anne Drost, Marni Hamilton, Marlene Van der Horst, Wendy Wiebe) 7:01.18.

Coxed Fours:
1986: 1 Canada (Tina Clarke, Tricia Smith, Lesley Thompson, Jane Tregunno, Jenny Wallinga) 6:50.13, 2 Australia (Debbie Bassett, Susan Chapman-Popa, Robyn Grey-Gardner, Marilyn Kidd, Kaylynn Fry) 6:54.31, 3 England (Joanne Gough, Elizabeth Callaway, Kate Holroyd, Patricia Reid, Alison Norrish) 7:06.02.

Eights:
1986: 1 Australia (Debbie Bassett, Susan Chapman-Popa, Margot Foster, Robyn Grey-Gardner, Urszula Kay, Marilyn Kidd, Vicki Spooner, Annelies Voorthuis, Kaylynn Fry) 6:43.69, 2 England (Fiona Johnstone, Alison Bonner, Katherine Grose, Pauline Bird, Kate Holroyd, Elizabeth Callaway, Joanne Gough, Pauline Reid, Alison Norrish) 6:45.62, 3 Canada (Jane Tregunno, Kathryn Barr, Tina Clarke, Marilyn Campbell, Jenny Wallinga, Tricia Smith, Andrea Schreiner, Lesley Thompson, Barbara Armbrust) no time taken.

TEN PIN BOWLING

Ang and Heng have a fling

Given more or less free rein to choose whatever sports they wanted, it was perfectly understandable that the Malaysian organisers of the 1998 Games should go for something in which their country had a very good chance of winning gold medals. As it happened, Tenpin Bowling fully justified its inclusion with 15 countries entering the various events and five of those countries getting medals.

World Championships had first been held in 1923 and there had been two Commonwealth winners at the 17 Men's Singles competitions over the years - David Pond, of Great Britain, in 1967 and Marc Doi, of Canada, in 1995. Great Britain had also won the Men's Doubles three times between 1967 and 1983 and Australia had done so twice. Debby Ship, of Canada, had been Women's Singles champion in 1995 and was succeeded by Australia's Cara Honeychurch the next year.

1998 Games Highlights

The 1000-plus daily crowds were excitable - to say the very least - and gave their players enormous and cheerfully partisan support, but if the intention was to put off the redoubtable Australian women visitors it did not work. Cara Honeychurch and Maxine Nable opened the competition by winning the Women's Doubles with 130 pins to spare over their Malaysian rivals and the rest of the opposition a long way behind.

In the Men's Doubles the same day the Malaysians got their wish as Kenny Ang and Ben Heng won by an imposing 223-pin margin from Bermuda. The next day's Mixed Doubles provided further success for Cara Honeychurch in partnership with Frank Ryan, though the margin was a narrow one over England and Canada.

In the Women's Singles the tireless Ms Honeychurch was always in command from the qualifying round onwards, including in her aggregate one perfect score of 300, and she stretched her lead to 378 pins over her team-mate, Maxine Nable, with Malaysia taking the bronze. In the Men's Singles Kenny Ang won his second gold medal from two Canadians who had oddly finished only 8th in the Doubles.

TEN PIN BOWLING MEDALLISTS

First held 1998

Men's singles:
1998: 1 Kenny Ang (Mal) 6046, 2 Bill Rowe (Can) 5946, 3 Warren Rennox (Can) 5850.

Men's doubles:
1998: 1 Kenny Ang & Ben Heng (Mal) 3552, 2 Antoine Jones & Conrad Lister (Ber) 3329, 3 Michael Muir & Frank Ryan (Aus) 3229.

Women's singles:
1998: 1 Cara Honeychurch (Aus) 6406, 2 Maxine Nable (Aus) 6028, 3 Lai Kin Ngoh (Mal) 5920.

Women's doubles:
1998: 1 Cara Honeychurch & Maxine Nable (Aus) 3678, 2 Lai Kin Ngoh & Shalin Zulkifli (Mal) 3548, 3 Pauline Beck & Gemma Burden (Eng) 3273.

Mixed doubles:
1998: 1 Cara Honeychurch & Frank Ryan (Aus) 3605, 2 Pauline Beck & Richard Hood (Eng) 3560, 3 Jane Amlinger & Bill Rowe (Can) 3536.

WATER POLO

1950: Australia beat New Zealand in a series of three matches 11-4, 13-2, 5-2.

Note: This event is included in the Australian Commonwealth Games Federation's retrospective compilation of gold medals won by Australian competitors, but was not listed as an official event in the report of the 1950 Games published in New Zealand and is not included in the New Zealand Olympic Committee's list of medal-winners published in 1998. It would seem that water polo should be regarded as having been an exhibition sport at the 1950 Games. It has not been contested in subsequent Games.

The Australian team was as follows: John Amadee, Peter Bennett, Herman Doerner, Owen Doerner, Colin French, Malcolm Hastie, Percy Johnston, James McKay.

OFFICIAL COMMONWEALTH GAMES BOOKS FROM
The Parrs Wood Press

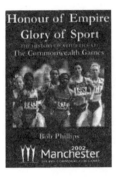

Honour of Empire, Glory of Sport
THE HISTORY OF ATHLETICS AT
THE COMMONWEALTH GAMES
by Bob Phillips
FOREWORD by David Moorcroft O.B.E.
Hardback - 320 pages - 40 colour/b&w photographs
ISBN: 1 903158 09 5 - £20.00

Bob Phillips' masterly study of athletics at The
Commonwealth Games, highlighting some of the great
rivalries and performances that have taken place since the
Games' inception.

The Iron in His Soul
BILL ROBERTS AND MANCHESTER'S
SPORTING HERITAGE
by Bob Phillips
FOREWORD by Roger Black
Hardback - 260 pages - 40 b&w photographs
ISBN: 1 903158 32 X - £16.95

Salford-born into a working class family Bill Roberts, who
died last December aged 89, became an athletics hero in
the 1930s, winning gold at the Berlin Olympics in 1936 in
the 4 x 400m relay and following it up to become
Commonwealth 440 yards champion in Sydney in 1938.
His story is bound up with the history of sport in
Manhcester.

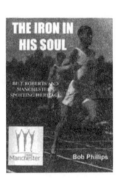

Both books available from all good bookshops,
or at their cover prices POST FREE (UK only) from:

The Parrs Wood Press
FREEPOST
Manchester M15 9PW

CREDIT CARD ORDERS: 0161 226 4466